Louisville

DIAMONDS

The Louisville Major-League Reader 1876-1899

PHILIP VON BORRIES

TURNER PUBLISHING COMPANY

TURNER PUBLISHING COMPANY

Turner Publishing Company Staff:
Publishing Consultant: Douglas W. Sikes
Designer: Herbert C. Banks II

Library of Congress Catalog Card Number: 96-61627

ISBN: 978-1-56311-323-9

Additional copies may be purchased directly from
Turner Publishing Company.

Limited Edition.

TABLE OF CONTENTS

DEDICATION 6

INTRODUCTION 7

Chapter One
LOUISVILLE DIAMONDS:
LOUISVILLE AND THE BIG SHOW, 1876–1899 8

Chapter Two
LOUISVILLE'S MAJOR–LEAGUE GALLERY I:
THE FIRST NATIONAL LEAGUE YEARS, 1876–1877 36

Chapter Three
PETE BROWNING:
THE ORIGINAL LOUISVILLE SLUGGER 39

Chapter Four
LOUISVILLE'S MAJOR–LEAGUE GALLERY II:
THE AMERICAN ASSOCIATION YEARS, 1882–1891 61

Chapter Five
LOUISVILLE KINGS:
LOUISVILLE AND THE 1890 WORLD SERIES 76

Chapter Six
LOUISVILLE'S MAJOR–LEAGUE GALLERY III:
THE SECOND NATIONAL LEAGUE YEARS, 1892–1899 88

Chapter Seven
THE LOST CITY OF HISTORICAL BASEBALL:
LOUISVILLE'S MAJOR–LEAGUE FIRSTS, RECORDS AND NOTABLE ACHIEVEMENTS 95

Chapter Eight
BIG–LEAGUE NAMES OF LOUISVILLE:
LOUISVILLE'S ALL–TIME MAJOR–LEAGUE & SEASONAL ROSTERS, 1876–1899 100

Chapter Nine
LOUISVILLE'S BIG SHOW NUMBERS:
LOUISVILLE'S PRINCIPAL MAJOR–LEAGUE STATISTICS, 1876-1899 124

Appendixes
EXTRA INNINGS:
LOST STARS: THE HALL–OF–FAME CASE FOR THE AMERICAN ASSOCIATION'S PREMIER STARS 132

LINGO: THE LANGUAGE OF BASEBALL 140

KENTUCKY IN THE MAJORS: ROSTER OF KENTUCKY–BORN MAJOR–LEAGUERS 145

KENTUCKY BASEBALL TRAVEL SITES 158

LOUISVILLE & KENTUCKY MINOR–LEAGUE HIGHLIGHTS 164

Bibliography 182

Index 184

Team card of 1885 Louisville American Associaiton club. Notable figures include Guy Hecker (#5), Pete Browning (#6), and Chicken Wolf (#13). (National Baseball Library and Archive, Cooperstown, NY)

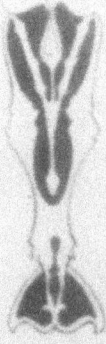    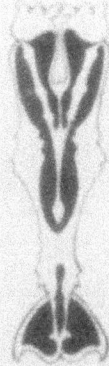

JACK KERRINS
Catcher

"The Old Gladiator"
PETE BROWNING Left Field

PAUL COOK
Catcher

EWING
Pitcher

RED EHRET
Pitcher

TOM "Toad" RAMSEY
Pitcher

STRATTON
Pitcher

GUY HECKER
Pitcher

TOMNEY
Short Stop

GLEASON
Short Stop

ESTERBROOK
First Base

VAUGHN
Catcher

SHANNON
Second Base

WEAVER
Center Field

JIMMY WOLF
Right Field

1888-1889 team card. (University of Louisville Photographic Archives)

DEDICATION

To Mickey Mantle, whose star shines as bright in the heavens as it did on earth; to Jamie Milliken and Christina Kearns, both shining hopes for a better tomorrow; to Uncle Milton and Aunt Lib, quite simply the best; to Father Michael Milliken and Kent Brown, who both know why; to Standiford Caldwell (b/d 1881), Mary Caldwell (1889-1890) and Virginia Caldwell (1898-1899), who make sure I find Pete Browning every time I go to Cave Hill Cemetery; to Frank "Dixie" Davis, a star pitcher for the Louisville Colonels in the minors and the St. Louis Browns in the majors; to Mary Gail, Eugenia, Brenda, Beverly, Cathy, Mary Bo and Pam – solid gold all the way; to Stan Starks, a multiple Eclipse Award-winning director who runs second to no one in my book; to Richard Topp, whose name matches his baseball talents; to Bill Williams, Executive Director of the Louisville Slugger Museum – one of baseball's best; to Walter and Mary Barney – for their indispensable help; to Cotton Nash, an All-American who made a young autograph seeker feel the same way a long time ago; to Kid Nichols, Ty Cobb, Babe Ruth, Walter Johnson, Lefty Grove, Roy Sievers, Robin Roberts, Al Kaline, Ernie Banks, Sandy Koufax, Joe Morgan, Johnny Bench, Tony Perez, Sparky Anderson, and Kenny Lofton (Willie Mays incarnate); to Ray Chapman, who left us way too soon; to all the other native sons of Kentucky who made it to the bigs; to the 1975 World Series; to old Crosley Field in Cincinnati, where I first learned why baseball is the greatest game on the face of the earth; to David Nemec, who helped a rookie break into the big show; to Dan Gutman, my other favorite baseball writer; to my late father, Frank, who believed in defense; to Todd Schrupp, Racing Television's brightest star; to Andy Stith, Raymond Cassidy and Christoper Blanco – all future greats; and to the golden remnants of great baseball days gone by – a Trapeze glove, baseball hats with cards stuck in them, and "the Mick."

INTRODUCTION

This book is a sequel to *Legends Of Louisville: Major League Baseball in Louisville, 1876-1899*. Published in October of 1993, 'Legends' broke new ground on two fronts. It was the first book ever done on Louisville's epic major–league stars, days and teams. It also was the first book ever done on any segment of Louisville's colorful baseball history.

Though I might have had the first word to say about Louisville's opulent major–league days in book form, there are obviously many more words to be written about that extraordinary history. Thus, this book.

It is based upon extensive research that I have been doing on Louisville's major–league years since 1983 (when I started out with a simple piece on Pete Browning that grew to 20 pages, and in time, became the genesis for both books).

Some of that research came after 'Legends' was completed. The other part came before 'Legends', but for various logistical reasons, could not be incorporated into 'Legends'.

One final note. While the two books are similar, that is all there is to it. 'Legends' was a media guide of sorts, an introduction to a vast, previously uncharted area. That area having now been settled, *Louisville Diamonds: The Louisville Major–League Reader (1876-1899)* enters now to develop that area.

Enjoy.

CHAPTER ONE
LOUISVILLE DIAMONDS:
LOUISVILLE AND THE BIG SHOW, 1876-1899

William Ambrose Hulbert *(National Baseball Library and Archive, Cooperstown, NY)*

PRELUDE

*L*ouisville's baseball heritage is wondrous and immense.

Its first boxscore (under the rules of Hall–of–Famer Alexander Cartwright, the true father of baseball who some 150 years ago promulgated the basic rules the game still uses today) dates to 1858.

It played against the historic Cincinnati Reds of 1869–1870, baseball's first professional club.

And, since the turn of the century (that timeframe including several brief hiatuses), Louisville has been a sanctuary of minor–league baseball.

And, the thread that binds those two eras is Louisville's magical 20–year major–league history, an era that indelibly stamped it as a grand American baseball city.

Louisville's birth as a major–league town, remarkably enough, coincided with the birth of the esteemed National League, this country's oldest, continuously–active major–league loop which inaugurated play in 1876.

The 'twin births' were no accident, but rather the product of design, since Louisville was not only a charter member of the National League, but played an instrumental role in the establishment of the "senior loop" as well.

This latter fact has been obscured — buried in some quarters — for many years by revisionist historians, but that does not change the facts of the National League–founding matter one scintilla.

In early December of 1875, William Hulbert — of the Chicago club in the National Association — travelled to Louisville.

There, he met with representatives of three other clubs, which along with his club, represented the "western" portion of his proposed National League. Besides Chicago, the group included Cincinnati, St. Louis and Louisville.

Armed with their proxies, he then met with representatives of the four "eastern" teams — Boston, Hartford, Philadelphia and New York — the following February in New York City. The result was the birth of the National League, its list of charter members including Louisville.

No one questions those facts. What has become warped over the years is the truth regarding the nativity of the National League.

Though New York City has long heralded itself as the birthplace of the National League, nothing could be further from the truth.

In point of fact, that statement has as much validity as the claim that Abner Doubleday invented baseball in Cooperstown, New York.

(Indeed, about the only thing that these two specious claims prove beyond the shadow of a doubt is that when it comes to historical claimjumping, New York has no peer — absolutely none whatsoever — as the game's greatest historical thief.)

Having dispensed with the falsehood that New York City founded the National League, that leaves two other options standing, both of them interesting and with great merit.

Many contend that Louisville and New York City share the honor. That is, they are co-founders, that based on the solid, logistical precept that the National League founding could not have been done without both of them (absolutely true).

However, there is a third belief about the National League's founding, which is perhaps the most hardline of all. That is the contention that Louisville was the outright founder of the National League.

A notable advocate of that viewpoint is the renowned baseball writer and scholar, Harold Seymour, who averred in his classic work, *Baseball: The Early Years*:

At Louisville, Hulbert and (St. Louis owner Charles) Fowle were appointed a committee with full power to act for the Western clubs and given the job of going east to negotiate with the Eastern teams they wanted to include. Louisville, therefore, was the real birthplace of the National League, not New York City.

(This is not an isolated quote. Part of a baseball item from the Sunday, March 27, 1892 issue of the Louisville Courier–Journal says: "It is not well known that the first meeting of the National League was held in this city, at the Louisville Hotel.")

For the record, Hulbert almost became as big a casualty as Louisville in the matter of the National League, Hulbert's muscular replacement for the decrepit, erratic and crooked National Association (the National League's predecessor).

In a shrewd political move designed to insure acceptance of his plan, Hulbert recommended that an easterner, Morgan Bulkeley, be the first president of the National League. As a logistical consequence, Bulkeley — a mere figurehead in the National League story — was one of the first persons elected to the Hall of Fame. By vivid contrast, Hulbert — the genius behind the National League, this country's oldest major league — did not make it into Cooperstown until 1995.

And, in the matter of the "lost history" of the Louisville/National League story, no discussion would be complete without a look at one Mr. Larry Gatto, whose two principal passions in life were his saloon business and baseball.

By any standards, Gatto was an unqualified success at both ventures. At the time of his death in Louisville at age 54, Gatto (1856-1910) was reported by the Louisville Courier-Journal to be the wealthiest saloonkeeper in the city.

Much of his success had come from "an oyster with each drink", a marketing tool which made him nationally famous. Another part of his success was the fact that Gatto ran a clean operation. Simply put, the saloons operated by this devout Catholic were just that, and no more.

Gatto did not serve minors, nor did he serve patrons who had had too much. Nor, did he allow any funny business with the fairer sex in his establishments. Lending further stature to his high rank as a

businessman, citizen and family man was Gatto's well–known generosity to a variety of charities.

Without a doubt, Gatto had not come easily to his prosperity, which at the time of his passing was reported by the Louisville Courier-Journal to be in the neighborhood of a quarter of a million dollars.

Born on Christmas Day in Genoa, Italy, Gatto had immigrated to this country with his family. Initially settling in Boston, they moved to New Orleans before finally staking roots in Louisville.

To help the family make ends meet, Gatto was forced to leave school at an early age. It was reported by the Louisville Courier–Journal, in its obituary of Monday, April 18, 1910, that Gatto began life with a bundle of newspapers under one arm and a bootblack's kit over his shoulder. He was the classic Horatio Alger rags–to–riches story in every way.

A man whose saloons were considered to be a model in that business, and hailed as a pioneer in modern saloon methods, Gatto was also a baseball enthusiast of the highest order.

His friends in that sport numbered in the dozens, and included some of the most prominent figures of the day. On the local level, Gatto owned parts of several of Louisville's major-league teams, one of them the 1890 co-World Champions.

Prior to that, Gatto had acted as the unofficial business manager of another Louisville major-league team in the 1880s, travelling with the team, paying bills, and buying and releasing players. And, for years there was an amateur nine in Louisville named after him.

That splendid baseball resumé, say some historians, included another major item, one which requires a brief backgrounding.

According to a Louisville Courier-Journal account dated December 6, 1875, Hulbert and the other western representatives were headquartered at the Louisville Hotel, located at Main and Seventh. (The aforementioned 1892 news item also specifically names the Louisville Hotel, which was razed in 1921.)

These newspaper accounts certainly refute the long–held belief by some historians that the Hulbert group met at the famed Galt House. (Still in existence today, the Galt House — a venerable trademark of the city — was then located five blocks east of the Louisville Hotel.)

Still subject to final interpretation, however, is another location mentioned over the years in some historical quarters as being the site of the Louisville/National League meetings. That is Larry Gatto's saloon, which was located on Green Street (now Liberty Street). This might be stretching it some when Gatto's age is factored in. At best, Gatto would have been 18 at the time of the National League meetings in Louisville; still, that is one of two logistical possibilities involving Gatto's saloon (based upon the little information currently extant about Gatto's early years.)

The other scenario involving Gatto's saloon is slightly more convoluted, but also more feasible.

That is the possibility that Gatto's saloon served the Louisville Hotel in an ancillary manner, thus making the opulent Louisville Hotel and Gatto's gregarious saloon the co-sites of Hulbert's historic Louisville meetings (though admittedly for vastly different reasons).

The former would have provided quality lodging and allowed for the orderly conduction of important business in a formal, respectful manner. The latter would have provided a convivial, relaxed atmosphere for the conduction of more business in an informal setting.

Moreover, there was an advantage attached to the saloon. The back room of a tightly-run saloon would have afforded more privacy than a hotel could ever guarantee (these men, after all, were in the process of overthrowing the National Association, the game's first major–league circuit). Also, Gatto's saloon wasn't just any saloon; it was run by an adamant baseball man who could well see the advantage that could accrue to his city and its baseball fortunes with the success of these meetings.

And, it is worth noting that the American Association — the National League's first great competitor, of which Louisville was also a charter member — was founded in November of 1881 in a Pittsburgh saloon. (Along this line, it should be remembered that many an American political candidate — including a number of American Presidents — have been chosen in the proverbial crowded, smoke-filled backrooms.)

What exact part, if any, that Gatto played in the Louisville/National League story may never be known. Documented beyond question, however, are all the other aspects of Gatto's mighty baseball life, a colorful page rather than a fleeting footnote in Louisville's fabled major–league history.

Thus, it is only right and fitting that such a baseball man get recognition worthy of his deeds and lifelong support of the game. Therefore, justice has now been served for one Mr. Larry Gatto, one of Louisville's many big–time baseball giants of yesteryear.

THE FIRST NATIONAL LEAGUE YEARS: 1876-1877

*L*ouisville's first stint in the National League lasted but two years, 1876 and 1877, before being terminated by the pennant-throwing scandal of 1877. It was a tough pill to swallow for the proud baseball city, a charter member and co-founder of the league.

From the get–go, there were problems, however, since the seeds of the game's first great scandal actually had been sown in the 1876 season.

The winner of the inaugural National League flag was the game's first great dynasty — Chicago. After a brief hiatus, a revised Chicago squad came back in the 1880s behind an array of stars like Cap Anson, George Gore, Billy Sunday, King Kelly, Larry Corcoran, John Clarkson, Jim McCormick and an infield called "The Stone Wall" (that included Louisville native Fred Pfeffer), and in the space of seven years, churned out five flags.

A fearsome power that first National League season, Chicago had the league's champion pitcher (Albert Spalding); four of the circuit's top five batsmen, including titlist Ross Barnes; and Anson, who would become the first player to log 3,000 career hits. They clinched the flag on September 26 and went on to win the flag by six games. An unimpressive fifth was Louisville, whose season that year ended on October 5 with an 11-2 loss to Hartford at home. (The batboy on that year's team, reportedly, was one John McCloskey, who is profiled — as is the 1876 National League Louisville Grays club — in Chapter 2.)

Though no one certainly was going to deny Chicago that season, Louisville might have done better had it not been for a meaningless player who was a harbinger of vile things to come.

His name was George Bechtel, and in late June, following an investigation of several questionable games, Louisville officials gave Bechtel the option of resigning or being expelled. He adamantly denied any wrongdoing and chose to fight it out.

Certainly, the contests in question had no bearing on the pennant race. Nonetheless, at stake was one of

the cardinal principles behind Hulbert's establishment of the new league—unimpeachable honesty on the parts of all concerned. After all, this was the National League, not the National Association (Bechtel's old stomping grounds, where thievery was the rule, not the exception).

As time would quickly prove, however, the Bechtel incident was merely a prelude to the game's first great scandal, the 1877 National League pennant-throwing scandal.

In late August, Louisville appeared to be a lock to take the National League flag, then went into a tailspin. Chief competitor Boston took full advantage of the situation, their comeback work highlighted by a torrid win streak in the final weeks of the season. Taking over

Cap Anson *(University of Louisville Photographic Archives)*

first place in early September, they clinched the loop's second flag in late September and by season's end, stood as the National League champion by a mammoth margin of seven games.

(One of Louisville's losses during that period, incidentally, was a 1–0 defeat at the hands of Cincinnati hurler Bobby Mitchell, the first southpaw to pitch in the National League. The winning margin was provided by teammate Lipman Pike, described as the first star Jewish ballplayer in the National League, who homered.)

Although the sudden collapse was initially attributed to poor hitting and star pitcher Jimmy Devlin's bout with boils, Louisville officials didn't buy it. Piece by piece, they put the puzzle together, the main block being telegrams that contained the code word "sash" (indicating that a game would be thrown).

The upshot was that at the end of October, the club announced the suspensions of pitcher Jimmy Devlin, left fielder George Hall, utility player Al Nichols and shortstop Bill Craver. (Devlin's part in the fix had a chilling aura since his name had cropped up during the Bechtel investigation the year before. The Louisville club, however, had completely exonerated Devlin of any wrongdoing.)

The team's action was followed by a more grievous penalty some five weeks later. At a National League meeting on December 4, 1877, the circuit banned the quartet — as well as Bechtel — from the game for life.

✎

"Indeed, if there was a centerpiece of the Louisville team in those years, it was Delvin, who literally was their only pitcher both seasons."

✎

The ramifications of the bans were felt the following year on March 7 when the Louisville directors voted not to field a team for the 1878 season, in their words "being unable to secure a team sufficiently strong to cope with the other nines."

The resignation was accepted by the league on April 2, but that was a sham since Louisville had not been included on the league's 1878 schedule, which had been released earlier.

Certainly, the 1877 scandal was a gut-wrenching affair for Walter N. Haldeman — one of the city's most prominent citizens — in more ways than one.

Publisher of the renowned Louisville Courier-Journal and president of the National League Louisville Baseball Club, he had been encouraged by his son, John Avery Haldeman, to give more space in the newspaper to baseball. (This was not strictly partisanship. The 1877 Louisville Grays, buoyed by the additions of such players as Hall, Craver, first baseman Juice Latham, center fielder Bill Crowley and right fielder Orator Shaffer, sported a new look that made it—in the eyes of many—a major contender for the flag.)

And ironically, it was the younger Haldeman — briefly a member of the 1877 Louisville National League outfit — who broke the story of the scandal.

Jimmy Devlin (The Louisville Redbirds Baseball Club)

Nichols was no great loss. A utility infielder who batted .211, he had a history of association with gamblers. He later defied his ban by playing some minor-league baseball, then faded into obscurity. The other three, however, were an entirely different matter.

Craver was a quality shortstop who batted .265. The only mark against the 33-year-old player was his age.

The losses of Hall and Devlin were the most devastating. Both were 28, in the prime of their careers, and in their respective entities, genuine stars with bright futures.

The runner-up in the 1876 inaugural National League batting race with a .366 average, Hall had led the neophyte league that year in home runs. His 1876 work also included runner-up positions in total bases, slugging average and triples. The kind of sterling power hitter that is the lifeblood of a successful team, the British native came back in 1877 to rank among the league leaders with a .323 average.

Devlin was no less a great one.

Indeed, if there was a centerpiece of the Louisville team in those years, it was Devlin, who was a one-man staff both seasons, that mammoth work a reflection of the early years of the game.

A 30-game winner with Louisville both years he pitched for them (30–35 off Louisville's 69 game schedule in 1876 and 35–25 off Louisville's 61 game schedule in 1877), Devlin also led the team in hitting in 1876 with a .315 average. That year, he also topped the league in games pitched (68, that total including three ties), complete games (66), strikeouts (122) and innings pitched (a gargantuan 622). In addition, he finished second in the ERA race (1.56) and he was fourth in wins (30).

Regarding the 1876 season, Devlin might have done better had he not lost a major–league record 14 shutouts (he was 5–14 in such contests). And for the record, Devlin still holds the major–league mark for most losses in a season by a rookie pitcher.

The next year, in 1877, Devlin again led the National League in games pitched (61, including one tie), complete games (61) and innings pitched (559).

He also finished second in wins (35), win percentage (.583) and strikeouts (141), and his 2.25 ERA was the third-highest in the league.

The last years of Devlin, a man who literally threw away a fabulous pitching career, were perhaps the most anguished and pathetic of the scorned quartet. Following the ban, Devlin made numerous pleas for reinstatement. He was denied it every time. Devlin returned to his native Philadelphia, where oddly enough, he became a policeman. He died there in 1883 of tuberculosis. He was 34.

❦

The 1877 flag-pitching fiasco was a startling contrast to the elegant home of the 1876 and 1877 Louisville National League club, a ballpark which had been modelled after the handsome Hartford Ball Club Grounds.

During its two decades in the major leagues, Louisville used three ballparks. In a sidebar note that is reflective of Louisville's bizarre major-league history, all three of them were either catastrophically damaged or destroyed.

Louisville's first two major-league teams (the 1876 and 1877 squads) played at a ballpark located at St. James Court. Later, that area served as the site of the 1883 Southern Exposition. Opened by President Chester A. Arthur on August 1, 1883, the fabulously successful exposition ran through 1887.

A palatial mansion district since the 1890s, St. James Court today is one of the finest examples extant of Victorian architecture.

Known as Louisville Baseball Park as well as St. James Court, the ballpark was located just a few blocks south of downtown Louisville. Its boundaries were Magnolia, Fourth, Hill and Sixth Streets (home plate was at the intersection of Fourth and Hill).

In mid-April of 1876, the ballpark's grandstand was heavily damaged by a tornado. The violent storm, however, did not delay the season opener and the city's major-league debut.

That took place, as scheduled, on April 25, 1876, with Louisville losing 4-0 to Chicago — the inaugural National League champion. The loss was the first shutout in National League history. Just over a week later, on May 3, Louisville posted its first major-league victory, crushing St. Louis 11-0 at home.

Eclipse Park, Louisville's second big-league ballpark, was used by the city during its entire American Association membership (1882-1891) and briefly during its second National League stint. Located at 28th and Elliott on the city's west side, it was destroyed by fire in late September 1892.

The city's third and last ballpark, also called Eclipse Park, was located at 28th and Broadway, across the street from the original Eclipse Park. Used by Louisville during the bulk of its second National League tenure (1892-1899), it too fell victim to a fire, the blaze occurring — ironically enough — during Louisville's last major-league season.

Like the two before it, Louisville's last major-league ballpark disaster was a direct product of the wooden style that characterized the game's early sporting edifices. The cost of the conflagration was enormous. Because of the fire, the Louisville club was forced to play the last six weeks of its final major-league campaign on the road.

Though long gone with the ages, the second Eclipse Park (also known as League Park) is historically significant. It was there that the last major-league game in Louisville, indeed in Kentucky, was played. The date was September 2, 1899, and Louisville hammered Washington 25-4.

For the record, Louisville was officially known as the "Louisvilles" during all but two years of its big-top membership. The exceptions were the 1882 and 1883 seasons, when the franchise was known as the Louisville Eclipse, retaining the name of the city's crack semi-pro club that reigned supreme in the city before Louisville became a member of the American Association. (Most likely, the name was a reference to a famous 18th-century racehorse and sire.)

Frequently referred to as the "Falls City" team, Louisville had a host of nicknames during its major-league years, the most popular of which was the "Colonels."

Other nicknames included the "Grays" (1876 and 1877), believed to be a reference to the gray uniforms the South had worn during the Civil War; the "Cyclones", after a violent windstorm that cut up the city in 1890, the year Louisville captured its only major-league pennant; the "Night Riders", a reference to Kentucky's tobacco wars of the 1890s (during that time, tobacco companies gave unusually low prices for tobacco; some farmers struck back at the big tobacco interests, their battles including "night raids" against fellow tobacco farmers who went along with the pricing system of the tobacco companies); and the "Wanderers", in 1899, when the team spent the last month and a half of the city's final major-league season on the road after fire destroyed the city's ballpark.

❧

Louisville's position as a great American city — and by extension, a major-league baseball town — was the product of sound geography.

Founded in 1778, it was named Louisville the following year in honor of Louis XVI, the French king who had aided the cause of the American colonies during the Revolutionary War. (Granted "city" status by the Kentucky Legislature in 1828, it became Kentucky's largest city two years later, and remains so today.)

Located on the Ohio River, just above the point where that river pours into the Mississippi, Louisville was originally a frontier settlement. Its growth was directly related to westward expansion (due to the Ohio River, a major conveyor of people and goods.)

The first big break for Louisville was the Louisiana Purchase of 1803. That freed navigation to the sea (the lower Mississippi and New Orleans), a major shipping lane which had been previously held by the Spanish. That in turn made Louisville a vital link in the shipping of goods between the deep South and the big cities of the North.

That was firmly realized in 1830 with the construction of the Portland Canal, opening the way for free and unrestricted traffic from Pittsburgh to New Orleans (prior to that, boats had disembarked in Louisville, then re-entered the Ohio River below the Falls of the Ohio). As a result, Louisville was transformed from a frontier outpost to a booming river town which was an essential port city along the heavily-trafficked Ohio River.

The city grew substantially more with the advent of railroads in the mid-1800s. That form of transportation changed the face of the country, sparking a slow shift of the nation's major transportation mode from water to land. Goods could be transported much more quickly and directly via railroads, and Louisville was a part of it all via the L&N (Louisville & Nashville) Railroad, founded in 1850 so that Louisville could maintain its mercantile economy.

A logical consequence of this commerce was growth, and at one time, Louisville ranked as one of America's biggest cities. This, of course, helped its cultural and sporting growth. By the end of the 19th century, though, Louisville had levelled out, bypassed by such cities as Cincinnati (a major competitor for southern trade and at one time the pork capital of the world); Chicago, still the railroad crossroads of America, and at one time a major venue for stockyards and steel mills; Pittsburgh, an industrial giant nicknamed "Iron City"; and St. Louis, yet another mid–America mecca via its location at the doorsteps of the Missouri and Mississippi Rivers.

THE AMERICAN ASSOCIATION YEARS: 1882-1891

*I*f a person was looking for a simple, definitive reason why Louisville did so poorly in its 20 years of major-league play (they had only six winning seasons), the answer would be "dynasty."

In 1876, its first major-league season, Louisville ran straight into a Chicago club that would be a few years later — with a substantially different cast — the game's first dynasty, winning five National League flags in the span of seven years (1880–81–82–85–86). Its outstanding members during those years included Hall–of–Famers Cap Anson, John Clarkson and King Kelly, as well as such stalwarts as George Gore, Fred Pfeffer, Larry Corcoran, Jim McCormick, Ned Williamson, Tommy Burns and Abner Dalrymple.

In 1882, Louisville rejoined the majors via another charter membership — this time in the colorful American Association. Over the span of its 10-year operation (1882-1891), that loop would be governed by the game's second great dynasty.

That was the St. Louis Browns, who during the American Association's existence, picked off four straight pennants (1885-1888); finished second three times and ran third once.

Transferring back to the National League in 1892 after the collapse of the American Association, Louisville found itself at the hands and mercy of not one, but two dynasties, who, during Louisville's last eight years in the majors, took the National League flag seven times. Those were the Boston Beaneaters (1892-1893 and 1897-1898) and the Baltimore Orioles (1894-1896).

This, of course, is an oversimplification.

Every other team in those same leagues faced the same predicament. Still, it gives one an idea of the competition Louisville faced. It allowed no room — absolutely no margin — for error.

In short, one had to be at its best to compete, and Louisville — a marginal franchise all those years —

1886 Chicago National League Championship Team (National Baseball Library and Archive, Cooperstown, NY)

had no chance. Its mercurial ability to lose was exceeded only by the number of different ways it found to rip apart the franchise. The examples abound.

There was the 1877 scandal, predicated on Louisville's misfortune to find the most talented pitcher in the league, who also happened to be one of the league's most dishonest players.

There was Louisville's uncanny ability to trade away high-quality players like Icebox Chamberlain and Patsy Donovan, to name but a few.

It knew nothing about the concept of balanced pitching, as witness the 52–win season of Guy Hecker in 1884. It was a wonderful piece of work, but Hecker was never the same pitcher again. That might have been different had the other three Louisville pitchers contributed more than 16 wins.

And then there was the case of having their major-league franchise run by people like Mordecai Davidson; and finding a way to lose despite the presence of megastars, such as the 1884 squad did with Hecker, Browning and Wolf, and the 1897-1899 squads, which included Hall-of-Famers Fred Clarke and Honus Wagner. All things considered, it's amazing that Louisville even won one major-league pennant.

The one consolation was that Louisville had a lot of company during those years, teams that suffered likewise at the hands of those dynasties.

The 1882 season was exciting and glamorous if for no other reason than the fact that major–league baseball had returned to Louisville after an absence of four years.

Rookie Pete Browning got the American Association batting title (.378), Tony Mullane had a wonderful one–time run (30–24) with the club, and the club got on–the–road no–hitters from Mullane and budding star Guy Hecker within about a week of each other (Mullane no–hitting Cincinnati 2–0 on September 11, Hecker no–hitting Pittsburgh 3–1 on September 19). In the end, though, Cincinnati prevailed by 11 1/2 games over Philadelphia to take the American Association's first flag.

The playing leader of the Cincinnati ship, ironi-

1888 St. Louis Browns American Association Championship Team (National Baseball Library and Archive, Cooperstown, NY)

cally, was former Louisville Grays player, Charles "Pop" Snyder, a catcher on the 1876 and 1877 Louisville squads. And, as the winning margin suggested, they were done with their season pretty early.

On September 18, the Louisville Courier–Journal said that the Cincinnatis were "the crowned champions beyond the peradventure of a doubt". That was a $50 way of saying they had blown the competition out of the water. Louisville, who closed its season on October 1, ran in the middle of the pack (third in the six–team league).

The following year was the exact opposite, as the American Association race was as close as a razor, Philadelphia winning by one game over St. Louis (with a 66–32 record to a 65–33 mark).

Though Louisville wound up fifth in the eight–team league, it nonetheless had a say in who the champion was — Philadelphia or St. Louis.

The traditional account has it that a wild pitch by Guy Hecker in a critical late–season contest versus the Athletics gave Philadelphia the American Association flag.

This is true, but only in a general sense. The specifics are much more complicated.

Louisville played their last four games of the season at home against Philadelphia, who needed only one victory in that series to take the American Association pennant. Few, including the Louisville Courier–Journal, expected a sweep by the Eclipse.

Louisville almost pulled it off, though, taking the first two games 7–5 and 6–3 via Sam Weaver and Hecker respectively, and the series finale 10–5 courtesy of Hecker.

This was remarkable work from the sore–armed pair, two of the three bright spots for Louisville that year (Pete Browning was the other with a .338 batting average). Hecker was the staff ace that year with a 28–25 slate; Weaver was the other major gun with a 24–20 ledger that constituted the balance of Louisville's 52–45 mark in 1883.

The fly in the ointment, however, was the third game, which the Athletics won 7–6 in 10 innings. The winning tally was posted by Harry Stovey, though it was not via a wild pitch off Hecker (whose sheer guts carried him through this crucial four–game set with Philadelphia.)

In fact, Stovey walked, took second on a wild pitch by Hecker, advanced to third on Lon Knight's single to left, then came home with the pennant–clinching run when Mike Moynahan singled to left center.

As for the other part of the story, the facts are in line.

The loss was a bitter and costly defeat, because — so the story goes — St. Louis Browns owner Chris von der Ahe had promised each Louisville member a new suit if they beat the Athletics. So angry were Louisville players over that loss that six years later, in 1889, when Hecker sought the managership of the Louisville club, he was emphatically denied it.

This is amazing when you consider the extraordinary Louisville career of Hecker, still today the only pitcher ever to lead a major–league circuit in both wins and batting average.

But there you have it. Petty revenge knows no boundaries.

The 1884 campaign was a topsy–turvy one for Louisville. In early June, they tied New York for the lead. A month later, they slipped by New York into the first place slot. Several weeks later, they yielded it to Columbus. In late September, Louisville moved up to second, but a week later fell back to third, where they stayed for the rest of the season.

That they finished no better than they did, with a 52–game winner (pitching Triple Crown winner Guy Hecker) and a .336 slugger (Pete Browning) leading the way, identified the team's true character and problems. It was, in essence, a two–man club with a one–man pitching staff. Their 68–40 slate (and a .630 win percentage that was exceeded only by their .667 pennant work of 1890 off an 88–44 tabsheet) was good enough for show money in a 13–team loop. Incidentally, they were managed by Mike Walsh, who the year before had been an American Association umpire.

The champion was New York, who took the flag by 6 1/2 games over Columbus behind the sterling work of first–baseman Davey Orr and pitchers Tim

Keefe and Jack Lynch. Though no one knew it at the time, it would be a while before a team other than the St. Louis Browns would wear the American Association crown.

Of worthy note that season was Louisville's May 1 opener at home, which saw them beat Toledo 5–1. That game marked the career debut of catcher Moses Fleetwood "Fleet" Walker, generally acknowleged as the first black major–league ballplayer (his brother, outfielder Welday Wilberforce "Weldy" Walker, became the second later that season).

Walker's big–show entrance was anything but memorable as he went zero–for–three and made all four of his team's errors in the defeat. Still, it was better than an August 21, 1881, game in Louisville between the Eclipse and the White Sewing Machine Company (of Cleveland) when Walker was not allowed to play. The action was decried in numerous quarters, by the Louisville Courier–Journal, the fans and even a Louisville baseball executive. Stripped of their best player, they lost 6–3.

The Walker brothers — who had starred on their baseball team at Oberlin — are epic figures in baseball history. After the 1884 season, no blacks played major–league baseball again until 1947, when Jackie Robinson re–integrated baseball.

It is interesting to note Kentucky's strong connections with both these black pioneers: Fleet Walker, for the aforementioned reason, and Robinson, via Kentucky native/Dodger teammate/future Hall–of–Famer Pee Wee Reese, who did so much to ease Robinson's transition into

1892 Boston National League Championship Team
(National Baseball Library and Archive, Cooperstown, NY)

1894 Baltimore Orioles National League Championship Team
(University of Louisville Photographic Archives)

pro ball. (Moreover, Robinson's entrance into the big show was affected by another Kentuckian and another future Hall–of–Famer, then–Baseball Commissioner Albert Benjamin "Happy" Chandler.)

While Fleet Walker lasted only one season (as did his brother), he nonetheless was a high–class player. He batted .263 that year, 23 points higher than the league average. And, the backup catcher on that Toledo team that season was none other than Deacon McGuire, a rookie

Albert Benjamin "Happy" Chandler
(University of Kentucky King Library, Special Collections and Archives)

Moses Walker (middle, far left) and brother Welday Walker (rear, second from right), members of the 1881 Oberlin College baseball team. (National Baseball Library and Archive, Cooperstown, NY)

The 1885 season was over before it began. Led by the bone–crushing pitching of Bob Caruthers (40–13) and Dave Foutz (33–14), the St. Louis Browns took the American Association lead for good on May 7 and cruised to the flag by 16 games over Cincinnati.

It was a joke, but not to teams like Louisville, who closed their season on October 1. They tumbled to a 53–59 slate (.473), work that earned them a fifth–place tie in the revamped eight–team loop. Its major performers were Pete Browning, who took his second American Association batting crown with a .362 mark, and Guy Hecker, who reeled off a 30–23 mound tab.

The 1886 race was a little closer, but the end result was still the same, as the Browns took the American Association flag, this time by 12 games over Pittsburgh (for the record, their winning margins during their skein of four straight AA pennants from 1885 through 1888 were 16, 12, 14 and 6 1/2 games respectively). So easy was the Browns' second successive American Association flag that von der Ahe began negotiating in early September for a return World Series bout with the Chicago White Stockings, a fellow dynasty who themselves were headed for a repeat in the National League.

As for Louisville, it had three bright spots — Guy Hecker, Pete Browning and Toad Ramsey, but the latter two were impaired ballplayers whose major–league careers were inordinately compromised by alcoholism.

who went on to spend a record 26 years in the majors (the standard is now 27, held by Nolan Ryan.)

The highly-regarded but lowly-treated Walker, by the way, was the subject of a small poem that went:

> *There is a catcher named Walker,*
> *Who behind the bat is a corker.*
> *He throws to a base,*
> *With ease and grace,*
> *And steals 'round the bag like a stalker.*

Harold "Pee Wee" Reese
(University of Louisville Photographic Archives)

Jackie Robinson
(University of Louisville Photographic Archives)

Ed Brown
(Keeneland Library)

Toad Ramsey
(National Baseball Library and Archive, Cooperstown, NY)

Hecker, the only pitcher ever to win a major–league batting title, took the 1886 American Association title with a .341 average (and went 26-23 on the mound). One of his brighter days during the 1886 season was a six–for–seven performance that established a major–league mark for runs scored in a game. By the time the versatile Hecker completed his career, he would own major–league pitching, hitting and fielding marks (see Guy Hecker profile in Chapter 4).

Browning contributed a .340 batting average and Ramsey was the ace with a blazing 38–27 mound slate that included 499 strikeouts. However, the numbers could have been even better for this pair of chronic drunks, whose wild habits did nothing to help a team that finished four games under the .500 mark.

The 1887 season was another monster one for St. Louis, who by early September had amassed a lead of nearly 20 games. They wound up taking their third

Pete Browning (University of Louisville Photographic Archives)

Isaac Murphy (third from right) at 1892 clambake in upstate New York. (Keeneland Library)

Elton P. "Icebox" Chamberlain
(National Baseball Library and Archive, Cooperstown, NY)

straight American Association flag by a 14–game margin over Cincinnati.

Led by Pete Browning (who batted a career–best .402, but *still* did not win the batting title) and Toad Ramsey, who went 37–27 and polished off a league–leading 355 strikeouts, Louisville finished fourth in the eight–team league with a 76–60 mark (.559).

Another member of that team was rookie Lafayette Napoleon "Lave" Cross, who wrapped up his 21–year career in 1907 with a career .297 batting average and over 2,600 hits.

ᗏᗸᗩ

Also on the scene that year in Louisville was another major–league club, the Louisville Falls Citys. They were the town's entry in the short–lived National Colored Base Ball League. This country's second black big–top circuit, it opened in early May and was done before the end of that month. (For the record, the first black American major–league circuit — the Southern League of Colored Base Ballists — lasted some-

what longer, opening in June 1886 and holding on until August. These two loops were forerunners of the fabled 20th–century Negro Leagues, in which Louisville had five entries between 1930 and 1954.)

Playing their games at both Eclipse Park and their own grounds (Falls City Park at Sixteenth and Magnolia on the city's west side), the Falls Citys — one of Louisville's top clubs (formed in 1883) — were part of a circuit according to local newspaper accounts that included the Boston Resolutes, the Lord Baltimores, the New York Gorhams, the Philadelphia Pythians and the Pittsburgh Keystones.

One eye–catching ball-player for the Falls Citys was the elegantly–named Napoleon Ricks. Though he did not appear in the Saturday, May 7, 1887, opener, which the Falls Citys dropped to the Boston Resolutes 10–3, Ricks was a subsequent force in a number of games after that.

Existing boxscores show him with games of two–for–five in an 8–2 win over the New York Gorhams on Sunday, May 8, 1887; three–for–five in an exciting 12–11 loss to the Gorhams on Monday, May 9, 1887; and four–for–seven (including one triple) in a 27–9 demolition of the Gorhams on Tuesday, May 10, 1887.

Overall, that made him nine–for–17, a sizzling .529 batting average, solid indication that he could hit. When his position (shortstop, the single most impor-tant one on the defensive spectrum) is factored in, it can be safely said that here was a quite a marvelous wonder, a fine ballplayer.

Indeed, his name and his limited numbers conjure up exquisite visions of a slick ballplayer, possessed of magical hands that could turn a double play as easily as they could slap out a single.

It is our loss — an egregious loss — that we do not know him better today.

At this point, it should be noted that Ricks was one more shining example in Louisville's extraordinary black sporting history.

A stellar example is the world–famed Kentucky Derby, long the world's most coveted Thoroughbred classic, which in its early years was virtually owned by black reinsmen. Indeed, 15 of the first 28 Derbies (1875–1902) were won by black jockeys.

That contingent includes the inaugural 1875 Kentucky Derby (Oliver Lewis), plus the stellar trio of Isaac Murphy, Willie Simms and Jimmy Winkfield.

The first man to win three Kentucky Derbies (1884, 1890 and 1891), a record not broken until 1948 by the peerless Eddie Arcaro, Isaac Murphy was America's first, great black athlete. His work in the Louisville–hosted Kentucky Derby also includes the honor of being the first rider ever to take successive editions of the Kentucky Derby.

Like Murphy, Simms is also a member of the Hall of Fame. A man who won both Derbies in which he rode (1896 and 1898), Simms is known today also as the man who introduced the crouched style of riding to the British turf. Winkfield, the second man to take back–to–back Kentucky Derbies (1901 and 1902), had an extraordinary career that included race-work in Russia and Europe. It also saw him escape from the Bolsheviks in World War I and the Nazis in World War II.

And, the Kentucky Derby history book carries the name of five black trainers — all in the 19th century, who saddled Derby victors. The most prominent, unquestionably, was Ed Brown — like Murphy and Simms a member of the National Racing Hall of Fame.

❧❧

In 1888, the St. Louis Browns garnered their fourth straight American Association flag, finishing 6 1/2 games in front of runner-up Brooklyn.

What made this pennant so remarkable, however, was the fact that the Browns dynasty continued despite the jettisoning of star pitchers Bob Caruthers and Dave Foutz. Angered by the 1887 World Series loss to the Detroit Wolverines, the eccentric von der Ahe had dispatched the pair to Brooklyn.

Normally, when one sells off a duo that has won 198 games for you in three years — every one of those years bringing you a flag — you pay for it. Not in von der Ahe's case, whose trio of Silver King, Nat Hudson and Icebox Chamberlain (sold to him courtesy of Louisville) picked up where the old duo had left off.

Zack Phelps (The Filson Club, Louisville, KY)

Louisville went in the opposite direction, landing next–to–last in the eight–club circuit with a 48–87 (.356) mark that was a sign of even worse things to happen.

The team leaders were pitcher Icebox Chamberlain (14–9) and Pete Browning, whose .313 average would have been much bigger had it not been for repeated drunkeness and several suspensions.

The reign of the St. Louis Browns finally ended in 1889. In early September, they yielded the lead to Brooklyn, who went on to win the American Association flag by two games over St. Louis. Helping to deny St. Louis their fifth straight American Association pennant were a pair of familiar figures — Bob Caruthers (40–11) and Dave Foutz (.277 batting average).

At the opposite end of the spectrum, wildly so, was Louisville, who struggled through its worst major–league season ever, posting a 27–111 record (and a wretched .196 win percentage). Part of that ledger included a 26–game losing streak (May 22-June 22) that still stands as a major–league record.

The team leaders gave evidence of how bad the situation was. The top pitcher was Red Ehret with a 10–29 mark; Farmer Weaver and Chicken Wolf led the Louisville offense with .291 batting averages.

Weaver's and Wolf's numbers, however, were far ahead of the average of Pete Browning, who batted .256 for the season (he was suspended for the final two months). It was both a career low and the first sub–.300 mark for Browning.

It was even worse for pitcher John Ewing, a brother of future Hall–of–Fame catcher Buck Ewing, who posted a horrendous 6–30 mark.

That season also marked the debut of one of the game's greatest–hitting pitchers, Jack Stivetts, who significantly enough, got the first win and first hit of his major–league career in a 12–7 win over Louisville on June 30, 1889. When he concluded his 11–year career in 1899, he exited the game with a 204–131 pitching slate, a .297 batting average, and membership on four Boston National League championship squads (1892–93–97–98).

The next season was even more unbelievable.

A three–league war diluted the quality of both the National League and the American Association, as the newly–formed Players' League drew a substantial amount of its major talent from the two older circuits.

As a result, Louisville won the American Association flag. In the process, they also became the first team in major–league history to vault from last to first in the space of a single season (there is something wacky about this feat; when it was duplicated 101 years later, in 1991, it involved not one, but *two* teams).

The only major–league flag of their 20–year big–top existence, Louisville got it courtesy of Chicken Wolf, the American Association batting champion that year with a .363 average, and a pair of top–notch pitchers in Scott Stratton (34–14 and a record 16–game win streak) and Red Ehret (25–14).

Led by this trio, Louisville rolled up an 88–44 record, a mark greatly aided by a blistering 35–8 run during the months of July and August. (The 1890 season, though, proved to be an optical illusion, as it turned out to be the only winning season that Louisville had during the 1890s.)

In the 1890 World Series, Louisville met National League titlist Brooklyn, whom they gallantly played to a seven–game standoff (each team registered three wins, three defeats and one tie) before horrible weather terminated the series.

⚜

Of worthy note at this juncture is the name of Zack Phelps, the American Association president during Louisville's 1890 flag–winning season and another "lost" Louisville baseball giant in the vein of Larry Gatto and John McCloskey.

Born in Hopkinsville, Ky., on July 17, 1857, Phelps came to Louisville at an early age with his parents. A brilliant student, Phelps was determined to become a lawyer.

However, his studiousness and drive — according to a Courier–Journal article the day after his death — forced him to relocate to Salt Lake City, Utah, for reasons of health. After two years of reading law, he was granted a diploma, and in 1880 — his health renewed by his protracted tenure in the West — Phelps returned to Louisville to practice.

On January 1, 1881, Phelps formed a law partnership with a Judge William Jackson. On the same day, he was married to Miss Amy Kaye. Phelps was fond of saying in years afterward that that day was the beginning of two grand partnerships — one with a graceful lady for life, the other with a good business friend that lasted until Jackson's death.

A highly successful criminal lawyer, Phelps had upwards of 300 cases on the docket at the time of his untimely demise. A man who numbered friends in all walks of life (upon learning of his death, minstrel Al G. Field left the stage of Macauley's Theatre and declined to go on during the remainder of the evening program), Phelps was busy also in many other ways, as one might expect one of the town's most distinguished citizens to be.

He was a member of several fraternal groups, and he was closely identified with several city charities. Phelps also was an ardent Democrat, who espoused the

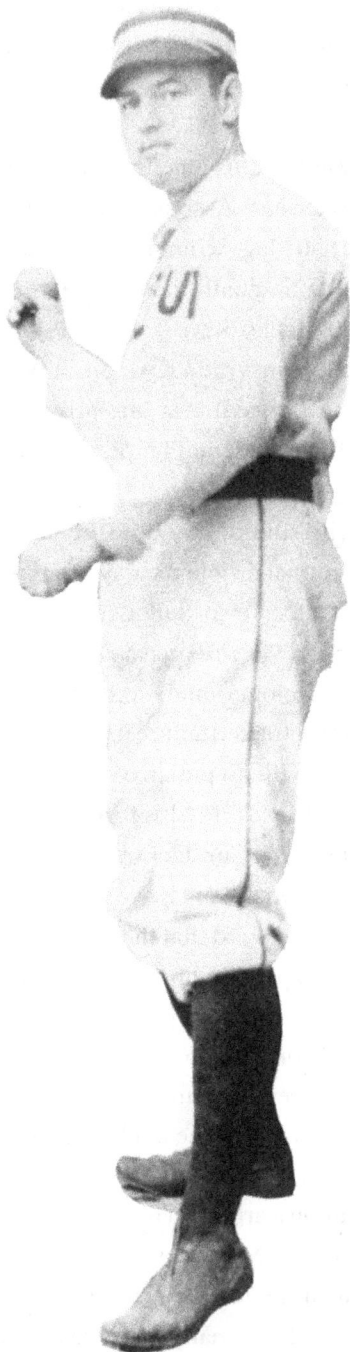

Tip O'Neill
(National Baseball Library and Archive, Cooperstown, NY)

causes of a number of political figures. Unquestionably, the most prominent was the ill–fated William Goebbel (the only Governor–elect ever assassinated in this country, Goebbel was shot down on January 30, 1900 by an unknown assailant outside the Kentucky statehouse).

Phelps' baseball resumé was something, too. From 1885 through 1887, he was the president of the Louisville American Association club. That tenure included some celebrated run–ins with the hard–hitting and hard–drinking Pete Browning (interestingly enough, Phelps' grave in historic Cave Hill Cemetery overlooks that of Browning's).

In 1890, Phelps served as the president of the American Association (a position he reassumed late in the 1891 season as the loop began its trek into oblivion). One of the best–known baseball men in the country, he was also an attorney for the National League for a number of years.

Pneumonia claimed Phelps on August 29, 1901, after a 16-day siege, and his passing marked the exit of one of Louisville's and baseball's greatest patrons. Phelps is buried on a lot owned by his wife's family (sadly enough, his widow — Amy Kaye Phelps — followed her husband to the grave some 10 weeks later).

Zack Phelps' final resting place is a white marble cross over a granite circle with an inlaid ivy bed; his name, lifedates and an inscription are in raised letters.

The inscription reads: "One who loved his fellow men."

It is a worthy epitaph to be sure, yet as is the case all too often with summations for fine, productive men, it is an understatement.

❧

In their final season in the American Association (which folded up after the 1891 campaign), Louisville finished next-to-last in the nine–team league. At the top of the heap was Boston, who took the concluding American Association flag by 8 1/2 games over St. Louis.

The latter was nothing short of one of the greatest clubs ever seen in major–league history.

In 10 years of American Association membership, St. Louis rolled off four straight pennants (1885-1888), a trio of seconds and a third, and turned out such stellar players as Charlie Comiskey (a future Hall–of–Famer), Bob Caruthers, Dave Foutz, Curt Welch, Silver King, Tip O'Neill, Arlie Latham, Nat Hudson, and Tommy McCarthy (another future Hall–of–Famer).

Louisville did not have much to show for the 1891 season. One standout was Patsy Donovan, a .321 hitter (and star for Brooklyn versus Louisville in 1890 World Series) who was released in September 1891 for both physical (an injured leg) and personal reasons (he was accused of criticizing Manager John Chapman).

It proved to be one more extraordinary mistake by Louisville management as Donovan went on to post big numbers while in the bigs (a .300 batting average, over 2,200 hits and 518 stolen bases during a 17–year career that ran through 1907).

Another top member of Louisville's last American Association squad was future Hall–of–Famer Hughie Jennings, a shortstop on the National League dynasty Oriole teams (1894–95–96) and later the manager of the Detroit Tigers (1907–1920), where he took American League flags in his first three seasons.

Overall, the 10–year American Association membership proved to be the most productive years of Louisville's major–league existence, as they got five winning seasons and one pennant (which included their only trip to the World Series). In addition, Louisville also turned out four batting titlists (Pete Browning had two crowns, Guy Hecker and Chicken Wolf got one each) and one Triple Crown champion pitcher (Hecker).

It made no difference, though. The end was near for the volatile franchise. Indeed, by the time the 1890s concluded, Louisville was a major–league ghost town.

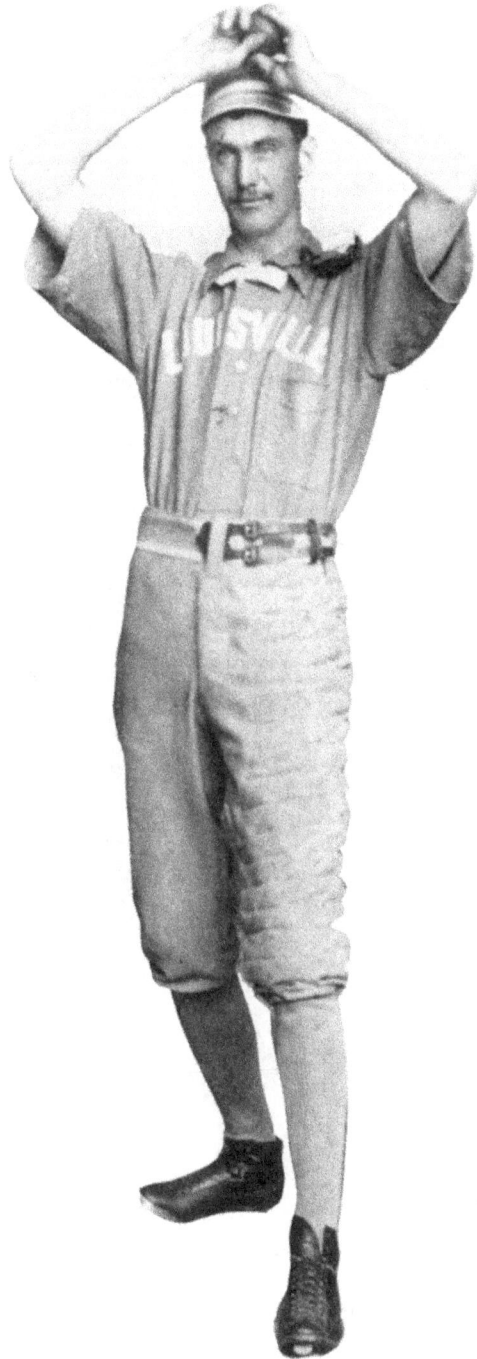

John Ewing
(National Baseball Library and Archive, Cooperstown, NY)

William Van Winkle "Chicken" Wolf
(National Baseball Library and Archive, Cooperstown, NY)

Guy Hecker
(National Baseball Library and Archive, Cooperstown, NY)

THE SECOND NATIONAL LEAGUE YEARS: 1892-1899

*L*ouisville's final eight years in the big show (1892–1899) — their second National League stint — were the worst of their major–league history.

Three times they finished in the cellar, twice next–to–last, and never higher than ninth in the re–organized National League, which expanded following the collapse of the American Association after the 1891 season. (The lone saving grace for Louisville baseball during that timeframe was the glittering cast of stars — fading and future — seen on its stage during that time.)

The competition was fierce . . . and with good reason.

Two dynasties so completely ruled the National League grounds during that period that they took seven of eight flags (the 1899 Brooklyns captured the other one).

The first dynasty were the Frank Selee–managed Bostons, an outfit which included Kid Nichols, Hugh Duffy, Tommy McCarthy — all future Hall–of–Famers — and Bobby Lowe. They copped the 1892 and 1893 National League flags.

The former was a split–season format, and Boston — the first–half victors — beat second–half winner Cleveland in the ensuing series. The following year, Boston bested runner-up Pittsburgh by five games.

Though powerless in the face of such a giant, Louisville still had some bright spots both seasons. The 1892 assemblage included Louisville native Fred Pfeffer, one of the two great second–basemen of the pre–modern era (see Chapter 6) and sure–armed outfielder Tom Brown (a solid batter and superb base stealer whose only shortcoming was striking out).

Team leaders included Scott Stratton (21–19) and

Deacon Phillippe
(National Baseball Library and Archive, Cooperstown, NY)

Honus Wagner
(University of Louisville Photographic Archives)

Willie Keeler *(University of Louisville Photographic Archives)*

Curt Welch
(National Baseball Library and Archive, Cooperstown, N.Y.)

Jimmy Collins
(National Baseball Library and Archive, Cooperstown, NY)

Fred Clarke
(National Baseball Library and Archive, Cooperstown, NY)

utility man Harry Taylor (.260). Another good one was Ben Sanders, who no–hit Baltimore 6–2 at home on August 22 that season. This was the third of four Louisville big–top no–hitters (Tony Mullane and Guy Hecker were the first to do so, in 1882; rookie Deacon Phillippe was the last, no–hitting New York 7–0 at home on May 25, 1899).

Standouts on the 1893 Louisville club included pitcher George Hemming (18–17) and outfielder Willard Brown (.304). The club also included three notables — Jerry Denny, Matty Kilroy and Curt Welch — closing out their careers.

An ambidextrous third–baseman, Denny was the last position player not to wear a glove, spending his entire 13–year career (1881–1894) bare–handed.

Kilroy had a worksheet that included an all–time record 513 strikeouts in 1886 as a 20–*year–old rookie* for Baltimore in the American Association.

Welch, a star outfielder on the fabulous St. Louis Browns American Association dynasty, endures today in baseball for "Welch's $15,000 Slide" (supposedly the amount of money the winners earned when Welch scored on a wild pitch in the tenth inning of the deciding game of the 1886 World Series against the Chicago White Stockings).

The next three years belonged to the last great dynasty of the pre–modern (pre–1900) era, the Baltimore Orioles, who annexed the 1894, 1895 and 1896 National League flags. Managed by Ned Hanlon (a 1996 Hall of Fame inductee), that crew included Hall–of–Famers Wee Willie Keeler, Hughie Jennings, Wilbert Robinson and John McGraw.

These were hardly glory years for Louisville, who finished last (of 12 teams) in the senior circuit all three years.

However, their 1894 team included future Hall–of–Famer and rookie Fred Clarke (see Chapter 6), the club's top batter in 1895, 1897, 1898 and 1899.

Topsy Hartsel
(National Baseball Library and Archive, Cooperstown, NY)

Dummy Hoy
(National Baseball Library and Archive, Cooperstown, NY)

And, their 1895 team included four players of note: future Hall–of–Famer Dan Brouthers, a five–time batting titlist; high-class shortstop Jack Glasscock, who called it quits after that year; Jimmy Collins, a rookie on that outfit who eventually earned Cooperstown laurels for defining the way third base should be played; and strong–armed pitcher Gus Weyhing (see Chapter 6 profile).

Of singular interest on the 1896 team was pitcher Charles Emig, whose life was as long as his big–top career was brief. Louisville's oldest surviving major–leaguer, Emig made his last pitch at age 100 in Oklahoma in 1975.

Boston returned to their National League flag–winning ways in 1897 and 1898, besting Baltimore both times, that group including old stagehands Nichols, Duffy and Lowe, plus recent additions and future Hall of Famers Billy Hamilton and Jimmy Collins.

On the Kentucky side, Hall–of–Famer Honus Wagner (see Chapter 6 profile) began his career in 1897 with Louisville, as did another Hall–of–Famer, Rube Waddell, although the two were total opposites.

Wagner was the complete professional; Waddell, a fun–loving manchild and a 191–145 lifetime hurler, drove every manager he had to despair. His tragic death in 1914 at age 37 from tuberculosis seemed to underline the lost talents of this man who loved chasing fire engines, tending bar, playing sandlot baseball with kids, and fishing as much as he did throwing a baseball.

The 1898 team included such standouts as deaf–mute Dummy Hoy, a gifted outfielder and hitter whose handicaps — according to some historians — led to the practice of umpires "calling" strikes by emphatically raising their arms in the air; future home run king Harry Davis; pitcher Nick Altrock, who enjoyed World Series suc-

Jack Glasscock
(National Baseball Library and Archive, Cooperstown, NY)

Jerry Denny
(National Baseball Library and Archive, Cooperstown, NY)

Tommy Leach
(National Baseball Library and Archive, Cooperstown, NY)

Rube Waddell
(National Baseball Library and Archive, Cooperstown, NY)

cess with "The Hitless Wonders" Chicago White Sox after the turn of the century and later become one of the game's most beloved clowns; Topsy Hartsel, a consummate leadoff man who would enjoy his greatest success with Connie Mack's pennant winners in the early 1900s; and third–baseman Tommy Leach, who very nearly became the first man to play 1,000 games at two positions — third and outfield (only three men to date have done that — Babe Ruth, Ernie Banks and Rod Carew). The team pitching leader was Bert Cunningham, with a splendid 28–15 mound ledger.

Though Louisville finished ninth in its final two major–league seasons, it was on an obvious upswing, posting .464 and .493 win–percentage marks in 1898 and 1899 respectively.

Much of that success was directly attributable to the foursome of Clarke, Wagner, Leach and pitcher Deacon Phillippe, the latter a rookie hurler with the 1899 National League Louisvilles, whose work that year included a no–hitter and a 21–17 record.

Their greatest work, however, came in the colors of the Pittsburgh Pirates, where the powerful quartet landed up when Louisville was one of four teams dropped by the National League after the 1899 season.

Under the aegis of Barney Dreyfuss (their old boss at Louisville who bought half of the Pittsburgh franchise, then wound up the sole owner of the Pirates shortly thereafter), the dynamic crew spearheaded a team that took three straight National League flags (1901–1902–1903) and one World Championship (1909).

As for Louisville, it had become a roaring minor-league town by then, its major–league years, teams and players memories of the past.

Some of those memories from Louisville's grand major–league days can be seen in the following pages.

CHAPTER TWO
LOUISVILLE'S MAJOR-LEAGUE GALLERY I:
THE FIRST NATIONAL LEAGUE YEARS, 1876-1877

*From left to right, the 1876 Louisville National League club are (**RECLINING**) George Bechtel, outfield; Johnny (John J.) Ryan, left field; (**SEATED**) John Carbine, first base and outfield; Bill Hague, third base; Chick Fulmer, shortstop; Manager John Chapman, outfield; Joe Gerhardt, first base; Art Allison, right field; (**STANDING**) Scott Hastings, center field; Jimmy Devlin, pitcher; and Charles "Pop" Snyder, catcher. (The Louisville Redbirds Baseball Club)*

THE 1876 LOUISVILLE GRAYS

*T*his is where it all began.

Glorious despite its obvious age, the opposite page gem is a photograph of the city's first major-league outfit.

Except for second-baseman Ed Somerville, who died the following October of a lung hemorrhage, all the principal players from the 1876 club, plus several reserves, are pictured.

Five players on this team are particularly noteworthy. Bechtel and Devlin were part of a quintet banished from the game for life the following year for shady playing.

Chapman, who was closing out his playing days, was embarking on a long managing career that climaxed in 1890 with the American Association flag for Louisville.

Charles "Pop" Snyder later coached the Cincinnati club which won the inaugural 1882 American Association flag.

And, Johnny Ryan — who in his lone career pitching start on July 22, 1876, threw 10 wild pitches, a major-league record that still stands today—later became a policeman. He was kicked to death in 1902 by a criminal he was attempting to arrest.

LOUISVILLE CURIOS

Both Jimmy Devlin and Bill Hague resided at the St. Cloud Hotel during the 1877 season. Young John Avery Haldeman, briefly a member of the 1877 team and the journalist who broke baseball's first scandal, lived at 289 Sixth.

JOHN MCCLOSKEY

A king without a crown, John McCloskey was a trailblazing pioneer who spent his entire life spreading the gospel of baseball throughout the country.

Though long forgotten by the game to which he gave his entire life, McCloskey produced a body of baseball work that was both magnificent and enduring.

Nicknamed "The Father of the Texas League," McCloskey either founded or helped establish numerous other minor-league operations during his life (1862-1940). Besides the Texas League, that group included the Pacific Northwest League (the forerunner of the modern-day Pacific Coast League) and the Southern League. All three endure today in powerful fashion, a sterling tribute to the baseball genius of McCloskey and his indefatigable work at the grass roots of the game.

A generous man who often used his own money to sustain struggling ballplayers, clubs and circuits, McCloskey is reputed to have established more professional baseball leagues than any other man in history of the sport.

Though he never played in the majors, McCloskey managed several big-top clubs, including his hometown's National League aggregation in the mid-1890s. It was one of nearly four dozen major- and minor-league teams (at all levels) he managed during his venerable career ,a figure believed to be a record (Additionally, one source reports he managed nearly every season between 1888 and 1932).

Possessed also of a strong eye for baseball talent, McCloskey discovered a number of fine players over the years, including Fred Clarke, Jimmy Collins, Joe Tinker, Joe "Iron Man" McGinnity, Herman Long, Red Ehret and Jack Pfiester.

Nicknamed "Honest John", McCloskey — who died on November 17, 1940 at age 78 — began his extraordinary diamond career as the batboy for the 1876 Louisville National League team. By the time he had retired in the 1930s, McCloskey had held every major position in the game — player, coach, manager, scout and executive.

Buried in Louisville's Calvary Cemetery, within sight of the final resting place of another Louisville great — pitcher Gus Weyhing, McCloskey is watched over by a two-sided marker. On the front is his name and lifedates; the reverse contains his name, nickname ("Honest John") and a mighty inscription that reads: "This tribute of grateful memory is dedicated by the youth and manhood of America, benefited by his life spent as a player, manager and league organizer of his beloved game, baseball."

It is a great epitaph for a giant of the game, a man who was truly the "Johnny Appleseed of baseball."

John McCloskey (National Baseball Library and Archive, Cooperstown, NY)

Chapter Three
PETE BROWNING:
The Original Louisville Slugger

J.F. Hillerich & Son Company, circa early 1900s. (University of Louisville Photographic Archives)

PETE BROWNING

*T*he player most synonymous with the epic American Association, the National League's heartiest 19th-century competitor, Louis Rogers "Pete" Browning was Louisville's first major-league superstar.

The first rookie to win a batting crown, Browning made his major-league debut in 1882 in the newly-formed American Association, leading that circuit with a towering .378 batting average.

His banner rookie season also included a loop-leading .510 slugging average for his native Louisville in the neophyte league, which during its brief decade-long existence (1882-1891) gave the sport a host of innovations and "firsts" including Sunday baseball; beer at the ballpark; the popularization of "Ladies Day" as a standard baseball promotion; the game's first two black major-leaguers — brothers Moses and Welday Walker; league control of umpires; the percentage system of determining pennant winners; standardized contractual procedures; and an appearance (Cincinnati versus National League Champion Chicago) in the first World Series (an aborted affair in 1882 that was terminated after one game due to the animosity of American Association president Denny McKnight).

A three-time batting champion, Browning picked up his second crown in 1885, again leading the American Association in the colors of his home town with a .362 average.

Only one of three pre-modern players (along with Ross Barnes and Hall-of-Famer Dan Brouthers) to take batting crowns in two separate leagues during the 19th century, Browning took his third and last batting title with Cleveland in 1890, when he headed the Players' League with a .373 tab.

Overall, during a spectacular 13-year career (1882-1894) spent primarily with Louisville in first the American Association and later the National League, Browning nine times either led or was ranked among the top-four hitters in his league.

His personal best was a .402 mark in 1887, which remarkably enough, ran a distant second to the .435 average of Triple Crown winner Tip O'Neill, whose work included the second-highest average ever com-

Pete Browning (The Hillerich & Bradsby Company)

John A. "Bud" Hillerich at the lathe during the 60th anniversary of the Louisville Slugger bat in 1944. (University of Louisville Photographic Archives)

an apprentice in his father's wood-turning shop to watch the game.

Hillerich offered to make a replacement for Browning, and the pair retired to the shop where Hillerich selected a length of sturdy white ash, still the most prized wood for batmaking because of its resiliency and whipping action.

Repeatedly turning it on the lathe finally produced a suitable replacement that accidentally turned out to be the first modern baseball bat, a Louisville Slugger.

The next day, so the story goes, Browning used the custom-made stick to garner three hits in a game. Browning's secret of success did not stay a mystery very long, as first members of the local club and later players from other professional teams showed up at the shop looking for similar bats.

Initially, the elder J. Frederich Hillerich wanted no part of the new fad, for his business was booming with orders for wooden butter churns, bedposts and handrails. Only begrudgingly did he allow his son Bud to continue the bat-making activity.

The bat making, however, proved to be the Hillerichs' salvation at the turn of the century when progress dried up the market for wooden butter churns. Instead of going under, the firm smoothly switched to manufacturing bats, all stamped with the trademark that had been registered in 1894, Browning's last major-league season.

On September 1, 1905, nine days before Browning died, the firm made modern endorsement-advertising history by signing a contract for its first autographed model with future Hall-of-Famer Honus Wagner (the first major-leaguer to have his name on a bat, Wagner had inaugurated his major-league career with Louisville in 1897).

piled in single-season play (Hugh Duffy's .438 ledger for the 1894 Bostons remains the all-time record).

As wild as that loss was, it paled in comparison to the battle the year before, 1886, when Browning became the only man in major-league history to ever lose a batting title to a pitcher. That came at the hands of Guy Hecker, a teammate no less, who nipped Browning .341 to .340.

Despite the freakish events that cost him a pair of batting crowns, though, Browning remains today one of the game's greatest hitters.

The possessor of the twelfth-highest lifetime batting average in the history of the game, his .341 mark also stands as the game's fifth-highest average by a right-handed stickman.

Off the field, Browning made history, too.

In 1884, he broke his favorite bat during an early spring game. That was no small matter in baseball's pre-modern days when teams rarely carried more than a handful of bats, which they used until broken beyond repair.

In the stands that day, however, was John Andrew "Bud" Hillerich, who had sneaked off from his job as

In 1916, the business changed its name to Hillerich & Bradsby, a few years after Frank Bradsby—previously a buyer for Simmons Hardware in St. Louis, the firm's first national outlet—came to work for the company.

Though the broken-bat story has gained a mythical quality over the years in the eyes of some historians, there is substantial evidence to verify this incident, including the word of John Andrew "Bud" Hillerich, who maintained its accuracy to the end of his life at age 80 in 1946.

Certainly, the results that the new bat produced are absolutely indisputable.

Though it was not the first time a round, barrel-shaped bat had been used in professional play, John Andrew Hillerich's bat revolutionized the game.

Instantly popular, the custom-made bat quickly became the rage of the game, the standard by which all other bats were to be judged in the future. And, in short order, it birthed the world's most famous batmaking company.

Left in the historical wake of the Louisville Slugger bat were the flat sticks and crude round bats of previous years, suddenly and permanently, relics of the past.

The Louisville Slugger bat incident, no doubt, accounted for much of Browning's prolific success as a batsman. And, not surprisingly, the 1884 episode has also contributed mightily to the enduring legend of Pete Browning.

Nicknamed "The Gladiator" by the lively sporting press of his day for his battles with them, flyballs and liquor, Browning was a constant source of news—and amusement—his entire career.

Illiterate ("Oh yeah, what

league was he in?", he reportedly asked an astonished reporter who told him President Garfield had just died from an assassin's bullet), deaf, defensively a liability and a chronic alcoholic ("I can't hit the ball until I hit the bottle," he frequently exclaimed during his career), he was eccentric as well.

Indeed, his eccentricities alone ensured the Browning legend, that contingent including — but not limited — to his refusal to slide; his one-legged defensive posture; naming his bats (many of them after Biblical figures) and then "retiring" them after they had produced their quota of hits; computing his average daily on his cuffs; and increasing the "power" of his eyes ("lamps" he called them) by staring directly into the sun.

That legend was further solidified by a hard and early death.

In June of 1905, Browning's life — and peaceful retirement — fell apart. Years of hard drinking and a

The center of attention, unquestionably, in this antique photograph of the 1877 Louisville Eclipse, is the city's up-and-coming baseball wonder, Pete Browning (middle row, second from left). Louisville's top semi-pro outfit for years, the Eclipse went major-league in 1882 when the town joined the American Association. Team members are (STANDING) John Reccius, pitcher; J. Pfeiffer; T. Lehan; and W. Zimmerman, right field; (SEATED) Quinlan, substitute and catcher; Browning (possibly seen in his first photograph as a player);, M. --- (name indecipherable); and Coleman, catcher; (FOREGROUND) Charles Pfeiffer, left field; and C. Arny, centerfield. (Univeristy of Louisville Photographic Archives)

LOUISVILLE CURIOS

A bachelor, Pete Browning lived his entire life with his mother at his birthplace, 1427 W. Jefferson.

He is buried in Lot 549, near the intersection of what used to be called Virgilia and Hovenia Avenues, on the southwest side of Cave Hill Cemetery.

In the June 1982 issue of "Twilight Zone" magazine, Browning was the subject of a magical short story by David Nemec entitled "Browning's Lamps".

And, in 1989, it was confirmed that Pete Browning was the uncle of Tod Browning (1880-1962). A vaudeville actor, the younger Browning became a noted film director. His work included the 1931 horror classic, "Dracula", which shot Bela Lugosi to stardom; the controversial "Freaks"; and a number of top films with Lon Chaney, known as "The Man Of A Thousand Faces". Interestingly enough, Tod Browning learned his craft from another native Kentuckian, the legendary D.W. Griffith.

Apocryphal stories about Browning abound; here are three examples.

On one occasion, Browning thoroughly outwitted John McGraw, who was known to hook his hand inside the belts of baserunners tagging up at third on fly balls (that delay often being just enough to get them out at the plate). Browning, however, was wise to the maneuver and surreptitiously loosened his belt. When a flyball was subsequently hit to the outfield, McGraw found himself holding an empty belt as Browning — much to the amusement of the crowd — crossed the plate holding his pants up.

Another was the 'Aity Ate' episode. This 1885 mishap at the Lindell Hotel in St. Louis, recounted in David Nemec's ground-breaking book on the American Association, The Beer and Whisky League, demonstrated the problems Browning had with words and numbers. Leaving a message for teammate Guy Hecker telling him what room the pair were staying in, Browning wrote "Aity Ate" (88).

And, it was reported that Browning — during his days in the American Association — thought nothing of stepping off a train as it came into a station and loudly proclaiming himself to all congregated as the famed champion batsman of that circuit.

Browning, who batted right and threw right, was six feet tall and weighed 180 pounds.

The bats Browning reportedly favored were as big as his career numbers: 37 inches in length and 48 ounces in weight.

crudely-treated mastoid infection (the root of all his personal, professional and physical problems including his illiteracy, deafness and alcoholism) had resulted in irreversible brain damage.

Exhibiting erratic behavior, he was judged insane and committed to a state asylum at nearby Lakeland, Ky., where he remained for a few weeks (it has been reported that he died in this insane asylum; this is not true). Following his release, Browning spent the last few months of his beleaguered life in and out of old City (now University) Hospital in Louisville, where he died at age 44 on September 10, 1905.

Buried in historic Cave Hill Cemetery (founded 1848), the final resting place for many of Louisville's old-time major-leaguers, Browning was honored in September 1984 during the centennial anniversary of Hillerich & Bradsby.

Joining with the city of Louisville (Harvey I. Sloane, Mayor), the company helped fund and dedicate a new four-and-a-half-foot tall marker that fully detailed Browning's legendary career achievments... and correctly spelled his name.

THE LIFE AND TIMES OF PETE BROWNING

FEBRUARY 15, 1849

Browning's parents, Samuel Browning (1814-1874) and Mary Jane Sheppard (1826-1911) are married in Jefferson County, of which Louisville is the county seat. Pete Browning is the youngest of eight children born to them — four sons (Charles, Henry, Louis and Samuel, Jr.) and four daughters (Blanche, Fannie, Florence and Ida May).

JUNE 17, 1861

Pete Browning is born in Louisville; lives entire life at 1427 W. Jefferson on near west side of Louisville with his mother, who dies there at age 84 in early April of 1911, having lived there for more than a half century.

OCTOBER 1874

Browning's father, a prosperous merchant, dies in mid–October at age 59 from injuries received in a cyclone.

APRIL 13, 1877

In what is thought to be Browning's career debut (his first known boxscore appearance) in organized baseball, he goes zero–for–four as the National League Grays decimate the Eclipse 22–1. Browning has three putouts and one error at third base.

The Grays are paced by Juice Latham (five–for–six). Three other Grays get four hits each — third baseman Bill Hague, right fielder George Shaffer and center fielder Bill Crowley.

Devlin throws a three–hitter against the Eclipse, who get their lone run in the ninth via a pair of errors.

JULY 17, 1877

Browning pitches the Eclipse to a 24–8 bombing of the Amateurs. Browning's work also includes a three–for–six performance at the plate and four runs scored. He is 16 years and one month old.

JULY 25, 1877

Playing third base for the Amateurs, Browning goes zero–for–four as the Mutuals defeat Amateurs 15–10.

JULY 27, 1877

This game is thought to be the contest alluded to in Browning's obituaries in the Louisville Courier–Journal and the Louisville Times — the game that gained Browning his first major baseball attention.

Using a fine curveball and deceptive change of pace, Pete Browning pitches the Eclipse to a 4–0 shutout win over the National League Grays. His strikeout victims that day, notably enough, include George Hall and Jimmy Devlin, two of the four participants in that season's National League pennant–fixing scandal.

The clearly–irritated Courier–Journal runs only a note on the game, reporting in its lead paragraph that "the Grays were thrashed yesterday afternoon by the Eclipse nine."

The concluding sentence of the "homer" story gives clear indications of Browning's pitching skills that day: "The last inning came with the score of 4 to 0 against them, and, as the Grays went out in striking order, the figures remained unchanged."

AUGUST 3, 1877

Browning is the losing pitcher as Frank Lafferty of the Grays no–hits the Eclipse 14–1. The latter gain their only run in the fifth inning via a missed third strike, a bad throw to second and a flyball between second baseman Joe Gerhardt and right fielder George Shaffer which is allowed to drop.

The hitting star for the Grays is George Hall, who rips off four hits — two singles, a triple and a home run.

The opening paragraph of the Louisville Courier–Journal story the following day (Saturday, August 4, 1877) is a doozy: "Yesterday afternoon, the Grays sat down on the boys from the West End; in fact, squashed them rather badly."

AUGUST 28, 1877

Browning drops a tough decision to the Amateurs,

who score twice in the ninth to beat the Eclipse 9–7. They score their winning runs on "muffed flies." Browning, who manages to blow a 7–1 lead, has only himself to blame, however. Browning goes one–for–five (a double) in the sloppy 20-error contest (12 by Browning's team).

SEPTEMBER 1, 1877

Batting lead–off and playing second base, Browning gets two of four hits for the Liberty in their 7–6 win over the Amateurs. The contest is riddled by errors on both sides — 10 for the Amateurs, 11 for the Liberty.

SEPTEMBER 7, 1877

Batting second in the order and playing second base for the Amateurs, Browning goes two–for–four as the Amateurs defeat the Mutuals 6–3. One of Browning's hits is a double; he also scores one run and plays some fine defense. According to the Courier-Journal, Browning is robbed of a third hit by Mutuals' third baseman T. Daily, who makes "a rattling line catch close to the ground" of a ball hit by Browning.

SEPTEMBER 8, 1877

Browning — with three singles in four at–bats — does his job as the lead–off man. Still, the second baseman's efforts are in vain as the Libertys fall to the Amateurs 7–3.

SEPTEMBER 11, 1877

Browning, playing second and batting third in the lineup, goes zero–for–four as the Amateurs are defeated by the Louisville National League Grays 12–7.

SEPTEMBER 12, 1877

Batting first and second respectively in the lineup, first baseman John Haldeman and Browning — at shortstop — team up to destroy a team from nearby Anchorage. Haldeman and Browning get five hits each, and score five runs apiece in the game which is called on account of darkness after eight innings.

Browning's work includes a pair of triples. The plate work of Haldeman, who will in a few months

expose the black work of "The Louisville Four", includes a double and a triple in the 21-2 romp.

SEPTEMBER 25, 1877

In a 13–4 triumph over the Amateurs, Browning goes four–for–six for the Eclipse, scoring twice and doubling once. Stationed at first base, he bats fourth in the lineup; fifth in the order is the shortstop, an "H. Browning", believed to be his brother Henry, who goes one–for–six.

1880

Shifted to third base in the lineup of Eclipse club, the city's top semi-pro club, to give his potent bat a place in the daily lineup.

1881

Signs first professional contract for $60 a month.

In September 1881, lays groundwork for lifelong battle with the press. Informed of President James Garfield's death from an assassin's bullet received two and a half months earlier, Browning queries an astonished reporter: "Oh, yeah? What league was he in?" Later as a major-leaguer, he will gain the monicker of "The Gladiator" for his battles with the press, flyballs and his pathological alcoholism, best phrased by another memorable quote ("I can't hit the ball until I hit the bottle!").

Illiterate, deaf, eccentric and defensively a liability, he is the classic baseball legend. Years later, it will be discovered that the mastoiditis which rendered him deaf as a young man lies at the root of his personal and professional problems. That major historical discovery will go a long way in correcting the previously-held conception of him.

MAY 2, 1882

Playing third base and hitting in the lead–off spot, makes major–league debut at St. Louis. Goes zero–for–four in 9–7 loss.

MAY 3, 1882

In 6–4 loss at St. Louis, gets first major–league hit.

Two–for–three performance includes a single, a triple, a walk and two runs scored.

MAY 5, 1882

Garners first major–league hits at home. Goes two–for–three in 2–1 win over St. Louis. Work includes a single, a double and a walk. His double is described thusly by the Louisville Courier–Journal:

The boss hit of the day was made by Browning, who sent the sphere clear over (Oscar) Walker's head, in center field, and he was playing far out, too. The ground, however, was so soft that it hit almost dead, and Browning only reached second.

This phogotgraph (circa late 1800s) is of the J.F. Hillerich Company the forerunner of the Hillerich & Bradsby Company. Second from left is J.F. Hillerich. Son John A. "Bud" Hillerich stands in the right side of the doorway, holding a bat and flanked by a butter churn and a bedpost. At far left is H.W. Bickel, a long-time employee who eventually became superintendent of the Hillerich & Bradsby Co. (University of Louisville Photographic Ar-

1882

Captures first of three major-league titles with .378 average in the American Association. He becomes the first rookie in major-league baseball history to take a batting title. He is all of 21. During that same season, Louisville meets an independent outfit from Atlantic City, a squad that has defeated every other team in the American Association that year. Fully aware of his hitting prowess and nervous about the short fences there at the seaside resort, the home team adopts a rule that any ball hit over the fence is a double, not a home run. Later running out what he thought was a home run, and sent back to second, Browning in succeeding years says that his "two-bag home run" was the "longest hit I ever made, an all-around-the-world hit, and it's still going yet."

MAY 2, 1883

The Louisville Courier–Journal concludes their Thursday, May 3, story of a 13–6 Eclipse win versus

Columbus with this remarkable sentence: "Browning was very ill last night and hardly able to play, but managed to hold up his end at the bat, making three singles and one double."

Batting second and playing third base, Browning also manages to score two runs in the contest. It is a stunning performance, whether his illness was alcohol–related or not.

SPRING 1884

In the early spring of the year (many accounts say mid-April), Browning makes history off the field. Having broken his favorite bat, he heeds the offer of a young woodworking apprentice, John A. "Bud" Hillerich, to make him a new bat. Hillerich custom-makes a new bat for the slugger, and unwittingly makes history. Browning is the recipient of the first "Louisville Slugger" bat, a revolutionary bat that forges modern batmaking via the firm of what later becomes Hillerich & Bradsby.

MAY 4, 1884

According to a Louisville Courier-Journal news story, Browning performs an heroic rescue of a child.

Browning saved a boy from being run over by a street-car at 17th and Marinet last night. The little fellow was trying to cross the track, when the mules struck him and knocked him under the car. Browning was standing by, and pulled him out in time to save his life.

During this season, Browning also submits for the first time to surgery for mastoiditis (an inflammation of the mastoid process, which is located behind the ears). The surgery affords only temporary relief, and for the rest of his life, Browning will be plagued by the mastoidal problems, which will be a major factor in his early death.

SEPTEMBER 6, 1884

Loses about a week because of a knee injury with Louisville involved in tight pennant race. Louisville finishes third as New York — with whom it had battled for first–place honors earlier in the season — goes on to take American Association flag.

1885

Captures second major-league batting title with .362 average in the American Association. Championship work also includes league-leading 174 hits. That

Browning Can Write.

A statement has been going the rounds to the effect that Pete Browning could not write. This caught the eye of the tall center-fielder, and in refutation he has sent the following autograph, with his compliments to the base-ball editor:

Pete Browning's signature and accompanying article in the Louisville Courier-Journal. (Philip Von Borries Collection)

same season, he is also switched permanently from infield to outfield.

JUNE 20, 1886

Browning's signature appears at the end of a short baseball item carried by the Louisville Courier-Journal. Headlined "Browning Can Write", the article reads:

A statement has been going around the rounds to the effect that Pete Browning could not write. This caught the eye of the tall center fielder, and in refutation he has sent the following autograph, with his compliments to the base-ball editor: (followed by Browning's illegible and misspelled signature).

JUNE 28, 1886

Browning is "suspended indefinitely" according to a story in the Louisville Courier–Journal. The main headline reads: "Pete Browning Laid Off." The secondary headline says: "The Great Center Fielder Falls A Victim To Dissolute Habits."

It is the first of two suspensions that season for drunkeness. The suspensions will prove costly in two ways.

At season's end, Browning is the runner-up in that year's American Association batting race as teammate Guy Hecker becomes the only pitcher in major–league history to win a batting title. The narrow loss to Hecker for batting honors (.341 to .340) denies Browning his second straight American Association batting title, and his third in five years. It is scarcely conjecture that without the suspensions, Browning would have been the runaway batting champion that year.

As for Louisville, they run a disappointing fourth, a finish unquestionably exacerbated by the absence of their fabulous hitting star.

EARLY JULY, 1886

Browning returns to lineup.

JULY 6, 1886

Browning hit with second suspension. The Courier–Journal reports: "Browning has again been laid off for incompetent playing." This suspension is substantially longer than the first, as Browning is out of action for approximately a month.

The 1886 season marks the first time that Browning misses a significant number of games. That year, Browning plays in 112 games, missing 26 games of a 138–game schedule (losing roughly one–fifth of the season).

However, his two worst seasons are yet to come. In 1888, he plays in just 99 contests, missing 40 tilts of a 139–game schedule (jettisoning roughly 30 percent of the season).

And in 1889, it reaches epic proportions when he plays in only 83 games of a 140–game schedule (the missed 57 games constitute approximately 40 percent of the season).

Totalled up, Browning will miss 160 games during his first eight years in the major leagues (1882–1889), all with Louisville, playing in 796 games of 956 contests. The 17 percent absentee rate is extraordinarily high for a player suffering from no visible injury, and makes the struggles of the Louisville franchise only that much more difficult.

AUGUST 8, 1886

Shortly after returning to the lineup, Browning celebrates in a big way by hitting for the cycle for the first time in his career. He goes four–for–five and scores two runs in an 11–6 win versus the New York Metropolitans.

SEPTEMBER 5, 1886

His attention diverted while leading off first base, Browning falls prey to an *unassisted* pickoff play by pitcher Dave Foutz, who races over and tags Browning out. Despite the mishap, Louisville still takes the home contest from St. Louis 8–2.

MAY 10, 1887

Browning, who had signed for $1,800 after a holdout earlier in the year, is the subject of a sterling piece in the Louisville Courier–Journal.

It begins by acknowledging that there are numerous stories about Browning, "and although the matter has been a little overdrawn, if anything, many of these tales have the merit of being founded on fact."

The article continues:

Such, at least, is claimed for the venerable incidents into which the names of Presidents Cleveland and Garfield are introduced, the mask story, the tale of the register in the street–car, the 'aty–ate' episode, and a few others which have been deservedly forgotten or buried long ago.

It then concludes with an endearing tribute from a teammate identified only as "a well–known and popular member of the Louisville Club."

Of course I know that they tell some rather queer stories about Pete, and altough some of 'em can be said to be a little hard on him, they do not convey a false impression of his character.

Browning would sooner play ball than eat pie, and outside his profession, if you want to call it that, he doesn't care for anything. He lets the events of the day slip by him without a single comment, and I believe if there was a war in the country to-morrow he would ask who was leading in the race. In fact, if he had to quit playing he would die of a broken heart in a month.

Browning was born and raised in Louisville, and has played ball since he was able to walk and without doubt will keep on playing until he is absolutely compelled to quit for want of physical strength. At the same time Pete has one of the biggest hearts in the world and is one of the easiest–going men I know."

MAY 11, 1887

This item on the travels — and travails — of Pete Browning appears in that day's (Tuesday's) "Baseball Notes" of the Louisville Courier–Journal.

Pete Browning was arrested late Monday night for

raising a disturbance in a streetcar at 13th and Walnut Streets. He persisted in paying his fare with checks, which are not good after 6 o'clock. Pete affirms that he was not drunk, but under the influence of quinine. He was fined by Manager (John) Kelly for being out at an undue hour. Browning had witnesses to prove that he was not intoxicated.

1887

Bats career-best .402, but does not win title, losing to Tip O'Neill's .435 average (second-highest ever in seasonal play).

At a post-season dinner party, Browning is presented a big gold watch. According to a local newspaper report, he finds himself wordless from the gift and the occasion, and facing a crowd crying "Speech! Speech!" Finally, he blurts out: "Where the hell's the gold chain?" The crowd explodes in laughter.

JUNE 22, 1888

The Louisville Courier–Journal runs this item on Friday morning under the headline, "Pete Browning's Fall":

Pete Browning is a blue–ribbon man no more. He fell from grace in Kansas City last Monday (June 18), and since then has been, apparently, endeavoring to make up for the time he lost while wearing the Murphy badge.

He got roaring drunk Monday, but was put to bed before he had a chance to show what a large sized ass he is when under the influence of liquor, but on Tuesday his sense of humor developed with each drink he took, and it was but a short time until he had purchased fishing tackle and begun fishing in the gutter in the front of the hotel. It had rained heavily and the gutter was full of water, and he couldn't resist the temptation to show how much he loved it — except as a beverage.

He made so much fuss about the hotel that he was put out of it, and came near landing in jail. He refused to go with the club to Cincinnati Tuesday night, and was left in Kansas City, where he probably is yet.

He is expected to become sober and penitent and to ask permission to rejoin the club. That is his usual way.

(For the record, the Kansas City fishing episode is one of the classic stories of Browning's colorful career; indeed, years later, when Browning dies, the Louisville Courier–Journal will recount it in their long article on him.)

Browning's escapade follows a successful series in Kansas City on Saturday, June 16 (a 6–5 win) and Sunday, June 17 (a 7–6 triumph). In both games, he goes three–for–four. His overall six–for–10 work is highlighted by three doubles (two on Saturday, one on Sunday).

JUNE 24, 1888

The Louisville Courier–Journal carries this delightful followup on Browning's fishing hijinks in Kansas City:

'The Lone Fisherman', as the small boys on the bleaching boards dubbed Browning, had returned from Kansas City. He was nervous and pale, but his time off had evidently had a good influence upon him, for his batting average was .750 percent (he went three–for–four, one hit a triple).

He couldn't see a balloon in the field, however, and almost every hit in his territory got away from him.

The story added that a well–known saloonkeeper shouted, "Hurrah for John Barleycorn," following a triple by Browning. The game ended in a 10–10 tie, being called on account of rain and darkness.

The "Notes of the Diamond" in that Sunday's issue of the Courier–Journal also had this bit of news that was hardly surprising under the circumstances:

Peter Browning returned (to Louisville) Friday night (June 22) from Kansas City. He reported yesterday morning (Saturday, June 23) to President (Mordecai) Davidson, and was fined $100. Pete pleaded that it was his first backsliding this year, but Mr.

Davidson says the fine will have to go. It was imposed by Acting Manager (John) Kerins.

JUNE 29, 1888

The Louisville Courier–Journal carries this off–the–wall one–liner (though not necessarily for those times) in its Friday baseball notes: "Pete Browning and Guy Hecker are the only Republicans in the Louisville Club."

JULY 11, 1888

Pete Browning returns in a big way to the Louisville lineup, as he goes two–for–four (a pair of triples) in a 7–4 victory versus Cleveland. The Louisville Courier–Journal the next day (Wednesday, July 11, 1888) carries a fine story (headlined "The Gladiator Makes His Reappearance"), complete with a superb hand–drawn illustration. The piece is unquestionably emblematic of Browning's ability to gain almost instant forgiveness and grace — even in the wake of the greatest of excesses — by virtue of his baseball talents. The opening paragraphs read:

Pete Browning led in the work in the field for the Louisvilles. The Gladiator was himself again, and the friends of the club were glad to see him again in the old position in the middle field (center field).

No less than three of Browning's four put–outs were circus catches, and one was a great running catch of a ball knocked by (Ed) McKean in the third inning, which looked safe for three bases.

Recovering himself, Pete completed a neat double play by throwing out (Cub) Stricker, who had attempted to leave first base on the hit.

Browning lined out two terrifc three–baggers when men were on the bases.

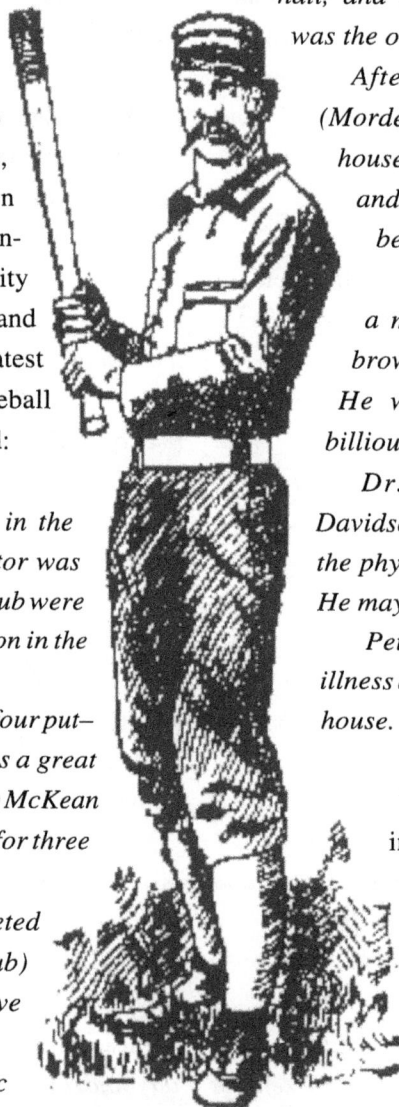

Pete Browning, late 1880s.
(Philip Von Borries Collection)

JULY 22, 1888

In its Sunday edition, the Courier–Journal carries a good–sized piece (headlined "The Gladiator Is Sick") on Browning, who had missed the preceding day's contest.

Pete Browning failed to show up yesterday (Saturday) afternoon for the game with St. Louis, and it was generally thought that the blonde center–fielder had gone off on a 'toot', whatever that word may mean.

(Outfielder Farmer) Vaughan was visiting his mother at her home on the Ohio (River) above Cincinnati, and consequently (Icebox) Chamberlain was the only man to be put in center–field.

After the game yesterday, President (Mordecai) Davidson went to the Gladiator's house to find out the cause of his absence, and found Petey stretched full length in bed.

The old hero's moustache had taken a melancholy curl and droop, and his brow was swathed in bandages and ice. He was suffering from an attack of billiousness and was in a high fever.

Dr. Edward Palmer satisfied Mr. Davidson that Browning is a sick man, and the physician has taken him under his care. He may not be able to play for several days.

Pete was unable to notify the club of his illness as he and his mother were alone in the house.

That medical verdict notwithstanding, however, Browning played on Sunday, July 22 (the day this story appeared), going two–for–four (one a double) and scoring two runs in a 5–3 loss to St. Louis.

AUGUST 5, 1888

The Louisville Courier–Journal carries this interesting baseball note (a pickup from the Philadelphia News) on Browning, who was described as being "crestfallen" the previous night.

"To think of it," said the tall center fielder, "that I left my home to travel with such an agitation as this here. Well, it serves me correct. I am not exprised. I hope I git my valise.

"Talk about luck. Wot you think I did in Baltimore? Slapped the ball in der mug, and it went a whistlin' over der left field fence, but hit der top of a house, bounded back and I cum mighty near being put out at second.

"That's wot I call hard luck — eh?"

AUGUST 25, 1888

The Louisville Courier–Journal carries a massive story on Browning, who is under suspension again. The story, which is headlined "Big Pete's Challenge" and sub–headlined "Browning's Friends Alarmed at His Condition Since His Suspension", is yet more proof of the beleaguered 1888 season of Browning.

A good story is now going the rounds on Big Pete Browning, the Louisville center–fielder, who has been suspended by President Davidson, and who seems rapidly approaching the time of a back number.

A prophet is not without honor save in his own country' is an old quotation, and while Pete's figure and carriage would be recognized on any street in Cincinnati or Philadelphia, thousands of persons meet the great ball player in this city and never know that he has been the idol of every small boy and base–ball enthusiast in America.

To this latter class belongs a prominent member of the board of Councilmen, who has never yet witnessed a game of base ball, although during Councilman William L. Lyon's regime, he carried a complimentary pass around in his inside vest pocket.

This councilman is fat and dignified, does not patronize saloons, is unfamiliar with saloon slang, and is altogether a dignified and respectable member of society.

One night recently while it was raining hard, a very dilapidated individual boarded, at Eighteenth street, a car on the East Market and Shelby streets line. The new passenger was ringing wet, his blonde mustache drooped and met under his chin. One of his eyes was black and blue, and he seemed to have been in trouble.

It was Pete Browning, and he shook himself like a water spaniel, and sprinkled the respectable Councilman, who was ensconced comfortably in a corner seat. Pete was chewing on the end of a wet and misshapen cigar stump, and seating himself next to the Councilman, began conversation.

Gimme a spark," said Pete. The Councilman's two–for–a–quarter regalia was handed over, Pete's stump was lighted, and then was given the command:

"Throw it away!"

The Councilman looked at his fragrant cigar, the fire of which was well under way, but Pete looked dangerous and the cigar was thrown away. The center fielder's coat was thrown open, and the passengers loked amused when it was noticed that Browning wore no vest, undershirt or shirt. A damp 5 cent cigar was pulled from a pocket, and the Councilman was comanded to smoke it. Both men puffed away in silence some minutes with more and less satisfaction.

"I don't believe you can beat two threes and three deuces," spoke up Pete.

"You are a stranger to me, sir, and I never played poker in all my life," was the somewhat timid rejoinder.

"I'll bet you $50 that you can't beat three deuces and two trays."

"I never bet."

"Oh! you never bet, hey! Old Pete didn't come from Morehead. You are looking for something soft, but I ain't no greener. I tell you what I'll do. I'll bet $50 you can beat two trays and three deuces, ponies out of the stable."

"I never bet," (the councilman said) very timidly.

At this, Pete flared up, assumed a dangerous scowl, jerked the street–car bell and, grabbing the Councilman, dragged him from the car and into a low saloon, where he compelled the Councilman to drink stale common beer and learn the mysteries of poker dice.

The Councilman was badly frightened, and didn't dare to resist Pete or to assert his dignity. He was the maddest man in town when he learned Browning's identity and that Big Pete was as harmless as a child.

Since his suspension Browning's friends are becoming alarmed at his condition, and many think that sorrow is causing him to lose his mind.

Pete's intellect, except on the ball field, was never of the strongest, and since his suspension he seems to be growing childish and playful.

He imagines that everybody he meets wants to shuck poker dice, and he holds out his ragged $50 bill and tries to get a bet that he can or he can't beat three deuces and two trays. He never varies this combination, but sticks religiously to his three deuces and two trays.

1888

Enjoys seventh straight season at .300 or better, batting .313. A folklore part of that campaign is a mid–summer game at Cincinnati, where story has it he catches a flyball off Bid McPhee's bat with his feet. Playing right field, Browning wobbles, then falls to the ground, a victim of sunglare (this being before the age of sunglasses). However, as he falls, Browning's feet come together and he catches the flyball. (Though the rules of the time allowed such catches, this story is suspect — very, very suspect — considering

Louisville Slugger bat display. (*University of Louisville Photographic Archives*)

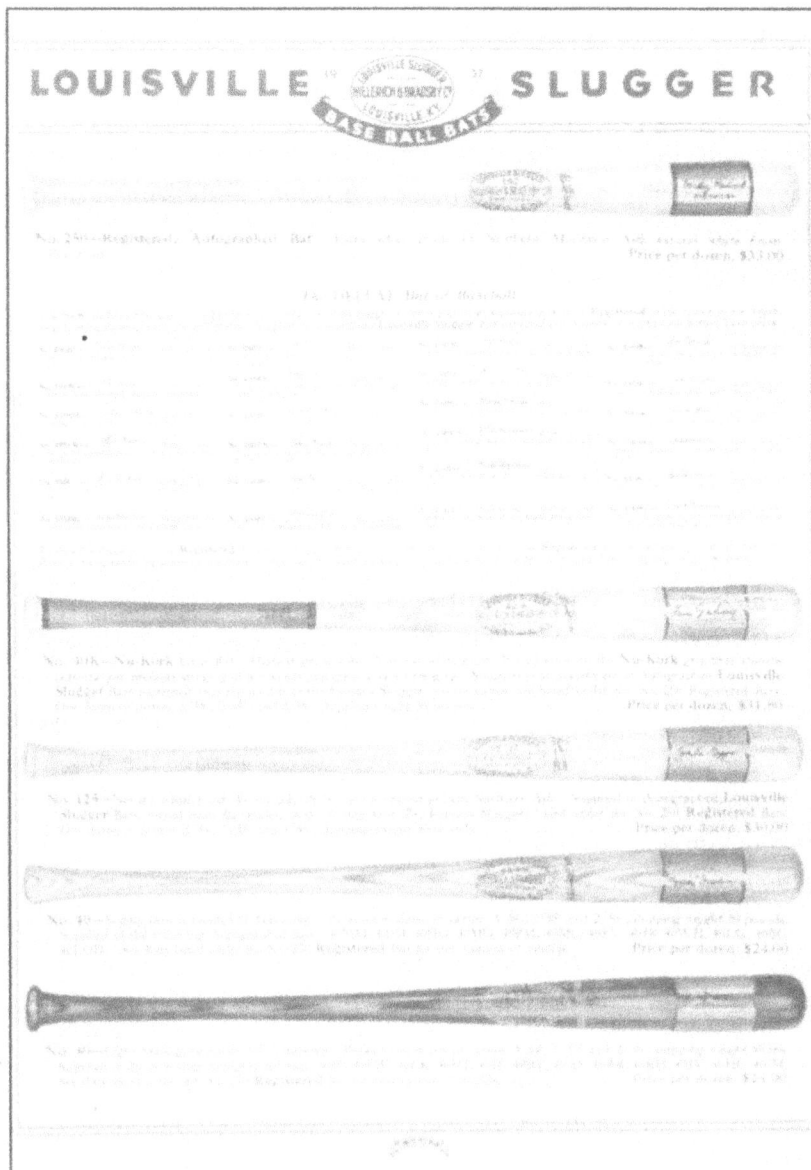

A Louisville Slugger advertisement. (Hillerich & Bradsby Company)

According to the story, Browning — an expert iceskater since childhood — can be often found at National Park skating rink (on West Main Street), where he "recently won a mile race of skates in very creditable time."

The listing on Browning begins thusly: "Peter Browning is keeping sober and rarely comes up town."

APRIL 9, 1889

Signs with Louisville for $1,600. Also delivers a signed pledge of abstinence sworn out before a local judge.

JUNE 7, 1889

Hits for cycle for second time in career (major–league record is three), but Louisville still falls to Philadelphia 9–7 in 11 innings. It is Louisville's 14th straight defeat. Streak will finally end at 26 straight losses, still the major-league record. Game is staged as a benefit for the survivors of the Johnstown flood one week before. Browning's five–for–six work includes a pair of singles, a double, triple and home run (plus two runs scored).

Browning's career defensive statistics, the overwhelming majority of which were done by hand).

But, the season is scarcely a picnic for owner–manager Mordecai Davidson, who spends much of his time dealing with the drunken escapades of Browning and pitcher Toad Ramsey. It is a safe bet that Browning would have had an even better season without the drink and the ancillary foolishness.

JANUARY 13, 1889

A colorful Sunday story in the Courier–Journal includes details of what the Louisville ballplayers are doing during the wintertime.

LATE JUNE – EARLY JULY 1889

Is part of players' strike against heavy-handed owner Mordecai Davidson. This is the first players' strike in major-league history. Is suspended for final two months of season because of drinking. Ends season with a .256 batting average, a career low.

OCTOBER 19, 1890

Comes home to Louisville, arriving the day after the second game of the 1890 World Series between American Association champion Louisville and National League titlist Brooklyn.

It is a bittersweet reunion, though, since both have enjoyed enormous success apart from one another after an eight–year partnership.

Signed by Cleveland for $4,480, Browning will wind up the batting champion of the Players' League with a .373 average (that includes circuit-topping 40 doubles). The downside, however, is that his native city has finally made its way into the World Series the year after letting their longtime star go. (Because of inclement weather, the Series will be called a draw after seven games, each team having a 3–3–1 record).

The Courier–Journal of Monday, October 20, 1890, reports the following:

Pete Browning, now the center–fielder of Al Johnson's Cleveland Brotherhood Club, arrived in the city yesterday from Cleveland.

The Gladiator's oldest friends would hardly know him from his present appearance. When seen by a reporter at the ball grounds yesterday, he was attired in a fashionable suit of clothes, the coat being a three–button cutaway of the latest style. A diamond pin adorned his scarf. He never looked better in his life, and he seemed to be in the best of health.

A long Browning quote then continues the story.

"I never was in finer condition," said he. "I told the people here that if I could get away from this town, I would show them how to play ball. Didn't I? Well, I did it. They said I couldn't keep sober. I fooled them. Not a drop did I drink this season. The people in Cleveland treated me splendidly, and old 'Pete' wasn't the boy to go back on them. See?

"You ought to have seen me line the ball out. I led 'em all. Dan Brouthers, Dave Orr, Mike Kelly, Roger Connor and all those sluggers were not in it with Pete, the Gladiator.

"Some of the Eastern papers are trying to put Dave Orr ahead of me, but they can't do it. My average is .391, and I have got the official averages at home. Dave Orr is a pretty good hitter, but he can't line them out like Old Pete. Al Johnson is the best man I ever

played under in my life. Nothing too good for us fellows."

Questioned about the Players' League (also known as the Brotherhood), Browning — the story related — "reached down in his pocket and pulled out a big roll of greenbacks."

"See this long–green?" said Pete. "Well, the Brotherhood is full of it."

The story concluded with this paragraph: "Browning will pass the winter in this city at the home of his mother. He says he expects to be transferred to the Cincinnati Club next season."

OCTOBER 21, 1890
Following the fourth game of the World Series, Browning gives his opinion of the World Series, spicing his remarks with more animosity over events of the previous year. They are carried the following morning (Wednesday, October 22, 1890) by the Courier–Journal.

"They ain't no telling how these games will come out," remarked Gladiator Pete Browning to some of the Louisville players in Director Larry Gatto's place last night. "All the Brooklyns might get killed in a wreck and then the Louisvilles will have to win; not that I mean that's the only way Pete's old club could win.

"You see, when Pete was here he wasn't nobody, and he had to go away from Kentucky to get recognition from the people. They didn't know Pete any more here.

"Now Pete comes back here, and everybody calls him 'Mr. Browning' and tell him he's fine as silk. 'Cause why? 'Cause he led Brouthers, Stovey, Orr, and Connor, and all them big batters, and got an average of .391, see?

"In 1882 and 1885, Pete was something here, but the papers pulled him down, and people called him 'Red Eye' and 'Distillery Pete', and hadn't no respect for him. But when he got with good people he got to be good people himself.

"In Cleveland, we all was the people, and Al Johnson's the boy to have at the head of a club. Look at this: every one of them 'long greens' is a fiver or tenner, and it's as big around as my arm. That's what the Brotherhood did. I'm going to play in Cincinnati next year. That's the best ball town in America next to Boston, and I hope I'll lead the hitters again and have as much money next year."

NOVEMBER 8, 1890

In its Saturday, November 8, 1890, issue, The Sporting Life (a weekly publication) carries an article headlined "Louisville Lines." The corespondent has this to say about Browning and his superior 1890 campaign with Cleveland in the Players' League:

The great form shown by Browning this year has had its natural result.

Some of the cranks are howling that he ought never to have been released by Louisville. This is all nonsense. Browning was no earthly good to Louisville. His only hope of accomplishing anything for himself or anybody else was by getting away from here, and fortunately for him, he went to Cleveland.

Pete, by the way, is very proud of his triumph this year. I met him on the street the other day and he talked very sensibly about it. He said that he had taken good care of himself, and early in the season he determined to show his revilers that there was some good left in him yet.

He did it, and he intends to do it again next season.

MAY 5, 1891

Bunts into triple play in top of the sixth inning; error in bottom of same inning allows Pittsburgh to lose to Chicago Colts.

MAY 7, 1891

The Louisville Post carries this pickup baseball note two days after Browning's May 5 fiasco: "Old Pete Browning writes to a local friend that he expects to lead the (National) League in batting as he did the Brotherhood (the Players' League) last year."

MAY 8, 1891

The Louisville Post, in its Friday edition, runs this note telling of Browning's popularity:

Pete Browning is still a favorite in Cincinnati. Wednesday it was so cold that the spectators shivered in great overcoats, but the old Gladiator warmed them into enthusiasm. The (Cincinnati) Enquirer says it will have to get several degrees colder than it was then to make the people forget him. Both the Enquirer and the (Louisville) Commercial–Gazette say Pete has not forgotten how to line 'em out.

MAY 10, 1891

This item appears in the Sunday edition of the Louisville Commercial.

A Pittsburgh man writes: Of the many thousands of ball cranks in this city yesterday there was not one half as happy as Pete Browning. Three hits on Friday, one of them a home run, a notification from the express office that a package was there in waiting for him.

When the charges were paid, it proved to be a small crate of ash bats, thoroughly smoke dried and almost black in color. Pete almost hugged the crate and tears stood in his eyes.

They were tears of joy, as he contemplated the elegant proportions of the different sticks and thought of the home runs, triples, doubles and singles they represented in the future.

JUNE 17, 1891

Browning is the subject of a feature article in Louisville Post entitled "Our Gladiator" (the sub–headlines read: "Pete Browning as He Appears to New Yorkers" and "New York Herald Gives the Louisville Slugger a Great Send–Off — A Model of Sobriety and a Much Slandered Citizen". Much of it is a pickup (reprint) of a New York Herald story, which begins thusly:

One of the distinguished citizens of Louisville is Mr. Lewis (note misspelling) Rogers Browning, the eminent exponent of the manly art of baseball. "Pete's" fame is co–extensive with the game of baseball — consequently he is known from coast to coast.

Further on, the sketch said of Browning:

Two years ago he was a confirmed drunkard; now he is a reformer, sober, hard–working and respected.

From the many stories that have been printed about Browning, the impression has gained ground that the "Gladiator" is ignorant and stupid. On the contrary, he appeared (to the writer) to be decidedly sensible and well–read.

According to the piece, the turnaround in his drinking came thusly:

In the autumn of '89 the Brotherhood revolt occurred (resulting in the Players' League of 1890) and Peter saw a chance to be free. Al Johnson, of Cleveland, offered him a good salary to play on his team, which was immediately accepted. Everybody laughed at this, because Johnson's men were generally inclined to "lush" more than to play ball, and "Pete" was regarded as quite an acquisition to their force.

But Browning had a genuine surprise in store for friends, enemies and the baseball world in general. The day he was suspended by the Louisville Club (in 1889) he decided never to touch a drop of liquor again.

The article followed with a long quote from Browning, who sounded like he had finally come to grips with his gargantuan drinking problem, if only for the time being.

"I merely did the right thing. I just quit it there forever, and I'll never drink again as long as I live. It was for my own sake and my family's. No man can help swearing off if he feels his position as I did, and every ball player that drinks should obey his conscience if he would save himself.

"Professional base ball puts more money into my hands than any other business ever could, and if I am fool enough to incapacitate myself from playing this game by drinking I deserve no sympathy at all."

"When I quit I didn't make any fuss and feathers about it. I just stopped right where I was and I haven't been in a saloon since then. My friends couldn't believe it at first and guyed me unmercifully, but as they gradually realized that I had quit sure enough, they let me alone. It will be two years now this August since I took the last drink. I feel better every way and know that I have been benefited very much.

"So many people have interviewed me and then made a 'monkey' out of me that I hope the Herald will set me right. I am not a lusher and never will be, and what is more, I want to deny all those ridiculous sayings that have been credited to me.

"They can call me 'Red–Eyed Pete', but I have some sense left and want the public to know it."

The article closed by noting that Browning is playing well for Pittsburg , and is one of J. Palmer O'Neill's "reliables."

JULY 7, 1892
In the twilight of his career, smashes out five hits (all singles) in six at–bats as Reds pummel Baltimore 21-2. Browning also scores four runs in Cincinnati rout.

The Louisville Times of the next afternoon, Friday, July 8, 1892, carries this good–sized pickup baseball note:

If Peter Browning were a horse he would be known as an 'in–and–outer', for, of all players in the world, Peter shows alternate good and bad form most frequently.

In the year of the Brotherhood League, or just before it, he was considered as almost useless. During the season of 1890, he proved to be one of the greatest of ball players.

Last year, the wheel turned down with him and once more he was considered worthless and was this year released by the Louisvilles. Now he is playing ball with Cincinnati, and Capt. (Charlie) Comiskey is charmed with his work, both at the bat and in the field.

The article closed with this paragraph on Browning's fine performance of the previous day: "Louis Rogers yesterday made five hits out of six times at the bat, two more than any other man in his team, although the total was 27."

APRIL 27, 1894

According to a baseball note in the Louisville Courier–Journal of Friday, April 27, 1894, Browning signs with future Hall–of–Famer's Mike Kelly's team, "Kelly's Killers", of Allentown, Penn. The colorful item reads:

Gladiator Louis Rogers Browning, better known as Pete, is no longer a baseball orphan. King Kelly has come to Peter's terms, and Browning will go to Allentown, Pa. Al Johnson is the principal backer of the club, and has always thought well of Pete. Browning declares he would much rather play there for $1,200 than here for $2,000, as they will not let him spend money there, and he will return home with a large wad of the long–green. He would have signed some time ago, but that Kelly wanted to think over a demand of $200 a month.

AUGUST 6, 1894

Browning plays the first of two games as a temporary replacement for St. Louis outfielder Fred Ely, who temporarily leaves team to attend to sick wife. Browning goes one–for–three in the 3–1 loss which takes place in his native city of Louisville.

Leaving no stone unturned, the Courier–Journal carries a majestic story the following morning (Tuesday, August 7, 1894) about the game:

Louisville and St. Louis played another fine game of ball yesterday afternoon. The Louisvilles won by the score of 3-1.

Just after the St. Louis team had begun to practice ball, a tall, lank figure of a man clad in a soiled gray uniform, with the words "Cincinnati" done in red lettering across the shirt front, walked out into center field and began taking care of the balls which were batted his way.

His cheeks were tanned and lean, and he wore a very sad expression. The uniforms of the St. Louis team are of very dark blue and the gray uniform in center made the wearer look like a stranger in a foreign land.

But the wearer of the gray suit was no stranger. He was at home. Those who looked closely, and remembered well, saw that Pietro Gladiator Browning, ex–champion batter of the world for several seasons, and until recently with Mike Kelly's Allentown aggregation, was to play center field for St. Louis. It was a great surprise to the spectators, and, if their expression of approval and cheers were evidence, it was a very pleasant one.

Browning has been engaged to play with St. Louis only temporarily. Ely's wife is sick, and he left for St. Louis yesterday morning. The team is short of players and Browning was signed to play until Ely returned.

Browning played well yesterday afternoon, accepting his only fielding chance handsomely. Browning also made the hit which was responsible for the only score made by the St. Louis team. He was heartily cheered for everything he did, and doffed his cap many times in response to loud calls.

Browning's first at–bat in the game evoked these lines later on in the Courier–Journal story.

Browning did not appear at bat for St. Louis until the third inning. He acted as if he wanted to make a hit very badly. He knocked two long fouls against the left–field fence, but ended by putting a high fly in Fred Pfeffer's hands.

The next–to–last paragraph of the story told the events behind the lone St. Louis run.

The only score made by the Browns was in the eighth inning. (Arthur) Twineham hit safely, and then it was Browning's turn at the bat. The Gladiator hit the ball hard, and it passed safely between Fred Pfeffer and (Danny) Richardson (at second and short respectively), Twineham taking third. Browning took second on the throw to get Twineham. (Pink) Hawley went out from Pfeffer to (Luke) Lutenberg, but Twineham crossed the plate.

AUGUST 7, 1894

Browning concludes his temporary stay with the St. Louis Browns. As in the other game, he plays center field and bats next–to–last in the order (in front of the pitcher). Though he goes zero–for–four, Browning scores one run and plays some fine defense as St. Louis beats Louisville 11–2.

The Courier–Journal of August 8, 1894, reports: "Browning, in center field for St. Louis, distinguished himself by a great running catch which looked to be good for three bases. He was applauded until he was very happy, and doffed his cap a number of times."

SEPTEMBER 30, 1894

It is a storybook ending to a fabled career. Browning's last major–league work comes as a right fielder for Brooklyn, for whom he goes two–for–two in the second game of a closing–day doubleheader. His work includes a pair of singles, a walk and one run scored. Making the story richest of all is the fact that it takes place in Louisville. Browning goes out a winner, as Brooklyn splits the doubleheader with a 12–4 laugher (called after five innings because of darklness).

The Courier–Journal reports the next day that Browning "was loudly cheered every time he walked to the plate."

OCTOBER 7, 1894

The Sunday edition of the Courier–Journal runs this baseball item in its seasonal recap story.

Pete Browning is watching the movements in regards to the new baseball association (a new version of the American Asociation) with as much care as as a mother looks after her most beloved child. He firmly believes that he will surely be a star in the new organization, if it really becomes an association in fact. He reads every paper that he can get his hands on carefully and he is enthusiastic when he talks of the

matter, as is a small boy when he discusses the circus. Browning says that he will probably sign with New York or Boston, though he has not settled as to the club as yet.

MAY 19, 1895

The Sunday edition of the Louisville Courier–Journal is enlivened by this baseball item on Browning:

P. Rodgers Browning, "Old Pete", as he is called now, finds time between the rushes of business at his saloon to witness every game that is played at the League Park.

In the afternoon that Louisville played such a bad game against Boston last week, Browning watched the wretched work between the meshes of the wire screen that extends in front of the benches under the grand stand.

"They need 'ole Pete' out there mighty bad," he remarked. "John McCloskey made me an offer the other day to play right field, but he didn't want to give me much. Must think I'm a Southern Leaguer, or a commons player, eh? But, I ain't — see.

"They all want 'ole Pete', for he is the boy who can line 'em out. This is the greatest year I ever saw to line 'em out. Why, the pitchers sail 'em over as big as bushel baskets and as slow as the Bloomfield accommodation train. It would be just a good thing to knock 'em all over the lot this year. Some of 'em going to offer Pete enough, and it won't be a week after that before I'm landing all the 'stickers'.

"My cellar down home is half full of as good sticks as you ever see — all oiled and rubbed.

"Pshaw, they don't remember what I am, they don't. But wait, I'll catch on.

"That's the team for you; the Bostons. They are the boys that can line 'em out, and play with their heads, too. Greatest on earth. Pennant? Well, I guess so. Mebbe fighters, but they'll take down the flag. It'll fly from a Boston pole next fall sure."

SEPTEMBER 25, 1895

In its Wednesday issue, the Louisville Courier–Journal reports that Browning will umpire a charity game.

"Pietro" Browning, the only Simon–pure "Gladiator" of the diamond, has consented to don the spangles again for sweet charity's sake and umpire the great game to be played next Thursday for the benefit of the Children's Free Hospital.

The contest, held between two teams of players from Louisville's National League club, sees the Reserves beat the Regulars 14–7. Propitiously-named Hercules Burnett goes four–for–four (two singles, a double and a home run) and scores four runs for the victors. The game raises about $250 for the hospital.

1896

Plays last recorded season of organized baseball at any level with Columbus of the Western League, batting .333 in 26 games.

LATE 1890s

Browning works as a cigar salesman, his bar — which was located near his residence at 13th and Market — having failed. Continues to be seen frequently at local baseball games, where he is — as in previous years — always well–received and well–remembered by the crowds.

JUNE 7, 1905

Declared a lunatic and committed to insane asylum at nearby Lakeland, Ky. The Courier–Journal story the following morning recounts Browning's prowess as a hitter. Toward the end of the piece, it relates Browning's secret for success as a batter during his playing days — daily washings of his eyes with buttermilk.

SEPTEMBER 1, 1905

Hillerich & Bradsby signs contract with Honus Wagner, who is the first man to have his signature on a bat. Modern endorsement-advertising history is made.

SEPTEMBER 10, 1905

Pete Browning dies at old City Hospital (renamed General Hospital, now University Hospital). Louisville Courier–Journal story announces his passing with headline that says: "Pete Browning 'Out' Of Game's Life". Headline for Louisville Times story reads: "Called Out For All Time On Life's Field". One of the major factors in his death was his alcoholism, which according to the Courier–Journal, dated to his early amateur days.

Old Pete was never known to take a drink until he played a game in this city with an amateur nine. He was asked to fill in for one of the players. On third base, a keg of beer had been placed, and those who reached the foaming fountain were entitled to a glass of lager. Pete knocked so many three–baggers and home–runs that little beer was left for anyone else.

Even allowing for some embellishment indigenous to sportswriters of that era, the story was a telling commentary on the extent of Browning's uncontrollable drinking.

SEPTEMBER 12, 1905

Buried in historic Cave Hill Cemetery, the final resting place of many of Louisville's grand old major-leaguers.

SEPTEMBER 10, 1984

On the 79th anniversary of Browning's death and during the centennial year of the Hillerich & Bradsby Company, the world's most famous batmaker joins with the city of Louisville to honor Browning with a new grave marker.

LOUISVILLE MAYOR HARVEY I. SLOANE
AND
HILLERICH & BRADSBY CO.
CORDIALLY INVITE YOU TO ATTEND
THE UNVEILING OF A NEW MEMORIAL FOR
PETE 'THE GLADIATOR' BROWNING,
LOUISVILLE'S FIRST BASEBALL STAR
WHO INSPIRED THE FIRST
LOUISVILLE SLUGGER BASEBALL BAT.
CAVE HILL CEMETERY
701 BAXTER AVENUE
11:00 A.M. MONDAY
SEPTEMBER 10, 1984

LEFT: Pete Browning's old grave marker. RIGHT: Pete Browning's new grave marker. TOP: Official invitation to the 1984 ceremonies for the dedication of the new Pete Browning grave marker. (All from the Philip Von Borries Collection)

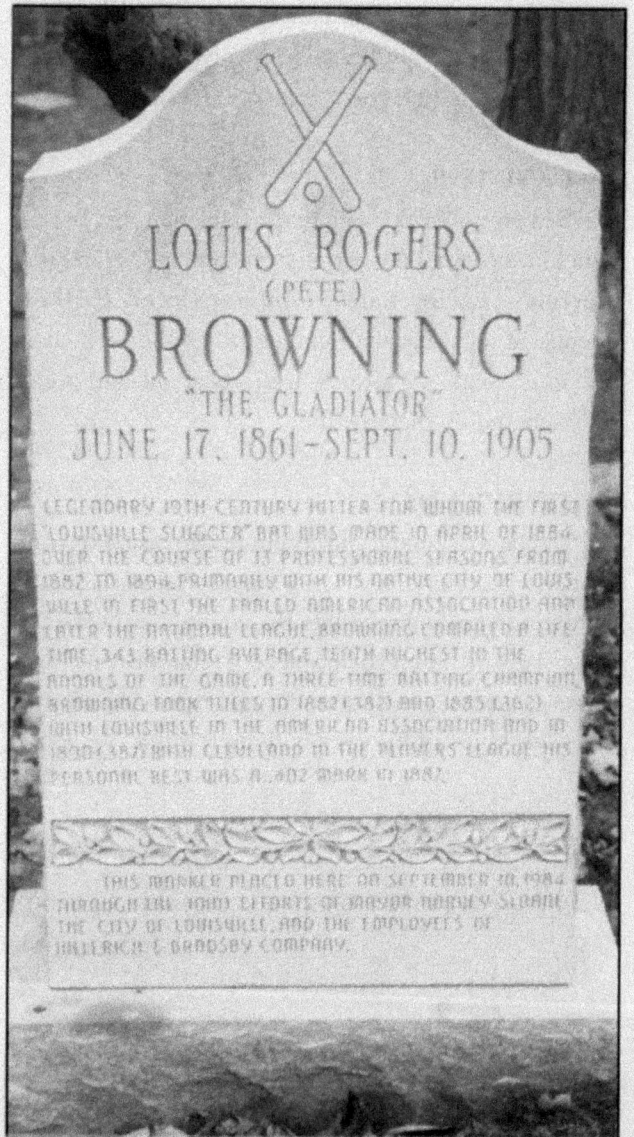

CHAPTER FOUR
LOUISVILLE'S MAJOR-LEAGUE GALLERY II:
THE AMERICAN ASSOCIATION YEARS, 1882-1891

The handsome photograph below is of the 1882 American Association Louisville Eclipse, whose forerunners by the same name were the most powerful semi-pro squad in the city and one of the best in the country. Among the players pictured are Louisville's three major-league batting champions: Pete Browning (American Association/1882 and 1885), Guy Hecker (American Association/1886) and Chicken Wolf (American Association/1890). Third in the 1882 American Association race, this is the club which brought major-league baseball back to Louisville after a four-year absence. Members of the team are (BACK ROW) Leech Maskrey, left field; Pete Browning, second base; Tony Mullane, pitcher; third baseman Bill Schenck (with Mullane's left hand on his shoulder); and utility player John Strick (far right, standing); (MIDDLE ROW) Dan Sullivan, catcher; Manager/shortstop Denny Mack; and first baseman/pitcher Guy Hecker (with Strick's right hand on his shoulder); (FRONT ROW) John Reccius, center field/pitcher; and Chicken Wolf, right field. (University of Louisville Photographic Archives)

TONY MULLANE

Five pitchers are known to have switch-pitched (thrown both right-handed and left-handed in the same game) in major-league history. The first was Anthony John "Tony" Mullane in a July 18, 1882, game versus Baltimore, which Mullane ended up losing 9-8 after Charlie Householder hit his only home run of the year in the American Association contest.

Besides Mullane, the group includes Larry Corcoran (for the 1884 Chicago National League White Stockings); John Roach

Tony Mullane (seated far left, middle row) and teammates of the 1888 Cincinnati American Association team. (National Baseball Library and Archive, Cooperstown, NY)

(the 1887 New York National League Giants); another Louisville pitcher, Elton "Icebox" Chamberlain, the only man to win a switch-pitched game (an 18-6 victory versus Kansas City on May 9, 1888); and Greg Harris (Montreal Expos, a 9–7 loss to Cincinnati on Sept. 28, 1995).

Handsome as well as talented, Mullane was known as "The Count" and "The Apollo of the Box" because of his smoldering good looks. That classic countenance led to the popularization of "Ladies Day" as a standard major-league promotion in the late 1880s when Mullane was pitching for Cincinnati in the old American Association.

Seeing that women flocked to the ballpark whenever the handsome Mullane pitched, team owner Aaron Stern began to shrewdly schedule Mullane against poor-drawing ballclubs, billing those games as "Ladies Day" events. The result was a major marketing tool for baseball that exists to this day.

Mullane, however, was more than just a great draw. He was also a great pitcher.

A 13-year veteran (1881-1894), Mullane posted a fabulous 285-220 career slate that included five 30-win and three 20-win seasons. That figure, incredibly enough, would have been even larger had Mullane not been suspended the entire 1885 season for contractural violations. That lost season almost certainly cost him a shot at 300 lifetime victories, a figure considered automatic for the Hall of Fame.

Mullane's first season, 1882, was with Louisville, where he gave a strong showing of the great career to follow. The ace of the staff, Mullane went 30-24 for the Eclipse.

The colorful Mullane died in 1944 at age 85. His death came exactly six decades after he pitched the game in which batterymate Moses Fleetwood Walker, major-league baseball's first black ballplayer, made his professional debut.

GUY HECKER

The only pitcher in major-league history to win a batting title did so in a Louisville uniform.

Nicknamed "The Blonde Guy" (a reference to the color of his hair), Guy Jackson Hecker led the American Association in 1886 with a .341 batting average. The work takes on greater form when the runner-up is factored in, legendary teammate Pete Browning, who just lost the batting crown that season with a .340 batting mark.

Given the specialization of pitchers (notably the relief pitcher) and the introduction of the designated-hitter rule in modern times, it seems highly unlikely that Hecker's precocious feat will ever be duplicated.

An extraordinarily versatile player who played first base when he didn't pitch, Hecker concluded his brief but brilliant nine-year career in 1890 with a 175-148 career hill slate and a .283 lifetime batting average.

That work included three other records of notable distinction.

In 1884, he turned out a Triple Crown pitching ledger comprised of a 52-20 mark, 385 strikeouts and a 1.80 ERA. He also led the league in innings (670.2); games pitched (76); starts (73); and complete games (72). And, for good measure, he batted .297.

The third highest win total ever posted in single-season play by a pitcher, behind the 60 wins of Hoss Radbourn for the National League Providence team in 1884 and the 53 triumphs of John Clarkson for the National League Chicago squad in 1885, Hecker's total was the highest ever compiled in the 10 years that the American Association operated (1882-1891).

It had its price, though. Hecker slipped in wins every year thereafter, his arm irreparably damaged as the result of the staggering work he shoulderd during his magnificent 1884 season.

Hecker's lifetime pitching tab also included a no-hitter on September 19, 1882, versus Pittsburgh. That came just days after the American Association's first no-hitter, which was pitched by Louisville teammate, Tony Mullane. In addition, Hecker on July 4, 1884 pitched both ends of a holiday doubleheader, beating Brooklyn 5-4 and 8-2 in a pair of American Association contests.

Hecker turned out another record in 1886, the year of his historic batting title.

In the finale of an August 15 doubleheader against Baltimore, Hecker scored seven runs off a flashy six-for-seven per-formance that saw him slug three home runs, drill three singles and reach base a seventh time via an error. His seven runs scored in a game still stands as the major-league record (the National and American League records are both six runs).

Hecker, incidentally, also picked up the win in the 22-5 smashing that completed a doubleheader trouncing of Baltimore.

And, on closing day of the 1887 season — October 7 — Hecker became the first man to play eight innings at first base without being offered a chance (as the visitors in the 2-0 loss to Cincinnati, Louisville had no ninth inning in the field after failing to at least tie the score in their final frame at bat).

Hecker called it quits at the end of the 1890 season, which he spent as a player/manager for a hapless Pittsburgh team that finished in the National League cellar with an abysmal 23-113 record.

After managing in the minors for a few years, Hecker returned to Oil City, Pa., where he had begun his baseball career, and entered the oil business.

Later opening a grocery store there, Hecker in 1931 was involved in an automobile accident that left the gallant right-hander's pitching arm so damaged he could not write except with a typewriter.

Issued a lifetime pass by the game in his final retirement years, Hecker later moved to Wooster, Ohio, where he died at age 82 on December 3, 1938.

LOUISVILLE CURIOS

In 1884, Guy Hecker lived at 1920 West Market in Louisville. And, for a portion of his major-league stay in Louisville (including the epic 1884 season), Hecker owned and operated the Hecker Baseball Supply Company, which was located at 445 West Jefferson.

Guy Hecker *(University of Louisville Photographic Archives)*

TOAD RAMSEY

If nothing else, Toad Ramsey certainly knew his worth.

So the story goes, Ramsey was once offered $100 to pitch a ballgame. He refused the offer, countering with his own proposal of $5 per strikeout, which was accepted. He then proceeded to strike out 24 batters, and landed up making $120!

Louisville's star hurler in 1886 and 1887, southpaw Thomas A. "Toad" Ramsey logged numbers both years that far exceeded the performances of his American Association teams.

In 1886, he went 38-27 with 499 strikeouts, losing that season's strikeout crown to Baltimore's Matty Kilroy, who set the all-time seasonal standard with 513 whiffs. (Ramsey's 1886 work also included a league-leading 588.2 innings pitched). In 1887, Ramsey came back with a 37-27 slate that including a league-leading 355 strikeouts.

Unfortunately, Ramsey was a hard drinker, and as a result, lasted but six seasons (1885–1890) in the major leagues, where he compiled a 114–124 lifetime slate. His mercurial career included a pair of 30–win seasons with Louisville, and a 24–17 mark in 1890 with St. Louis.

It also included an atrocious 8–30 mark in 1888 for Louisville, who went through a nightmare of a season.

THE 1885 AMERICAN ASSOCIATION LOUISVILLES. Most of the boys are here, and they look grand in this fabulous old-time team photograph (note the rather scattered arrangement of the players in this picture). By number, members of this team which finished in a fifth place tie with Brooklyn in the American Association that year are (1) Tom McLaughlin, second base; (2) Al Mays, pitcher; (3) Joe Miller, shortstop; (4) Leech Maskrey, left field; (5) Dan Sullivan, catcher; (6) Monk Cline, third base/outfield; (7) Jack Kerins, first base; (8) Philip Reccius, third base; (9) Pete Browning, center field; (10) Guy Hecker, pitcher; (11) Manager Jim Hart; (12) Norman Baker, pitcher; (13) Amos Cross, catcher; (14) Joe Crotty, catcher; and (15) Chicken Wolf, right field. The team leaders were Hecker, the staff ace with a 30–23 mark, and Browning, who captured his second American Association batting title with a .362 average. Also of interest in this photograph is Philip Reccius, whose older brother John Reccius is part of the 1882 Louisville American Association photograph. (University of Louisville Photographic Archives)

Looking to improve on their solid 76–60 mark of 1887, the franchise instead wandered aimlessly as Ramsey and Pete Browning — the team's top pitcher and top batter (a career–best .402) respectively of the preceding season — drove the outfit straight into east Hell with their wild drinking.

In its Thursday, July 26, 1888, issue, the Louisville Courier–Journal reported that Ramsey was in jail. Though simple in style, the story dramatically showed the depth of Ramsey's fall from grace. It began:

Tom Ramsey, the great left–handed pitcher of the Louisville Base Ball Club, stood in front of Hecker's saloon on Fifth Street yesterday (Wednesday) afternoon. It was understood that a constable, armed with several bail–writs, was looking for the left–hand hero of many a pitching battlefield, and that he was bravely standing on the sidewalk, alone and unprotected, created some surprise in those who happened to pass along.

An unlighted twenty-five cent cigar was stuck at an angle of forty-five degrees in the pitcher's mouth, and came in contact with the black stove–pipe hat which was rakishly tilted far forward over his eyes.

His freedom, however, was suddenly terminated when a "strong, firm hand grasped the collar of his silk–lined Prince Albert coat, and Tom was a prisoner to Constable Sam Webb, and was yanked off to jail."

To say the least, the situation was serious.

His entire salary for the season had already been drawn in advance, and the club could not help him immediately since owner–manager Mordecai Davidson was on an eastern road trip with the team. Thus, when no friends came to make bond for Ramsey, he was forced to remain in jail overnight because of $90.50 in debts to several saloons and the Fifth Avenue Hotel. Adding to Ramsey's woes — reported the Courier–Journal — were other creditors, who were expected to take a similar course of action unless those matters were resolved.

Interviewed that night in his cell, a pathetic Ramsey tearfully told a Courier–Journal reporter:

Toad Ramsey
(University of Louisville Photographic Archives)

"You see, I have no idea of the value of money, and that's why I am here. As long as a man has money in his pockets and has 6,000 people cheering him on the diamond, he has plenty of friends. To–night, I haven't got a friend in the wide world but John Kelly and my father and poor old mother. If I could prevent the news of my disgrace reaching home, I would give five years of my life most gladly. I will engage an attorney in the morning, and until then, I have no idea how I will be able to get out."

Things rapidly turned around, though.

The following day, through the financial help of a Louisville Evening Times reporter (and after taking the oath of insolvency), Ramsey was released from jail.

In relaying this news to the public, the Courier–Journal struck a firm blow for justice. Whether it was a serious defense, or just tongue in cheek, remains a mystery to this day, however.

The action of the saloon keepers in having Ramsey put in jail is condemned by nearly everybody who has the slightest acquaintance with Ramsey. He has spent hundreds of dollars in those very saloons and the profit from him alone must have been much greater than what the debts amount to.

Ramsey would not risk being blacklisted by the Louisville Club for such a small amount of money and would have been bound to return there after his suspension had ended.

Even if he had been transferred to another club then he could have been made to pay the debt by means of the bail writ when the club visited this city.

Ironically, Ramsey finished his life the way he had begun it: as a common bricklayer in his native Indianapolis, where he had been discovered as a teenager by future Louisville manager Jack Kerins.

ICEBOX CHAMBERLAIN

The only recorded winner of a switch-pitched game in major-league history, Elton P. "Icebox" Chamberlain concluded his 10-year major-league career in 1896 with a solid 157-120 lifetime ledger. That work included one 30-win campaign and a pair of 20-win seasons.

Nicknamed "Icebox" because of his coolness under fire on the mound (although another source attributed the monicker to his sulky, stand-offish ways, and yet another attributes it to his refrigerator-like build — short and squat), Chamberlain took an 18-6 win versus Kansas City on May 9, 1888, pitching both right-handed (his normal style of pitching) and left-handed.

Elton P. "Icebox" Chamberlain
(National Baseball Library and Archive, Cooperstown, NY)

He is one of four ambidextrous pitchers known to have hurled during the pre-modern era. Significantly, two of them were Louisville pitchers — Tony Mullane (1882) and Chamberlain. The quartet also includes Larry Corcoran (1884) and John Roach (1887).

Chamberlain, who began his career in 1886 with Louisville, occupies another spot in baseball history. On May 30, 1894, Boston's Bobby Lowe became the first man in major-league history to homer four times in a game. On the mound that day for Cincinnati was Chamberlain.

Chamberlain's first great season (25-11 in 1888)

was split between two teams. Louisville's ace (14-9) at the time the club (who would finish next to last that year in the American Association) traded him to St. Louis, Chamberlain supplied the latter with an 11-2 tab that helped that dynasty gain its fourth straight American Association flag.

The story behind Chamberlain's transfer was a classic example of the mismanagement which plagued the Louisville franchise throughout its entire major-league existence.

According to newspaper accounts, Louisville manager Mordecai Davidson and St. Louis owner Chris von der Ahe initiated the transaction during a train ride on August 31, 1888.

The deal was consummated the following day, when Davidson — who had asked to return home before making a final decision — wired von der Ahe with his okay. In short order, Chamberlain passed over to the St. Louis Browns for $4,000 cash.

Incredibly, the transaction had taken place because von der Ahe had managed to convince — a better word is conned — Davidson that the trade was a good one since Louisville had no chance to better their position. That was true of that season only, but not the future, which Davidson — in effect — sold a piece of at a staggering cost.

The following year, much because of no pitching, Louisville suffered its worst major-league season (complete with a major-league record 26-game loss skein).

Making the plundering worse was the fact that von der Ahe had had his choice of Louisville's top four pitchers — Chamberlain, Toad Ramsey, Scott Stratton and John Ewing.

The error of Davidson's deal was not lost on the Louisville Courier–Journal, who the day after the trade (September 2, 1888), responded with this item in its Base Ball Notes section:

Take (Lave) Cross, Chamberlain, (Jack) Kerins and (Hub) Collins out of the Louisville team, and the rest might well as be used for ballast. Just how it managed to win more games than Cleveland is something Philadelphia cranks can't understand. Goodbye, Colonels. You're a nice set of fellows, doubtlessly, but the rest of you have mistaken your vocations. Certainly baseball, as a regular thing, is something out of your line. (Note the absence of Pete Browning from the list of quality players; his hard drinking that year had put him — despite his .300 plus average — on the unwanted list, too.)

Emphasizing that opinion was another item in the Base Ball Notes section, which reported the Louisville manager turning down an offer for Cross and Collins because he wished "to strengthen his team, not weaken it."

On September 10, 1888, the Louisville Courier-Journal reported that Davidson had sold Chamberlain privately for a figure less than that offered by Baltimore. It was supposed that part of the St. Louis deal included standout Arlie Latham. However, the 1889 season found Latham with the Browns, proving that unlike Davidson, von der Ahe — the master of one of the game's earliest dynasties — was not a fool.

THE 1888 & 1889 LOUISVILLE AMERICAN ASSOCIATION TEAMS

*N*icknames don't win pennants, and the 1888 Louisville American Association outfit was proof paramount of that, finishing next to last in the circuit that year.

One of the many monickered players pictured here is Hubert B. "Hub" Collins (seated, far right), a classy–fielding second baseman/outfielder with a .284 lifetime batting average. Collins' fine career work included a .310 batting mark for Brooklyn against his native Louisville in the 1890 World Series.

Unfortunately, Collins' fine major–league career totalled only seven seasons; on May 21, 1892, at age 28, he succumbed to typhoid fever in Brooklyn, New York.

Besides his youth and the brilliant career that it abruptly terminated, another sad aspect to Collins' untimely demise was the fact that it came at a time when Collins was attempting to get his career back in good order. That career had been severely compromised by a collision on July 20, 1891 between Collins and outfielder Tommy "Oyster" Burns. In its May 23, 1892 story of Collins' death, the Louisville Courier–Journal reported:

A short fly had been hit to rightfield, for which both Collins and Burns ran. Owing to the noise made by locomotives passing the grounds, the two players did not hear the warning cries of the other men, and crashed together with frightful force.

Both were knocked senseless, and were carried from the field. Burns, the heavier man, was least hurt, and soon resumed his place on the team.

Collins, on the other hand, was unconscious for hours, and for some days his mind wandered. He

Members of the 1888 team in this grand ballpark photograph from yesteryear are (STANDING) Skyrocket Smith, first base; Guy Hecker, first base/pitcher; Pete Browning, center field; Jack Kerins, outfield/catcher; Paul Cook, catcher; Joe Werrick, third base; (SEATED) Toad Ramsey, pitcher; Icebox Chamberlain, pitcher; Bill White, shortstop; John Kelly, Manager; Scott Stratton, pitcher; Chicken Wolf, right field; and Hub Collins, left field. (The Filson Club, Louisville, KY)

Members of the 1889 club are (STANDING) Dan Shannon, second base; Farmer Vaughn, catcher/outfield; a man identified as Brown (most likely a club official of some kind); John Galligan, outfield; Chicken Wolf, right field; (SEATED) Farmer Weaver, center field; John Ewing, pitcher; Scott Stratton, pitcher; Red Ehret, pitcher; and Ed Flanagan, first base. Noticeably absent are five of the six principals in the strike (only Shannon is pictured): Pete Browning (left field), Phil Tomney (shortstop), Paul Cook (catcher), Harry Raymond (third base) and Guy Hecker (first base/pitcher). Note that with the exception of Farmer Weaver, all the other players in this photograph are looking away from the camera, perhaps at some action on the field (cynics might say for a way out of their wretched situation). (National Baseball Library and Archive, Cooperstown, NY)

finally got on his feet, but was unable to play during the remainder of the season.

Last spring (the spring of 1892), he joined the team and went South with it. A month in the South seemed to do him good, and he began the championship season in left field, where he did such good work, both in the field and with the stick, that (manager John Montgomery) Ward decided to keep him there. The collision had made Collins so timid he could not bring himself to play on the infield.

⌘

One of the worst teams in baseball history were the 1889 Louisvilles of the American Association, who reeled off 26 straight losses — still a major-league record — enroute to an abysmal 27-111 record and a last-place finish in the league that season.

Around the league, the club was the whipping boy for everyone. Locally, things were just as bad, if not worse, for the team, whose native city virtually treated them as pariahs.

In the midst of the disastrous road trip which produced 21 of the 26 straight defeats, the team was reported missing during the devastating Johnstown, Penn., flood. However, The Louisville Commercial displayed no concern for the team's plight in a June 4, 1889 article.

The Athletics failed to lower Louisville's average yesterday. The game scheduled to be played at Philadelphia did not take place because The Wandering Jays are waterbound somewhere between Columbus and the Quaker City. There is not much sympathy for them here. In fact, if the entire team had been standing in front of the Johnstown reservoir when it broke last

Friday evening, the majority of the people of Louisville would have viewed the calamity as a just visitation of Providence.

Certainly, they had their problems from all sides. Besides the record loss streak, there was the situation of superstar hitter Pete Browning, who was suspended for drunkenness the last two months of the season (violating a pledge of abstinence he had sworn out before a local judge on April 9 of that year). Not surprisingly, Browning batted a career low .256 that season, although the following year he came back with a .373 mark for Cleveland that earned him the batting championship of the Players' League.

Then, there was the brief players' strike that year in late June that followed on the heels of the end of the gargantuan loss skein. The first such strike in major-league history, it was precipitated by the heavy-handed tactics of owner Mordecai Davidson, who beleaguered the team's play and morale with illegal fines and pay dockings. (Shortly thereafter, Davidson turned the club over to American Association officials).

The history doesn't stop there, however.

The next year, this franchise became the first in baseball history to jump from last to first place in the space of one season when they took the 1890 American Association flag. That feat would not be turned out again until 1991 by the foes in that year's World Series — the Atlanta Braves and the Minnesota Twins.

LOUISVILLE CURIOS

The 1889 Louisvilles were the first major-league club to lose 100 games in a season. They had four managers that year. One of them was Dude Esterbrook, who committed suicide in 1901 aboard a train. At the time of his death, he was on his way to a mental institution.

RECORD 26–GAME LOSING STREAK OF THE 1889 LOUISVILLE AMERICAN ASSOCIATION CLUB

Date	Site	Opponent	Score	Pitcher	Loss #
5-22	Home	Baltimore	11-2	Ewing	1
5-23	Home	Baltimore	9-8	Ehret	2
5-26	Away	Cincinnati	8-7	Ewing	3
	Away	Cincinnati	16-4	Ehret	4
5-27	Away	Cincinnati	10-9	Stratton	5
5-28	Away	Cincinnati	13-12	Ehret	6
5-31	Away	Columbus	7-2	Stratton	7
6-1	Away	Columbus	8-3	Ramsey	8
6-2	Away	Columbus	11-4	Ewing	9
	Away	Columbus	12-3	Ehret	10
6-5	Away	Philadelphia	11-10	Stratton	11
6-6	Away	Philadelphia	5-2	Ramsey	12
	Away	Philadelphia	16-3	Ehret	13
6-7	Away	Philadelphia	9-7	Stratton	14
6-8	Away	Brooklyn	14-5	Stratton	15
6-9	Away	Brooklyn	12-2	Ramsey	16
6-10	Away	Brooklyn	7-5	Stratton	17
6-11	Away	Brooklyn	4-2	Ramsey	18
6-13	Away	Baltimore	4-2	Ehret	19
6-15	Away	Baltimore	4-2	Ramsey	20
6-17	Away	Baltimore	10-6	Ramsey	21
	Away	Baltimore	10-0	Ehret	22
6-18	Away	Baltimore	17-7	Ramsey	23
6-21	Home	St. Louis	7-3	Ramsey	24
6-22	Home	St. Louis	7-6	Hecker	25
	Home	St. Louis	3-2	Ewing	26

NOTES

The 26-loss skein was preceded by a three-game winning streak, the last an 8-4 victory over Baltimore on May 21 that placed Louisville's record at 8-20. The skid was finally halted on June 23, when Louisville topped St. Louis 7-3, and posted their record at 9-46.

During the streak (five at home, 21 away), Louisville was outscored by their opponents 245-118.

The biggest winner was Baltimore (seven victories). Cincinnati, Columbus, Philadelphia and Brooklyn (that year's American Association champion) all had four wins. The league runner-up, St. Louis, had three wins. Only Kansas City did not get a shot at Louisville during the horrendous streak.

Toad Ramsey was the losingest pitcher (eight defeats) during the skein. He was followed by Red Ehret (seven), Scott Stratton (six), John Ewing (four) and Guy Hecker (one).

The losing streak included five doubleheader defeats (May 26, and June 2, 6, 17 and 22) and three extra-inning losses (10 innings in first game of June 17 doubleheader, and 11 innings on June 7 and second game of June 22 doubleheader). The June 11 game was called after eight innings because of rain. The June 15 game was called after five innings because of rain.

CHICKEN WOLF

The third and last of Louisville's major-league batting champions, all of whom played in the American Association, William Van Winkle "Chicken" Wolf — along with Pete Browning and Guy Hecker — enabled Louisville to dominate the loop's hitter standings.

Between them, the trio logged four batting titles during the decade that the American Association operated (1882-1891), almost a title every other year.

Thought to be the only player to compete in the American Asociation all 10 years that it operated, Wolf was born in Louisville on May 12, 1862. Popularly known as "Jimmy", Wolf picked up his professional monicker in 1882 from another rookie, teammate Pete Browning.

In a pre-game lunch that year, Wolf gorged himself on stewed chicken despite his manager's orders that the team eat lightly before games. In that afternoon's game, Wolf made several errors. After the game, Browning loudly proclaimed that Wolf's bad performance was due to all the chicken he had eaten, and thus Wolf was rechristened.

Things were certainly never dull for Wolf, one of the American Association's — and the game's great stars — who played much of his career in Browning's

William Van Winkle "Chicken" Wolf
(University of Louisville Photographic Archives)

shadow. An August 22, 1886 game against Cincinnati was proof paramount of that. In that contest, a stray dog grabbed the pants of the Reds' centerfielder, Abner Powell, enabling Wolf to circle the bases and get a two-run home run that won the game for Louisville 5-3 in 11 innings.

Wolf's grandest moment came in 1890 when the speedy, solid-fielding outfielder took the 1890 American Association batting crown with a .363 mark. His work that year for a Louisville squad that won its only major-league pennant also included a circuit-topping 197 hits.

A career .290 hitter, Wolf carried his hot stick into that year's World Series against Brooklyn. leading his team with a .360 average (9-for-25) that included three doubles, one triple and eight RBIs.

Stripped of his vaunted speed toward the end of his career because of increasing weight, Wolf concluded his 11-year big-league tenure in 1892 with St. Louis of the National League.

After his retirement from baseball, he joined the Louisville Fire Department.

Wolf's last years were marked by tragedy and an end which mirrored that of Pete Browning. The downward slide began with a terrible accident.

Driving an engine to a fire, Wolf hit a candy cart broadside as he turned a corner (bystanders tried to warn Wolf of an upcoming obstruction, but the engine and team nonetheless ran blindly into the cart).

The impact caused the engine to become separated from the team. Hurled to the cobblestone street, Wolf suffered a head injury which left him "mentally unbalanced", according to his obituary in the Louisville Courier-Journal.

Wolf worsened when one of his children died shortly thereafter, and was finally committed to the state insane asylum at Lakeland in 1901.

Released in March of 1903, Wolf suffered a relapse several months later and died in old City Hospital on May 16, 1903. His end came four days after his 41st birthday.

Buried in Louisville's venerable Cave Hill Cemetery (Lot 5, Section 186), Wolf is one of several old-time major-leaguers buried there. That group notably includes Pete Browning, whose final days mirrored those of Wolf.

LOUISVILLE CURIOS

According to Louisville directories from that era, Chicken Wolf lived at 1908 West Walnut during his 1882 rookie season. In Louisville's American Association flag-winning year of 1890, Wolf was listed at 610 Myrtle. His profession was listed as "baseballist", as baseball players were called in those days. At the time of his death, he was living at 1922 West Walnut.

SCOTT STRATTON

One of three major guiding forces behind Louisville's only major-league pennant winner (Chicken Wolf and Red Ehret being the other two), Scott Stratton posted a brilliant 34-14 record for the American Association champs that year.

A foundation piece of that slate was a phenomenal win streak that tied the American League record and is just four short of the major-league standard.

LOUISVILLE CURIOS

In 1890, Stratton lived at the Phoenix Hotel. In 1892, he resided at the Waverly Hotel.

(Stratton's 16-game win feat, which for years has been reported as being just 15 successuive wins, is discussed in the section entitled "Lost Streak", which follows this profile).

The 1890 campaign was a career year for Stratton, who finished off his eight-year major-league stint in 1895. That work included a solid .274 lifetime batting average.

Oddly enough, in the 1890 World Series against Brooklyn, Stratton — the ace of Louisville's staff during the regular season — played second fiddle to Red Ehret. Stratton went 1-1 in three appearances, while Ehret—a 20-game winner during the regular season—emerged as the king of Louisville's staff during the post-season fray, winning two games and saving another.

LOST STREAK

Is one of the game's great pitching feats actually bigger — and better — than what is listed in the record books? It looks that way.

For years, the record books have listed pitcher Scott Stratton's 1890 seasonal win streak for the co-World Champion Louisvilles of the American Association at 15 straight.

Scott Stratton
(National Baseball Library and Archive, Cooperstown, NY)

the bottom of the sixth, and at the end of six complete innings, the score stood 6-3 (the final score).

Thus, Stratton should get the win, and Ehret — who pitched the final three innings — should get the save. This is in accordance with Baseball Rule 10.19A, part of the official scorer's section — Section X — which states: "Credit the starting pitcher with a game won only if he has pitched at least five complete innings and his team not only is in the lead when he is replaced but remains in the lead the remainder of the game."

Day/Date	Opponent (Site)	Pitching Summary and Score	Win #
6-28/SAT	Brooklyn (H)	*P6/6-3	1
7-1/TU	Brooklyn (H)	C/3-2	2
7-4/FRI	Rochester (H)	C/5-1#	3
7-8/TU	Philadelphia (H)	C/10-2	4
7-15/TU	Syracuse (H)	C/10-3	5
7-17/TH	Syracuse (H)	C/6-4	6
7-19/SAT	Brooklyn (H)	C/15-12	7
7-24/TH	Philadelphia (A)	C/7-6	8
7-28/MON	Rochester (A)	C/12-2	9
7-31/TH	Rochester (A)	C/8-3	10
8-6/WED	Brooklyn (H)	C/7-2	11
8-9/SAT	Syracuse (H)	C/11-2	12
8-14/TH	Rochester (H)	**P8/17-5	13
8-21/TH	Philadelphia (H)	C/2-1	14
8-23/SAT	St. Louis (A)	C/4-1	15
8-28/TH	Syracuse (A)	C/11-1	16

* Pitched six complete innings, Louisville scored four runs in bottom of sixth to push score to 6-3 (final score); Ehret pitches 7th, 8th, and 9th innings.
**Pitched eight complete innings, Louisvlle leading 17 - 4. Goodall pitches ninth inning. Louisville wins 17-5.
\# First game of the doubleheader.

However, boxscores and newspaper accounts put the streak at 16 straight. That discrepancy is significant since the revised total of 16 equals the American League record (shared by four hurlers), and is three short of the all-time major-league record held by a pair of National Leaguers.

The error surrounds the very beginning of the streak, a home game against Brooklyn on Saturday, June 28, 1890.

Stratton pitched six full innings. When Louisville (the home team) came to bat in the bottom of the sixth, they were down 3-2. However, they scored four runs in

NOTES

The last loss by Stratton before 16-game win streak began was a 10-7 defeat on Wednesday, June 25, at St. Louis.

Stratton's skein ended on Monday, September 1, with a 12-6 loss to Rochester. The game was the first part of a doubleheader defeat (12-6 and 10-5) for Louisville at Rochester.

Stratton lost a chance to run off 17-game win streak when he left after the first inning of a game on Saturday, July 5, against Rochester.

Stratton completed 14 of his 16 wins (noted by "C" in pitching summary).

During Stratton's streak, Louisville outscored its opponents 134-51.

Stratton's 16 wins included four wins each against Brooklyn, Rochester and Syracuse; three over Philadelphia; and one versus St. Louis. Eleven wins came at home, the other five on the road.

Stratton's 1890 win streak, the longest in American Association history, ties the American League record co–held by Walter Johnson (1912/Washington Senators), Smokey Joe Wood (1912/Boston Red Sox), Lefty Grove (1931/Philadelphia Athletics), and School-boy Rowe (1934/Detroit Tigers). And, it is three short of the major-league record shared by National Leaguers Tim Keefe (1888/New York Giants) and Rube Marquard (1912/New York Giants).

FARMER WEAVER

Yet another important part of Louisville's 1890 American Association championship squad was West Virginia native William B. "Farmer" Weaver, who batted .289 that season. In the World Series, the slick center fielder averaged a hit a game in the seven-game series.

Weaver's 1890 work also included a six-hit game (the major-league record of seven hits in a nine–inning game is shared by National Leaguers Wilbert Robinson/1892 and Rennie Stennett/1975). That fat game came at home on August 12, 1890, versus Syracuse. Hitting for the cycle as well, Weaver pounded out two singles, a double, two triples and one home run. Not bad for a day's work.

His six-hit game was the last of three by Louisville players, Weaver being preceded by Guy Hecker (three singles and three home runs in seven at–bats in an

Farmer Weaver
(National Baseball Library and Archive, Cooperstown, NY)

August 15, 1886, home contest against Baltimore) and Reddy Mack (six singles in six at-bats in a May 26, 1887 home game versus Brooklyn).

And, then there was the matter of a July 4 holiday game in 1893, in which Weaver shot the lights out of a flyball (Weaver was charged with nothing more than thoroughly entertaining the crowd during a thoroughly unentertaining season).

The July 5, 1893, item in the Louisville Courier-Journal read:

Weaver created a sensation in right field yester-

day in an appropriate manner. He is the possessor of a horse pistol that rivals the famous weapon of "Fighting Bob." He loaded the cylinder to the brim before the game yesterday and placed the weapon in his sliding pad. Someone knocked a high fly into his territory. Weaver ran under it, steadied himself and pulled his pocket cannon from his trousers. He fired five shots at the ball as it descended, knocked it back up in the air with the free hand and fired the remaining two shots at the ball as it descended for the second time. He then quickly dropped the weapon to the ground, catching the ball as it passed. He was heartily cheered for the successful performance of his original Independence Day feat.

Clearly, at bat or in the field, Weaver could make a lot of noise.

RED EHRET

Though reportedly blind in one eye, pitcher Philip Sydney "Red" Ehret didn't show it on the mound.

Part of the powerful tandem that hurled Louisville to the 1890 American Association championship and into the World Series, Ehret backed up staff ace Scott Stratton with a sparkling 25-14 record.

However, in the World Series that followed, Ehret was the kingpin of the Louisville staff with a 1.35 ERA garnered from a pair of wins and one save. His work was instrumental in Louisville getting a draw in the seven-game series (each club scored three wins and there was one tie game), which was called off in late October because of inclement weather.

Like teammate Stratton, the 1890 campaign was a career season for Ehret, a Louisville native who finished his 11-year major-league career — four of those seasons with Louisville — in 1898. After his playing days were over, Ehret became a minor-league umpire.

Undoubtably, the 1890 championship work was one of the grandest moments of a life that ended under hard circumstances.

One of Louisville's great baseball treasures, Ehret died destitute at age 71 in 1940. The end came in Cincinnati, for whom he had once hurled. A resident of the Hamilton County Home at the time of his death, Ehret was laid to rest in a section for the poor in the Baltimore Pike Cemetery. His gravesite remains unmarked.

Interestingly enough, Ehret — just days before his death, according to a Cincinnati Enquirer story — gave one of his few earthly assets to a friend.

It was a gold lifetime pass to the major-league parks.

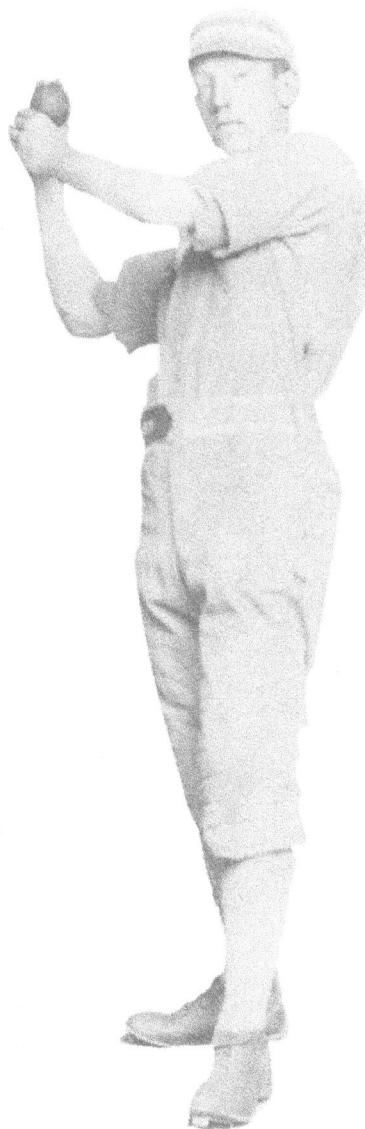

Philip Sydney "Red" Ehret
(National Baseball Library and Archive, Cooperstown, NY)

LOUISVILLE CURIOS

Red Ehret was so nicknamed because of the color of his hair. During the 1890 championship season, he resided at 2104 Logan.

CHAPTER FIVE
LOUISVILLE KINGS:
LOUISVILLE AND THE 1890 WORLD SERIES

For a brief moment, Louisville enjoyed baseball royalty and these were the Princes of the City. This recently-discovered photograph from a bygone era is of the 1890 American Association pennant-winning Louisvilles. And, though few realize it today, this picture is also of kings, the 1890 World Co-Champion Louisvilles, who played National League titlist Brooklyn to a standoff in that year's World Series. Grand, majestic and illustrious, this photograph is an invaluable addition to the legacy of both Louisville and American baseball. Note that the picture, which was taken in 1890 according to information on the photograph, is identified as the "1890-1891 Champion Louisvilles". That is a reference to the cancelled 1890 World Series which was to have been completed in the spring of 1891 (but never was). Three figures of interest (the only ones who can be postively indentified) are located in the middle row. One is Manager John Chapman. The playing manager of the city's first major–league team, the 1876 National League Grays, Chapman is refinely outfitted in a handsome suit and a derby hat. Seated second from the left in the same row is Chicken Wolf, that year's American Association batting champion off a .363 average that was nearly 75 points over his lifetime average. Shortstop Phil Tomney is fourth from the right in the center row. (University of Louisville Photographic Archives)

Louisville · Base · Ball · Club,
— 76 —
CHAMPIONS

I – 1890 LOUISVILLE AMERICAN ASSOCIATION CHAMPIONS – I

O ctober 6 may not be a holiday in Louisville, but in a small way, it should be, for it was on that date in 1890 that the city secured its only major–league pennant (and by extension, the only major–league flag for the state of Kentucky).

The pennant–winning triumph was a 2–0 win at home versus Columbus. It was Louisville's 83rd victory against 42 defeats of the magical 1890 campaign (which they would end at 88–44 by virtue of a closing–day 13–1 triumph over St. Louis at home on October 14).

The heroes of the flag–clinching game were pitcher Scott Stratton and center fielder Farmer Weaver.

Louisville's ace that year with a 34–14 ledger that included a record 16–game winning streak, Stratton held the eventual American Association runner-up to six hits.

Weaver, an important cog in the Louisville drive that year via fine defense and a solid .289 batting average, drove in one run and scored the other in the pennant–clinching contest. Both runs, incidentally, were posted in the first inning.

The magnificent event was reported the next day (Tuesday, October 7, 1890) by the Louisville Courier–Journal under a main headline that simply read: "Champions Now."

Two supporting headlines, however, were somewhat more effusive about the magnificent achievement, reading: "That Is What the Game of Yesterday Makes the Louisvilles" and "They Have That Silk, Even Were They To Lose Every Remaining Contest."

༝✕༝

The following Sunday's issue (October 12, 1890) of the Louisville Courier–Journal carried a long item about the arrangements of the impending World Series between American Association champion Louisville and National League titlist Brooklyn. Bannered "The World's Series" and sub–headlined "An Agreement Reached By Presidents Byrne and Parsons as to the Championship Games", it went as follows:

President Charles H. Byrne, of the Brooklyn club, arrived in the city last night from New York to complete the final arrangements for the world's series. He was met by President (Lawrence S.) Parsons, Vice President Sachs and Manager (John) Chapman at the Louisville Hotel soon after his arrival.

"The party adjourned to one of the parlors of the hotel and in a very short time arrived at an agreement for the series.

It had been intended by the clubs to play in Boston, Philadelphia, Chicago and New York besides in Louisville and Brooklyn, but on account of the lateness of the season and the lack of interest in the several cities mentioned resulting from the baseball war (the 1890 season saw three leagues competing against each other — the American Association, the National League and the Players' League), it was decided to play only in Louisville and Brooklyn. The agreement in full is as follows:

"It is agreed that the Brooklyn Club, of the National League, and the Louisville Club, of the American Association, having won the championships of their respective associations, will play a friendly series of games, not to exceed nine in number, to decide the World's Base Ball Championship.

"It is also understood that the club first winning a majority of such games shall be entitled to be called the World's Champions of 1891.

"The price of admission to all games shall be fifty cents, and to the grand stand twenty–five cents extra, and in case of the Louisville Club, the latter club is authorized to charge sixty cents for pavilion seats.

"The umpires agreed upon to officiate in this world's series are John McQuaid, selected by the Louisville Club, and Wesley Curry, selected by the Brooklyn Club, and it is also agreed that in the event of either of said umpires failing to report for duty at any game, the umpire present shall be and is hereby authorized to umpire said game. It is also understood

and agreed that all games of this series shall be played under and governed by the joint playing rules governing all National Agreement clubs.

"The following is the schedule of games we hereby intend to play, to wit: In Louisville, Thursday, October 16; Friday, October 17; Saturday, October 18; Monday, October 20; Tuesday, October 21, to be left as an open date. In Brooklyn, Thursday, October 23; Friday, October 24; Saturday, October 25, and Monday, October 27. If the ninth game is necessary to decide the series, the place and date will be determined hereafter, but the above schedule shall be followed precisely, as in a regular championship series. It is also understood that the courtesy of each ground is extended only to the press."

⚜

Because of rain, the 1890 World Series was delayed a day, the first game being played in Louisville on Friday, October 17, rather than Thursday, October 16.

The opener was a total disaster for Louisville, as The Sporting Life reported in its weekly edition of October 25, 1890, (the first four games of the 1890 World Series were covered in this issue). The opening paragraphs, which were as harsh as the 9–0 whitewashing Louisville sustained, went as follows:

The first game of the inter–league series between the champion clubs of the National League and the American Association, by courtesy called the "world's championship" series, was played at Louisville, October 17, before 5,600 people.

Excursion trains were run over all the roads entering in the Falls City, and many base ball cranks from all the large towns around Louisville were on hand to cheer the Cyclones on to victory. They were disappointed, however, as the game resulted in a score of 9 to 0 in favor of the Bridegrooms (the team got that monicker when a number of them got married following the 1887 season).

The day was an ideal one for ball playing. The sun came out quite warm in the forenoon, and by the time the game was called no traces of rain were visible.

(Bill) Terry's pitching and the fielding of the Brooklyns, especially (George) Smith's work at short, were the features of the play unless the amateur playing of the home team can be termed a feature.

They seemed to enter the game with a faint heart, and with the exception of Stratton seemed to expect defeat. The latter pitched a good game up to the fifth inning, when the ragged support of the home team caused him to give up.

Staked to a 3–0 lead in the first inning, Brooklyn never looked back, and was leading 9–0 at the end of eight innings, when the game was called on account of darkness. William "Adonis" Terry got the win and Scott Stratton the loss.

Louisville lost the second game of the 1890 World Series, held in the Kentucky city on Saturday, October 18, although the score was much closer this time: 5–3. The winning pitcher was Tom Lovett, the losing pitcher Ed Daily.

Down two games to none, and playing at home, Louisville badly needed a win in the World Series.

They almost got it in the third game, played on Monday, October 20, posting three runs in the eighth inning to knot the score at 7–7. However, that is where the game stayed as it was called after eight innings because of darkness.

The third game hurlers included Bill "Adonis" Terry, Scott Stratton and George Meakim. Terry went the distance for Brooklyn; Stratton worked three innings for Louisville, then was relieved by Meakim.

In the last game of the 1890 World Series held in Louisville, on Tuesday, October 21, Louisville finally got what it needed so desperately — a victory.

Striking for three runs in the first inning, Louisville held on for an intense 5–4 win behind the gutsy pitching of Red Ehret, who allowed seven singles. Tom Lovett of Brooklyn was tagged with the loss, the first by a Brooklyn hurler in the post–season lockup. It also marked the first of two victories by a team on its home grounds in the mercurial 1890 World Series (the other was the fifth game at Brooklyn).

The scenery for the World Series then changed, as

the pair of clubs left for Brooklyn early the following morning (at 2:50 on Wednesday, October 22).

Though the fifth game was due to have been played in Brooklyn on Thursday, October 23, rain forced its postponement until Saturday, October 25.

It was another Brooklyn triumph, and the 7–2 win put Louisville's backs completely against the wall, seemingly with no place to go and just one game from defeat in the fall tilt.

The winning pitcher for Brooklyn, who once again jumped off to an early lead they did not relinquish, was Tom Lovett. Ed Daily of Louisville was tagged with the defeat (he was the only starting pitcher in the 1890 World Series to go winless).

The series was renewed on Monday, October 27, and game six — a narrow 9–8 victory for Louisville — gave the Kentucky visitors some breathing room.

In addition, the Louisville squad finally yielded ace Scott Stratton his first World Series victory. It required some help, though, from Red Ehret. Working the final three frames, Ehret survived a rocky eighth inning —when Brooklyn scored three runs — to post the only save of the series.

Though it was an exciting game, only an estimated 600 fans witnessed the contest. That was a substantial dropoff from the 5,663 fans who had witnessed the series opener. The small crowd was a direct product of the cold and rainy weather that had gotten steadily worse since the arrival of the series in Brooklyn.

With no end to the inclement weather in sight, it was decided that game seven on Tuesday, October 28, would be the final contest of the 1890 World Series.

The intent was to conclude the series the following spring when weather permitted. This never happened, however, and that — for all intents and purposes — created co–World Champions out of Louisville and Brooklyn. That scenario would not have been possible had Louisville not taken to game seven so well.

Though Brooklyn led 2–1 at the end of the first inning, Ehret shut the door on them the rest of the way as Louisville ran off a 6–2 triumph in front of the smallest crowd of the series — an estimated 300 patrons.

The pitching star of the 1890 World Series, Ehret allowed just four hits in the concluding contest (in addition, Ehret aided his cause with a triple and a run scored).

The hitting star of the series was Brooklyn's Patsy Donovan, who had compiled a magnificent .471 ledger (eight hits from 17 at–bats, one of them a double).

Other final statistics for the 1890 World Series cast Tom Lovett and Chicken Wolf in a stellar light. Lovett was Brooklyn's top slinger in the series with a 2–2 record and a 2.83 ERA. Wolf was Louisville's primo stickman, posting a fabulous .360 average (nine hits in 25 trips to the plate) that included three doubles and one triple. (Clearly, Wolf's American Association batting title that year — gained off a brilliant .363 average — had not been a fluke.)

෬෯

In the November 8, 1890, issue of The Sporting Life, a correspondent discussed Louisville and the recently–concluded World Series under a "Louisville Lines" banner. The report was dramatically different in tone from the October 25, 1890, article which had likened the Louisvilles to amateurs.

Well, after all, the Brooklyns failed to win the world's championship from the Louisvilles, and it was because they couldn't.

When interviewed at Kansas City, Dave Foutz said that he thought his team would have no trouble with the Louisvilles, and I must confess that after the first game here, I was of the same opinion, but after they got over their buck ague the Colonels came very fast, and they made a rattling finish.

I now verily believe that if it had not been for their excessive nervousness in the first games, the Cyclones would have wiped up the earth with the Bridegrooms.

Taking it the season through, the Brooklyns excel the Louisvilles in one particular only, and that is batting. The Louisvilles are better fielders and base–runners, and have a better lot of pitchers; yet the world's championship series failed to develop the particular excellencies of each team, for the Louisvilles were strong in batting, where they expected to be weak, and weak in fielding, where they expected to be strong.

It is almost superfluous to say that the Louisvilles returned from the East in much better spirits than they were when they left. Manager (John) Chapman was in great good humor, for when he went away, he hardly expected his men to tie the series. The players also felt very good over the result, and are quite sure that if the schedule had been played out they would have beaten the Brooklyns.

It had taken a little doing, but Louisville had earned the undying respect of one of its harshest critics. Their World Series action, unquestionably, was the product of design, not luck.

Besides Wolf, other dramatic improvements on the Louisville team that year which led to the city's only major–league flag and World Series action major improvements on the Louisville team were those of pitchers Scott Stratton and Red Ehret. The former skyrocketed from a 3–13 ledger in 1889 to a 34–14 mark in 1890; the latter showed a similar strong turnaround, going from a 10–29 slate in 1889 to a 25–14 record in 1890.

Of such mighty feats are pennants made.

LOUISVILLE CURIOS

According to old-time address directories, Harry Raymond lived at the Commercial Hotel, and Farmer Weaver resided at 2430 Grayson during the 1890 season.

LOUISVILLE CURIOS

Four of the starters were Kentucky natives, three of them from Louisville — Ehret, Wolf and Hamburg. Stratton was from Campbellsburg.

The 1890 starting lineup was John Ryan (catcher), Scott Stratton and Red Ehret (pitchers), Harry Taylor (first base), Tim Shinnick (second base), Phil Tomney (shortstop), Harry Raymond (third base), Charlie Hamburg (left field), Farmer Weaver (center field), and Chicken Wolf (right field).

And, here are two curios from David Nemec's watershed book on the American Association, "The Beer and Whisky League."

Before the 1890 season, Tim Shinnick bragged that "he had never played on anything but championship teams since his days at Philips Exeter Academy in the mid–1880s."

To many at the time, Shinnick's streak looked to be in serious jeopardy, considering the team's record the year before coupled with the fact that the 1890 Louisville lineup did not include long-time stars Pete Browning and Guy Hecker.

And, Herb Goodall Louisville's superb relief pitcher that season with an 8–5 record — talked all season about quitting to become a doctor. He stayed on because the Louisville team was so good. However, the 1890 season turned out to be the only big–league campaign for Goodall, who indeed did leave the game for medicine.

II – 1890 LOUISVILLE AMERICAN ASSOCIATION CHAMPIONS – II

Here's an encore for the 1890 champions. This sketch appeared on the August 16, 1890, cover of The Sporting Life, and while not as polished as the photograph on page 76, it is still a remarkable reminder of one of the greatest teams in Louisville's venerable baseball history. Pictured are (TOP ROW) Michael Jones, pitcher; Charlie Hamburg, left field; Manager John Chapman; Herb Goodall, pitcher; Ned Bligh, catcher;. (MIDDLE ROW) John B. Ryan, catcher; Phil Tomney, shortstop; Dan O'Connor, first base; Tim Shinnick, second base; Red Ehret, pitcher; Farmer Weaver, center field; (BOTTOM ROW) Scott Stratton, pitcher; Chicken Wolf, right field; George Meakim, pitcher; Harry Raymond, third base; and Harry Taylor, first base. (Philip Von Borries Collection)

1890 LOUISVILLE AMERICAN ASSOCIATION CHAMPIONSHIP RECORD

Date	Opponent	Result	Score	Site	Date	Opponent	Result	Score	Site
APRIL					**JUNE (continued)**				
18	St. Louis	L	11-8	Home	14	Toledo	W	11-1	Home
19	St. Louis	W	5-3	Home	17	Columbus	W	4-2	Away
20	St. Louis	WF	0-0	Home	18	Columbus	L	6-4	Away
21	St. Louis	W	17-4	Home	19	Columbus	L	7-1	Away
22	Columbus	W	2-1	Home	20	Toledo	L	12-2	Away
23	Columbus	L	3-2	Home	21	Toledo	L	3-2	Away
27	Toledo	W	4-3	Home	22	Toledo	W	3-2	Away
28	Toledo	W	3-0	Home	23	Toledo	W	5-0	Away
29	Toledo	W	4-2	Home	25	St. Louis	L	10-7	Away
					26	St. Louis	L	3-0	Away
MAY					27	St. Louis	L	8-6	Away
1	St. Louis	W	6-3	Away	28	Brooklyn	W	6-3	Home
2	St. Louis	L	11-3	Away	29	Brooklyn	W	9-3	Home
3	St. Louis	L	10-6	Away					
4	St. Louis	W	11-2	Away	**JULY**				
7	Toledo	L	6-1	Away	1	Brooklyn	W	3-2	Home
8	Toledo	L	7-1	Away	2	Brooklyn	W	5-3	Home
10	Columbus	L	6-2	Away	4-DH	Rochester	W	5-1	Home
11	Columbus	L	10-0	Away	4-DH	Rochester	W	6-2	Home
12	Columbus	W	1-0	Away	5	Rochester	W	8-3	Home
16	Philadephia	L	8-6	Away	6	Rochester	W	13-5	Home
17	Philadelphia	W	8-5	Away	8	Philadelphia	W	10-2	Home
18	Philadelphia	W	5-2	Away	9	Philadelphia	W	3-1	Home
19	Philadelphia	L	11-3	Away	10	Philadelphia	W	12-3	Home
21	Brooklyn	W	4-2	Away	12	Philadelphia	W	8-4	Home
22	Brooklyn	W	15-8	Away	13	Syracuse	L	10-4	Home
23	Brooklyn	L	4-2	Away	15	Syracuse	W	10-3	Home
24	Syracuse	L	4-3	Away	16	Syracuse	L	9-3	Home
25	Syracuse	W	13-12	Away	17	Syracuse	W	6-4	Home
27	Syracuse	W	3-2	Away	18	Brooklyn	W	7-6	Home
28	Syracuse	W	5-0	Away	19	Brooklyn	W	15-12	Home
30	Rochester	L	4-3	Away	20	Brooklyn	W	7-6	Home
31	Rochester	L	4-1	Away	21	Brooklyn	W	11-4	Home
					23	Philadelphia	W	6-4	Away
JUNE					24	Philadelphia	W	7-6	Away
1	Rochester	W	3-0	Away	26	Philadelphia	L	7-1	Away
3	St. Louis	W	5-2	Home	28	Rochester	W	12-2	Away
4	St. Louis	L	9-2	Home	29	Rochester	L	6-3	Away
5	St. Louis	L	9-3	Home	31	Rochester	W	8-3	Away
7	Columbus	W	10-9	Home					
8	Columbus	L	10-5	Home	**AUGUST**				
10	Columbus	W	9-1	Home	1	Syracuse	W	6-5	Away
11	Columbus	W	4-2	Home	2	Syracuse	W	8-0	Away
12	Toledo	W	1-0	Home	3	Syracuse	LF	0-0	Away
13	Toledo	L	4-3	Home	5	Brooklyn	L	8-3	Home

Date	Opponent	Result	Score	Site	Date	Opponent	Result	Score	Site
AUGUST (continued)					**SEPTEMBER (continued)**				
6	Brooklyn	W	7-2	Home	28-DH	Syracuse	W	11-4	Home
7	Brooklyn	W	7-2	Home	29	Syracuse	W	6-1	Home
8	Brooklyn	W	7-2	Home	30	Baltimore	W	1-0	Home
9	Syracuse	W	11-2	Home					
10	Syracuse	W	8-5	Home	**OCTOBER**				
12	Syracuse	W	18-4	Home	1	Baltimore	T	5-5	Home
14	Rochester	W	17-5	Home	3	Columbus	W	5-3	Home
16	Rochester	W	9-7	Home	4	Columbus	L	6-3	Home
17	Rochester	W	8-2	Home	5	Columbus	T	0-0	Home
21	Philadelphia	W	2-1	Home	6*	Columbus	W	2-0	Home
23	St. Louis	W	4-2	Away	7	Toledo	W	6-3	Home
24	St. Louis	L	10-4	Away	8	Toledo	W	8-3	Home
25	St. Louis	L	13-2	Away	9	Toledo	L	7-0	Home
28	Syracuse	W	11-1	Away	10	Toledo	W	7-6	Home
29	Syracuse	W	10-9	Away	11	St. Louis	W	10-1	Home
					12	St. Louis	L	7-3	Home
SEPTEMBER					14	St. Louis	W	13-1	Home
1-DH	Rochester	L	12-6	Away					
1-DH	Rochester	L	10-5	Away					
2	Rochester	L	7-3	Away					

DH — Doubleheader
* — Pennant-clinching game

GRAND TOTALS:

Games	Wins	Losses	Ties	Pct.
136	88	44	4	.647

3	Philadelphia	W	10-4	Away
4	Philadephia	W	8-2	Away
6	Philadelphia	W	7-0	Away
8	Baltimore	L	3-1	Away
9	Baltimore	W	9-4	Away
12	Columbus	L	4-3	Away
13	Columbus	L	4-1	Away
14	Columbus	L	3-0	Away
15	Toledo	W	6-5	Away
16-DH	Toledo	W	6-1	Away
16-DH	Toledo	W	8-0	Away
17	Toledo	W	13-3	Away
19	Philadelphia	W	9-4	Home
20-DH	Philadelphia	W	22-4	Home
20-DH	Philadelphia	W	10-0	Home
21-DH	Philadelphia	W	12-4	Home
21-DH	Philadelphia	W	16-3	Home
23	Rochester	W	13-6	Home
24	Rochester	T	1-1	Home
26	Rochester	T	1-1	Home
28-DH	Syracuse	L	10-3	Home

Runs Scored: 820
Runs Allowed: 584
April record: 7-2 (includes one win by forfeit)
May record: 10-12
June record: 12-11
July record: 20-4
August record: 15-4 (includes one loss by forfeit)
September record: 17-8 (also had two ties)
October record: 7-3 (also had two ties)

Biggest losing streak was four defeats (happened twice); after June 21, never lost more than three straight games the rest of the season. As the summer got hotter, so did the Louisvilles. Records for July and August respectively were 20-4 and 15-4 (including one loss by forfeit) for a combined record of 35-8.

1890 WORLD SERIES LINE SCORES

GAME 1: Brooklyn 9, Louisville 0

(At Louisville, Friday, October 17, 1890)

```
                                    R   H   E
Brooklyn   300 030 30 - 9  WP - Terry      9  11   1
Louisville 000 000 00 - 0  LP - Stratton   0   2   6
```
(Game called on account of darkness)
Attendance - 5,663.   Time of game - 1:43.
Umpires - Wesley Curry and John McQuaid.

GAME 2: Brooklyn 5, Louisville 3

(At Louisville, Saturday, October 18, 1890)

```
                                    R   H   E
Brooklyn   020 201 000 - 5  WP - Lovett    5   5   3
Louisville 101 000 001 - 3  LP - Daily     3   6   5
```
Attendance - 2,800.   Time of game - 1:45
Umpires - Wesley Curry and John McQuaid.

GAME 3: Brooklyn 7, Louisville 7

(At Louisville, Monday, October 20, 1890)

```
                                    R   H   E
Brooklyn   020 130 10-7  Tie/ND - Terry    7  10   2
Louisville 001 102 03-7  Tie/ND -          7  11   3
                         Stratton & Meakim
```
(Game called on account of darkness)
Attendance - 1,253.   Time of game - 1:50.
Umpires - Wesley Curry and John McQuaid.

GAME 4: Louisville 5, Brooklyn 4

(At Louisville, Tuesday, October 21, 1890)

```
                                    R   H   E
Brooklyn   031 000 000 - 4  LP - Lovett    4   7   2
Louisville 301 000 10x - 5  WP - Ehret     5   9   2
```
Attendance - 1,050.   Time of game - 1:45.
Umpires - Wesley Curry and John McQuaid.

GAME 5: Brooklyn 7, Louisville 2

(At Brooklyn, Saturday, October 25, 1890)

```
                                    R   H   E
Louisville 010 010 000 - 2  LP - Daily     2   5   6
Brooklyn   210 200 20x - 7  WP - Lovett    7   7   0
```
Attendance - 1,048.   Time of game - 1:58.
Umpires - Wesley Curry and John McQuaid.

GAME 6: Louisville 9, Brooklyn 8

(At Brooklyn, Monday, October 27, 1890)

```
                                    R   H   E
Louisville 012 101 220 - 9  WP - Stratton  9  13   3
Brooklyn   100 004 030 - 8  LP - Terry     8  12   3
                            Save - Ehret
```
Attendance - 600 approximately.
Time of game - 2:00.
Umpires — Wesley Curry and John McQuaid.

GAME 7: Louisville 6, Brooklyn 2

(At Brooklyn, Tuesday, October 28, 1890)

```
                                    R   H   E
Louisville 103 000 020 - 6  WP - Ehret     6   8   3
Brooklyn   200 000 000 - 2  LP - Lovett    2   4   1
```
Attendance - 300 approximately.
Time of game - 1:30.
Umpires - Wesley Curry and John McQuaid.

Note: Best-of-nine series called after seven games because of inclement weather.

LOUISVILLE SUMMARY

1890 WORLD SERIES

BATTING

Player	BA	G	AB	H	2B	3B	HR	RBI	R	SB	BB	SO
Meakim p	.500	1	2	1	0	0	0	0	0	0	0	0
Ehret p	.429	3	7	3	0	1	0	0	1	0	0	0
Wolf rf-3b	.360	7	25	9	3	1	0	8	4	2	3	0
Taylor 1b	.300	7	30	9	1	0	0	2	6	3	2	3
Shinnick 2b	.292	7	24	7	1	1	0	3	3	2	2	2
Hamburg lf	.269	7	26	7	1	0	0	2	3	0	0	3
Weaver cf	.259	7	27	7	1	0	0	4	4	5	1	2
Stratton p-rf	.222	4	9	2	1	0	0	0	4	3	2	1
Tomney ss	.200	3	5	1	0	0	0	0	1	0	3	1
Raymond 3b-ss	.148	7	27	4	1	1	0	1	5	1	2	5
Daily p-rf	.136	6	22	3	1	1	0	3	1	2	1	2
Ryan c	.053	6	19	1	0	0	0	2	0	1	0	1
Weckbecker c	.000	1	4	0	0	0	0	0	0	0	0	1
Bligh c	.000	2	3	0	0	0	0	0	0	0	0	1
Totals	**.235**	**-**	**230**	**54**	**10**	**5**	**0**	**25**	**32**	**19**	**16**	**22**

PITCHING

Pitcher	W/L%	W	L	ERA	IP	H	ER	BB	SO	G	GS	CG	Sv	ShO
Ehret	1.000	2	0	1.35	20	12	3	6	13	3	2	2	1	0
Stratton*	.500	1	1	2.37	19	26	5	4	8	3	3	1	0	0
Daily	.000	0	2	2.65	17	12	5	8	5	2	2	2	0	0
Meakim*	.000	0	0	0.00	4	6	0	1	1	1	0	0	0	0
Totals	**.500**	**3**	**3**	**1.95**	**60**	**56**	**13**	**19**	**27**	**-**	**7**	**5**	**1**	**0**

*Totals include one tie game

BROOKLYN SUMMARY

1890 WORLD SERIES

BATTING

Player	BA	G	AB	H	2B	3B	HR	RBI	R	SB	BB	SO
Clark c	.667	1	3	2	0	1	0	1	2	0	0	0
Donovan rf	.471	5	17	8	1	0	0	3	5	3	2	1
Pinckney 3b	.357	4	14	5	0	2	0	3	4	1	2	1
Collins 2b	.310	7	29	9	0	1	0	1	7	2	3	0
Foutz lf-1b	.300	7	30	9	2	1	0	4	6	1	0	1
Smith ss	.276	7	29	8	0	2	0	7	3	1	0	3
Burns rf-lf-3b	.222	7	27	6	2	0	1	5	6	0	3	4
Daly 1b-c	.182	6	22	4	2	0	0	3	1	2	0	4
O'Brien cf	.125	6	24	3	0	1	0	3	3	3	1	5
Lovett rf-p	.067	5	15	1	0	0	0	0	0	0	0	4
Terry p-rf-lf-cf	.050	6	20	1	1	0	0	0	5	1	6	3
Bushong c	.000	2	6	0	0	0	0	0	0	0	0	1
Caruthers lf	.000	2	6	0	0	0	0	0	0	0	2	0
Totals	**.231**	**-**	**242**	**56**	**8**	**8**	**1**	**30**	**42**	**14**	**19**	**27**

PITCHING

Pitcher	W/L%	W	L	ERA	IP	H	ER	BB	SO	G	GS	CG	Sv	ShO
Lovett	.500	2	2	2.83	35	29	11	6	14	4	4	4	0	0
Terry*	.500	1	1	3.60	25	25	10	10	8	3	3	3	0	1
Totals	**.500**	**3**	**3**	**3.15**	**60**	**54**	**21**	**16**	**22**	**-**	**7**	**7**	**0**	**1**

*Totals include one tie game

LOUISVILLE'S 1890 WORLD SERIES ROSTER

(AMERICAN ASSOCIATION)

Bligh, Ned

Daily, Ed

Ehret, Philip "Red"

Hamburg, Charlie

Meakim, George

Raymond, Harry

Ryan, John

Shinnick, Tim

Stratton, Scott

Taylor, Harry

Tomney, Philip

Weaver, William "Farmer"

Weckbecker, Peter

Wolf, William "Chicken"

BROOKLYN'S 1890 WORLD SERIES ROSTER

(NATIONAL LEAGUE)

Burns, Tommy "Oyster"

Bushong, Albert "Doc"

Caruthers, Bob

Clark, Robert

Collins, George "Hub"

Daly, Tom

Donovan, Patrick "Patsy"

Foutz, Dave

Lovett, Tom

O'Brien, William "Darby"

Pinckney, George

Smith, George "Germany"

Terry, William "Adonis"

The 1890 Brooklyn National League Champions — (STANDING) George J. Smith, John Corkhill, William H. Terry, David Foutz, William D. O'Brien, Al Bushong, Thomas Burns; (SEATED) George Pinckney, Robert Caruthers, Hub Collins, William McGunnigle, Tom Daly, Robert Clark, Tom Lovett; and (FOREGROUND) Michael Hughes. (National Baseball Library and Archive, Cooperstown, NY)

CHAPTER SIX
LOUISVILLE'S MAJOR-LEAGUE GALLERY III:
THE SECOND NATIONAL LEAGUE YEARS, 1892-1899

Fred Clarke *(National Baseball Library and Archive, Cooperstown, NY)*

FRED CLARKE

On June 30, 1894, Fred Clarke gave signs of the Hall-of-Fame career that was to come with a splendid five-for-five career debut performance against Philadelphia in a 13–6 loss at home. The work, which included four singles and a triple, remains to this day the greatest debut in the game by a future Cooperstown member.

Elected to that pantheon in 1945, Clarke — one of the few bright spots for Louisville during its final major-league years — is credited by many historians with inventing flip-up sunglasses.

A playing manager for most of his career, Clarke was a champion on both sides of the lines.

As an outfielder, the fiercely competitive, always–hustling Clarke lasted over two decades in the majors (1894-1915), the first six of those with Louisville in the National League. He posted a career .312 batting average, and pounded out 2,675 lifetime hits. That platework included a 35-game hitting streak in 1895.

His best season was a .390 mark in 1897. That came the same season that the gifted Iowa native assumed the helm of the Louisville squad after manager Jimmy Rogers was fired by club president Harry Pulliam in mid-June. He was just 24. Clarke's contract that season called for a $2,400 salary, plus an additional $500 for managing.

As a manager, Clarke recorded a lifetime .576 win percentage. Most of his sixteen hundred-plus victories came with the Pittsburgh Pirates, whom he led to four National League pennants and one World Championship in the early 1900s.

LOUISVILLE CURIOS

During the 1897 season, Clarke resided at the renowned Galt House in Louisville.

FRED PFEFFER

A 16-year veteran whose professional tenure included four seasons with his native Louisville, Nathaniel Frederick "Dandelion" Pfeffer recorded a personal best .308 mark there in 1894.

But it was Pfeffer's glove that garnered him his fame.

One of the two greatest second-basemen of the pre-modern (pre-1900) era, Pfeffer made his name with Cap Anson's National League Chicago dynasty teams of the early- and mid-1880s, where he was a

Fred Pfeffer
(National Baseball Library and Archive, Cooperstown, NY)

member of an almost impenetrable infield known as "The Stone Wall."

He was exceeded in keystone-bag skills only by the great Bid McPhee of the Cincinnati Reds, although Hall-of-Famer Mike "King" Kelly — according to Daniel Okrent's and Steve Wulf's *Baseball Anecdotes* — called Pfeffer "the greatest second baseman of them all . . . he could lay on his stomach and throw a hundred yards."

Further evidence of Pfeffer's defensive prowess comes from Mike Shatzkin's *The Ballplayers*, which notes that Pfeffer "was the first infielder to cut off a catcher's throw to second base on a double steal attempt and cut down the runner at the plate."

(In some quarters and times, the McPhee–Pfeffer rivalry was a draw, as witness this item from the Louisville Commercial Gazette of Wednesday, May 6, 1891: "Association players to a man maintain that McPhee is the greatest second baseman in the profession, while the League men are inclined to favor Pfeffer, of the Chicagos." The article concluded by stating: "Louisville is, in this one instance, of the same opinion as the League.")

Pfeffer, a legitimate Hall-of-Fame candidate, also was a speedy baserunner who was once timed circling the bases in less than 16 seconds.

LOUISVILLE CURIOS

Pfeffer was a playing manager for Louisville in 1892. Pfeffer's family at one time, according to records, owned a saloon at 2524 Portland Avenue. (on the west side of Louisville).

And, one of Pfeffer's earliest and greatest performances came in a September 12, 1877 contest between the Louisville Amateurs and neighboring Anchorage. Though he went zero–for–five in the Amateurs' 21–2 pasting of Anchorage, he still earned plaudits from the Louisville Courier–Journal for his defensive wizardry.

"Pfeffer in particular distinguished himself by making a number of difficult running stops and throws. There is certainly not an amateur second baseman in the city who can equal him."

As intelligent as he was talented, Pfeffer midway through his successful career — in 1889 — became one of the game's first published players with a highly popular book, *Scientific Ball.*

After wrapping up his major-league work with Chicago in 1897, Pfeffer ran a celebrated bar there for years, which he sold for all of $1.50 in 1920 according to newspaper accounts. Later, he was in charge of pressboxes at several racetracks in Chicago, where he died in 1932 at age 72.

GUS WEYHING

Four times a 30-game winner and three times a 20-game victor, Gus Weyhing posted a career 264-235 ledger, much of it with also-rans between 1887 amd 1901. His career work included a no-hitter (a 4-0 victory) versus Kansas City in the American Association on July 31, 1888.

The big numbers were a stark contrast to the reed-thin 5-10, 145-pound hurler, who weighed only 120 pounds when he broke into minor-league ball.

"I was so skinny," he recalled years later, "you could see my heart beating through my chest."

The quote was pure Weyhing, whose ability to have fun and whose sense of humor were something else.

A perfect example of his fun–loving nature was this Louisville Courier–Journal story on October 23, 1890 (midway through that year's World Series between his home town and Brooklyn).

Though headlined simply as "Gus Weyhing In Town", the sub–headline was something else: "The Brotherhood Twirler Left Brooklyn Before a Constable Found Him With a Warrant". The article read as follows:

August Weyhing, the star pitcher of the Brooklyn Brotherhood (Players' League) team, arrived in the city yesterday, and will spend the winter with his parents, who live on Wenzel Street.

Like many other crack ball players, Weyhing got reckless and funny after the close of the regular base-

ball season, and left Brooklyn before a constable and a warrant could meet him. The warrant charges him with malicious mischief, and asks for $200 damages.

The saloon in Brooklyn most frequented by Weyhing and the other German players is kept by a German, and is a very fancy one. The walls are handsomely decorated and the frescoed ceilings are covered with pink cupids and winged angels.

Weyhing and his companions amused themselves by lathering slices of bread very thickly spread with butter and making bets as to who could stick the greatest number of slices on the faces of the pretty cupids upon the wall.

The frescoing was badly damaged and the saloon-keeper says Weyhing will have to pay for what he did, if he has to hold the warrant up until the base ball season opens next spring.

And from another source comes this classic story about Weyhing, who once owned a restaurant/bar establishment. When it failed, a sign was placed in the front window announcing the date that the business would be sold at public auction by the local sheriff. Below it, Weyhing hung his own announcement: "Attention, patrons. The first of July will be the last of August."

The first hurler to win 100 games in two different leagues (115 in the American Association and 119 in the National League), Weyhing truly could win in any league, as evidenced by his work of 1890 through 1892, when he won 30 or more games in three differ-

ent leagues (30–16 for Brooklyn in the Players' League in 1890, 31–20 for Philadelphia in the American Association in 1891, and 32–21 for Philadelphia in the National League in 1892).

Weyhing enjoyed most of his success with Philadelphia teams in both the American Association and the National League.

Perhaps the most prodigious of those teams were the 1894 Phillies, whose power-packed outfield included a trio of .400 hitters (Tuck Turner and Hall-of-Famers Ed Delahanty and Sam Thompson) and a fourth who batted .399 (Billy Hamilton, another Hall-of-Famer).

Nicknamed "Rubber-Winged Gus", Weyhing — who pitched for his native Louisville in 1895 and 1896 — attributed his lack of arm troubles and career longevity to constantly soaking his arm in hot water and keeping it out of the hands of trainers.

In 1951, he and another grand old-time Louisville player, "Strong-Armed" Bill Clingman (a shortstop and third baseman for Louisville's National League squads from 1896 through 1899), were special guests at a May 15 Golden Jubilee celebration (the 50th anniversary of baseball's present two-league structure) in Boston, where they watched the Boston Red Sox and Chicago White Sox play.

Weyhing, who in his later years worked as a night watchman for the Louisville Water Company, died at age 88 in 1955. He is buried in Louisville's Calvary Cemetery; his grave is near that of another Louisville-born great of the game — John McCloskey.

Gus Weyhing
(National Baseball Library and Archive, Cooperstown, NY)

THE 1897 LOUISVILLE NATIONAL LEAGUE TEAM

While the 1897 Louisville National League team was no giant, it was in fact a sleeping giant that would later awaken in Pittsburgh, where the Louisville franchise was transferred after the 1899 season.

One part of that giant-to-be was Hall-of-Famer Honus Wagner, a rookie infielder on the 1897 Louisville team. The pilot of that team was manager/outfielder Fred Clarke. They in turn would be joined by Tommy Leach in 1898 and pitcher Deacon Phillippe in 1899. That quartet would be the nucleus of the fine Pittsburgh teams of the early 1900s, which took four National League flags and one World Series.

The 1897 Louisville National League aggregation also included such notables as George "Rube" Waddell, Tom McCreery and Percival Wheritt "Perry" Werden.

Waddell began his storied and colorful Hall-of-Fame pitching career with Louisville in 1897 (see Chapter 1).

Right fielder McCreery caught everybody's attention with his work on July 12, 1897, when he established a major–league record that will probably endure forever by slamming three inside–the–park home runs against Philadelphia in a National League contest that Louisville won 10–7.

As for Werden, who batted a career–best .302 for Louisville in 1897, it remains a mystery today exactly why the Missouri native spent the bulk of his epic baseball career (1884–1908) in the minors. However, the numbers and talent of this 6–2, 220–pound slugger are undeniable.

Werden's major–league statistics include a lifetime .282 batting average; 150 stolen bases; the league lead in triples in 1890 with Toledo of the American Association (20) and again in 1893 (29) with St. Louis in the National League (evidence that the big man's batting prowess was complemented by superb speed);

Team members pictured are (BACK ROW) Joe Dolan, second base/shortstop; Albert "Abbie" Johnson, second base/shortstop; William "Still Bill" Hill, pitcher; Perry Werden, first base; Bill Wilson, catcher; Dick Butler, catcher; James "General" Stafford, shortstop; (MIDDLE ROW) William "Dad" Clarke, pitcher; Billy Clingman, third base; Fred Clarke, Manager/left field; Honus Wagner, outfield; Bill Magee, pitcher; (FRONT ROW) Roy Evans, pitcher; Bert Cunningham, pitcher; Charles "Chick" Fraser, pitcher; and Charlie Dexter, infield/outfield. (University of Louisville Photographic Archives)

and a 12–1 pitching mark (an indication of his athleticism) for the St. Louis Maroons, champions of the Union Association in 1884. His career minor–league work includes a .341 batting average; 350 stolen bases; one .400 season; and a number of offensive crowns (batting average, home runs and doubles).

HONUS WAGNER

Though awkward in appearance, the bowlegged, long-limbed and barrel-chested Honus Wagner had no discernible weakness on the diamond.

A lifetime .327 batter who laced out over 3,400 career hits, Wagner won eight National League batting titles between 1900 and 1911 for Pittsburgh, where he

Honus Wagner (University of Louisville Photographic Archives)

spent the majority of his career. Able to hit with power as well as for average, Wagner six times led his league in slugging percentage, seven times in doubles, three times in triples, four times in RBIs and twice in hits.

As a shortstop, he could make all the plays, many times the ball arriving at first base on a grounder with a flock of pebbles and dirt Wagner had scooped up as he quickly fielded the ball. Possessed of a powerful throwing arm, Wagner at one time held the major-league record for throwing a baseball the furthest distance (403 feet, eight inches in an Oct. 16, 1898 baseball throwing contest).

A heady baserunner as well, Wagner led the National League twice in runs scored and five times in stolen bases. Indeed, his major-league work includes the distinction of being the first man to steal second, third and home in the same inning under an 1898 rule that differentiated between stolen bases and advancing on the basepaths (in the fourth inning of an August 1, 1899 win against the New York Giants).

Considered by some to be the greatest shortstop in the history of the game, and by some the finest player ever turned out by the sport, John Peter "Honus" Wagner was a charter member of the Hall of Fame along with Ty Cobb, Walter Johnson, Christy Mathewson and Babe Ruth.

Wagner's links to Louisville are two-fold.

He began his Herculean 21-year career there in 1897, batting .338 in a part-time role, the first of 16 .300 seasons for "The Flying Dutchman" (many thought Wagner was Dutch; actually, he was German, the same descent as Richard Wagner, the composer of the opera after which Honus Wagner was nicknamed).

And, on Sept. 1, 1905, Wagner signed a contract with J.F. Hillerich & Son (the forerunner of Hillerich & Bradsby) that gave the firm the right to use Wagner's autograph on Louisville Slugger bats. The business agreement was doubly historic: Wagner became the first major-leaguer to have his signature on a bat, and modern endorsement-advertising was born.

THE 1899 LOUISVILLE NATIONAL LEAGUE TEAM

Despite a ninth-place finish in 1899, Louisville's National League team was clearly a club on the rise via an abundance of talent that included future Hall-of-Famers Fred Clarke, Honus Wagner and Rube Waddell, and such stars or stars-to-be as Dummy Hoy, Topsy Hartsel, Tommy Leach and Deacon Phillippe.

Much of that talent would be fully showcased not in Louisville, who was dropped from the National League roster after the 1899 campaign, however, but rather in Pittsburgh, which found itself with a dynasty of sorts in the following decade.

Team members shown in this photograph of Louisville's (and Kentucky's) last major-league team are (FRONT ROW) Malachi Kittridge (C), Billy Clingman (SS), Walter Woods (P), Fred Clarke (Manager/LF), Mike Powers (C), Henry Croft (2B), Dummy Hoy (CF). (MIDDLE ROW) Topsy Hartsel (OF, turned to right), Bill Magee (P), Tommy Leach (3B), Bert Cunningham (P), Honus Wagner (3B/OF), Charles Dexter (RF), Claude Ritchey (2B), Pete Dowling (P). (BACK ROW) Deacon Phillippe (P, between Leach and Cunningham), Rube Waddell (P), George Decker (1B), Fred Ketcham (OF), and pitcher Nick Altrock (sent to the minors before the season began). (University of Louisville Photographic Archives)

LOUISVILLE CURIOS

One of the members of the 1899 Louisville National League team was Charles "Chief" Zimmer (not pictured). A top-flight receiver, Zimmer was traded during the 1899 season to Louisville, for whom he batted .298. Zimmer, who ended his 19-year career in 1903 with a .269 batting average and over 1,200 hits, caught over 1,200 games in the big show.

The last figure is substantial since good catchers are like good tires. The generally-accepted "tread life" of the very best of catchers is some 1,500 games. Anything over that is nothing short of phenomenal.

And in 1903, Deacon Phillippe became the first pitcher in World Series history to win three games. His work came in a losing cause as Boston bested Pittsburgh in a best–of–nine series. The first modern–era World Series, it featured two former Louisville stars (and future Cooperstown residents) at the reins of the clubs — Fred Clarke for Pittsburgh, Jimmy Collins for Boston.

CHAPTER SEVEN
THE LOST CITY OF HISTORICAL BASEBALL:
LOUISVILLE'S MAJOR-LEAGUE FIRSTS, RECORDS & NOTABLE
ACHIEVEMENTS

Members of the 1874 Eagles (a semi-pro team) are (STANDING) Thomas Muir, third base; William S. Bodley, center field; Bors, first base; (SEATED OR RECLINING) Harry Thruman, second base; Prest Coleman (between two players holding bats), no position listed; W. Osborne, catcher; Allen Polk Houston (with banner around neck), left field; Allan McDonald, (in suit) right field; George Bayless (with cap on knee), shortstop; and Kenneth McDonald, no position listed. (The Filson Club, Louisville, KY)

LOUISVILLE'S MAJOR-LEAGUE FIRSTS, RECORDS & NOTABLE ACHIEVEMENTS

1. Louisville was a co-founder, along with New York City, of the esteemed National League. Louisville was also a charter member of this nation's oldest, continuously-active loop. The National League began play in 1876, the year after the first Kentucky Derby — the world's most famous horse race — was run.

2. The first shutout in National League history came at Louisville's expense, with Chicago whitewashing Louisville 4-0 at the latter's field (St. James Court) on April 25, 1876. (One month later, Louisville was involved in the first tie game — and extra–inning tie game — in major–league history. That was a 14–inning, 2–2 deadlock with Philadelphia that was called because of darkness.)

3. Johnny Ryan, of the 1876 Louisville NL club, still holds the major-league record for most wild pitches in a game. He uncorked 10 wild pitches in a July 22, 1876 game at Chicago. Another major–league record set in that game was most at–bats by two clubs in a nine–inning game — 106 (64 by Chicago, 42 by Louisville). Not surprisingly, Louisville lost 30–7.

4. Louisville was the site of the game's first great scandal, the 1877 National League pennant-throwing scandal that ultimately saw four players — Jimmy Devlin, Bill Craver, George Hall and Al Nichols — expelled from the game for life, and Louisville forced to leave the National League fold. Ironically, the fix was exposed by Louisville Courier-Journal reporter John Avery Haldeman, briefly a member of the 1877 team and the son of Walter

The 1892 Louisville Mutuals, an entry in the 1892 Louisville City League (an amateur circuit). Team members are (STANDING) Harry Fuller, third base; Henry Semple, pitcher; John Richter, shortstop; William Neal, first base/captain; Nick Reeder, second base; (SEATED) Joseph Fontana, left field; George Carnighan, center field; E.B. Stinson, Manager; William Preuss, right field; Phillip Vatter, catcher; (RECLINING) Fred Zahner, catcher; and Frank Redding, pitcher. (The Filson Club, Louisville, KY)

Members of an unidentified Louisville Eclipse professional team, circa 1883. (University of Louisville Photographic Archives)

Haldeman, publisher of the Courier-Journal and president of the Louisville National League Baseball Club.

5. Louisville was also a charter member of the fabled American Association, the National League's first major competitor which operated for 10 dynamic years (1882–1891). That colorful league gave major–league baseball such innovative and historic firsts as Sunday baseball; beer at the ballpark; the percentage system of determining pennant winners; league control of umpires; the development of "Ladies Day" as a standard baseball promotion; standardized contractural procedures; participation in the first World Series (an abbreviated affair in 1882); the sport's first black major–leaguer — Moses Fleetwood "Fleet" Walker; and the first players' strike in major–league history (1889 by Louisville).

6. The fabled Louisville stickman, Pete Browning, was the first rookie in major–league history to win a batting title –.378 for the Louisville Eclipse of the American Association in 1882. (See Chaper III profile)

7. Five pitchers have switch–pitched ballgames (hurled both right– and left–handed in the same game) in major–league history. Two of them, notably enough, played for Louisville. The first slinger to turn this feat was Tony Mullane for Louisville in a July 18, 1882, game versus Baltimore (Mullane lost 9–8 via a Charlie Householder home run). Other pitchers known to have done this include Larry Corcoran (1884/NL/Chicago White Stockings); John Roach (1887/NL/New York Giants); Icebox Chamberlain (1888/AA/Louisville); and Greg Harris (1995/NL/Montreal Expos). Chamberlain, by the way, is the only pitcher in major–league history to have recorded a switch–pitching victory (See Chapter IV profile). For the record, all but one of the ambidextrous quintet were right–handers by trade (Roach was a southpaw).

8. Louisville is the birthplace of the modern American baseball bat, the Louisville Slugger (a fact that entitles Louisville to be called "The City of the Bat" as well as "The Derby City". According to the time–honored story, legendary hitter Pete Browning broke his favorite bat during the spring of 1884. As a favor to the highly popular hometown star (whose glittering lifetime work includes three batting titles and a career .341 batting average). John A. "Bud" Hillerich custom–crafted him a bat — the first Louisville Slugger. The historical accident led to the creation of this country's most famous bat–making firm — Hillerich & Bradsby — and the world's most famous baseball bat, the Louisville Slugger.

9. Generally acknowledged as major–league baseball's first black ballplayer, Moses Fleetwood "Fleet" Walker made his career debut against Louisville on May 1, 1882, (as a catcher for Toledo in the American Association). It was a tough initiation for Walker, who went zero–for–three at the plate and made all four of his team's errors in a 5–1 loss. (See Chapter I)

10. The only pitcher ever to win a major–league batting title was Guy Jackson Hecker (Chapter IV), who took the 1886 American Association batting title with a .341 average for Louisville. Unquestionably, Hecker's best day as a hitter — that year and during his career — was an August game that saw him go six–for–seven (three singles and three home runs), and score a major–league record seven runs (he reached base a seventh time on an error in that game, which Louisville won 22–5).

11. Hecker's 52-win total in 1884 for Louisville is the best in American Association play and the third–best in major–league history (Old Hoss Radbourn got 60 for the 1884 Providence National League team, John Clarkson posted 53 for the 1885 Chicago National League club).

12. Hecker is one of three old–time Louisville major–leaguers to have gotten six hits in a game (the major–league record for hits in a game is seven, shared by National Leaguers Wilbert Robinson and Rennie Stennett). Hecker's work came in the second game of an August 15, 1886, doubleheader against Baltimore. He was followed by Joseph "Reddy" Mack and William B. "Farmer" Weaver, who also pulled off their feats in American Association play. Mack went six–for–six (all singles) on May 26, 1887 versus Brooklyn. Louisville won that game 27–9.

Weaver, in an August 12, 1890 contest against Syracuse, hit for the cycle… and then some. His numbers included two singles, a double, a pair of triples and a home run. Louisville took that contest 18–4.

13. Louisville still holds the major–league record for most consecutive defeats in a season (26 losses in 1889).

14. In 1890, Louisville of the American Association became the first team in major–league history to vault from last place to first place in the course of a single season. That feat was not duplicated until 1991 when the Atlanta Braves and the Minnesota Twins both pulled it off enroute to a memorable clash in that year's World Series.

15. Pitcher Scott Stratton (Chapter IV), the ace of the 1890 American Association pennant–winning club with a 34–14 mark, is officially credited with having posted a string of 15 consecutive victories that year. However, newspaper accounts put it at 16 straight, which equals the American League record (shared by Walter Johnson, Smokey Joe Wood, Lefty Grove and Schoolboy Rowe), and is just three short of the major–league standard (partnered by National Leaguers Tim Keefe and Rube Marquard).

16. In 1892, T.J. Dowse became the first player to play for four teams in a single season. His clubs included Louisville, Cincinnati, Philadelphia and Washington.

17. Fred Clarke's career debut for Louisville, on June 30, 1894, versus Philadelphia, remains the greatest ever by a future Hall–of–Famer. Clarke went five–for–five, that work including four singles and one triple. Clarke's fine work, however, went for naught as Louisville lost 13–6. (See Chapter VI)

18. On August 17, 1894, Louisville pitcher John Wadsworth set a major–league record that still stands when he yielded 36 hits to Philadelphia in a National League contest. Incidentally, Wadsworth went the distance in the 29–4 loss and pitched the following year for Louisville.

19. Louisville native Gus Weyhing (Chapter VI) is believed by historians to be the first slinger to win 100 games in two different historically– and statistically–recognized loops. His career totals include 115 victories in the American Association and 119 triumphs in the National League.

20. On April 6, 1896, Pete Cassidy of the Louisville National League Club became the first player in major–league history to be X–rayed (a splinter of bone was subsequently removed from his wrist).

21. This could be a record; at the very least, it's a rarity. On September 7, 1896, Louisville dropped a National League tripleheader to Baltimore (4–3, 9–1 and 12–1).

22. On June 29, 1897, Louisville lost a National League game 36–7 to Chicago. Chicago's total remains the record for the most runs ever scored by a winning team in a major–league contest.

23. On July 12, 1897, Tom McCreery of Louisville established a major–league record that will probably endure forever when he hit three inside–the–park home runs versus Philadelphia in a National League game. Louisville won 10–7.

24. The brilliant Tommy Leach, who began his major–league career with Louisville in 1898, got the first hit in modern World Series history (a triple for Pittsburgh

in the inaugural 1903 tilt against Boston). Along with Honus Wagner, Fred Clarke and Deacon Phillippe, Leach was part of the nucleus of the great turn-of-the-century Pittsburgh Pirate teams. A talented hitter (.270 lifetime batting average and nearly 2,200 hits), Leach was an equally adept gloveman who narrowly missed becoming the first man to play a thousand games at two different positions. The significance of what Leach — a third baseman, then an outfielder — almost accomplished cannot be overstated. In the history of the game, only three men have pulled off this feat: Babe Ruth, Ernie Banks and Rod Carew.

25. On August 1, 1899, future Hall–of–Famer Honus Wagner — who had begun his career with Louisville in 1897 — became the first man in major-league history to steal second base, third base and home in the same inning (under an 1898 rule that differentiated between advancing on the bases and stealing bases.) Wagner pulled off this historic "triple steal" in the fourth inning of a game against the New York Giants (Louisville won 7–1). In another historic event involving Louisville, Wagner on September 1, 1905, signed a contract with J.F. Hillerich & Son (the forerunner of Hillerich & Bradsby) that gave the firm the right to use his autograph on Louisville Slugger bats. The business agreement was doubly historic; Wagner became the first player to have his signature on a bat, and modern endorsement–advertising was born. And, finally, at one time, Wagner held the major–league record for throwing a baseball the furthest distance — 403 feet, eight inches. (See Chapter VI)

❦

Though this has nothing to do with Louisville's old–time major–league years, it is interesting to note that the two principals in major–league baseball's only on–the–field fatality, New York Yankees pitcher Carl Mays and Cleveland Indians shortstop Ray Chapman, were both Kentucky–born. Mays, a submariner whose pitch in a mid–August, 1920 game struck Chapman in the head, was born in Liberty, Kentucky. Chapman, who died of a skull fracture the day after the beaning, was born in Beaver Dam, Kentucky.

CHAPTER EIGHT
BIG-LEAGUE NAMES OF LOUISVILLE:
LOUISVILLE'S ALL-TIME MAJOR-LEAGUE & SEASONAL ROSTERS, 1876-1899

Dan Brouthers *(National Baseball Library and Archive, Cooperstown, NY)*

LOUISVILLE'S ALL-TIME MAJOR-LEAGUE ROSTER

Allison, Arthur Algernon
Born: January 29, 1849/Philadelphia, Penn.
Died: February 25, 1916/Washington, D.C.

Altrock, Nicholas
Born: September 15, 1876/Cincinnati, Ohio
Died: January 20, 1965/Washington, D.C.

Andrews, William Walter
Born: September 18, 1859/Philadelphia, Penn.
Died: January 20, 1940/Indianapolis, Ind.

Baker, Norman Leslie
Born: October 14, 1862/Philadelphia, Penn.
Died: February 20, 1949/Hurffville, N.J.

#Barnie, William Harrison
Born: January 26, 1853/New York, N.Y.
Died: July 15, 1900/Hartford, Ct.

Bassett, Charles Edwin
Born: February 9, 1863/Central Falls, R.I.
Died: May 28, 1942/Pawtucket, R.I.

Beard, Oliver Perry
Born: May 2, 1862/Lexington, Ky.
Died: May 29, 1929/Cincinnati, Ohio

Bechtel, George A.
Born: September 2, 1848/Philadelphia, Penn.
Died: Date and location unknown

Bell, Charles C.
Born: August 12, 1869/Cincinnati, Ohio
Died: February 7, 1937/Cincinnati, Ohio

Bligh, Edwin Forrest
Born: June 30, 1864/Brooklyn, N.Y.
Died: April 18, 1892/Brooklyn, N.Y.

Bohn, Charles
Born: 1857/Cleveland, Ohio
Died: August 1, 1903/Cleveland, Ohio

Boone, George Morris
Born: March 1, 1871/Louisville, Ky.
Died: September 24, 1910/Louisville, Ky.

Booth, Amos Smith
Born: September 4, 1852/Cincinnati, Ohio
Died: July 1, 1921/Miamisburg, Ohio

Borchers, George Bernard
Born: April 18, 1869/Sacramento, Calif.
Died: October 24, 1938/Sacramento, Calif.

Boyle, Edward J.
Born: May 8, 1874/Cincinnati, Ohio
Died: February 9, 1941/Cincinnati, Ohio

Brashear, Roy Parks
Born: January 3, 1874/Ashtabula, Ohio
Died: April 20, 1951/Los Angeles, Calif.

Briggs, Grant
Born: March 16, 1865/Pittsburgh, Penn.
Died: May 31, 1928/Pittsburgh, Penn.

Brouthers, Dennis Joseph
Born: May 8, 1858/Sylvan Lake, N.Y.
Died: August 2, 1932/East Orange, N.J.

Brown, Lewis J.
Born: February 1, 1858/Leominister, Mass.
Died: January 16, 1889/Boston, Mass.

Brown, Thomas T.
Born: September 21, 1860/Liverpool, England
Died: October 25, 1927/Washington, D.C.

Brown, Willard
Born: 1866/San Francisco, Calif.
Died: December 20, 1897/San Francisco, Calif.

Browning, Louis Rogers "Pete"
Born: June 17, 1861/Louisville, Ky.
Died: September 10, 1905/Louisville, Ky.

Burnett, Hercules H.
Born: August 13, 1869/Louisville, Ky.
Died: October 4, 1936/Louisville, Ky.

Butler, Richard H.
Born: Date unknown/Brooklyn, N.Y.
Died: Date and location unknown

Byers, Burley (born Christopher A. Bayer)
Born: December 19, 1875/Louisville, Ky.
Died: May 30, 1933/Louisville, Ky.

Cahill, Thomas H.
Born: October, 1868/Fall River, Mass.
Died: December 25, 1894/Scranton, Penn.

Carbine, John C.
Born: October 12, 1855/Syracuse, N.Y.
Died: September 11, 1915/Forest Park, Ill.

Carey, George C.
Born: December 4, 1870/East Liverpool, Ohio
Died: December 17, 1916/East Liverpool, Ohio

Carl, Frederick E.
Born: 1856/Germany
Died: May 4, 1919/Washington, D.C.

Cassidy, Peter Francis
Born: April 9, 1873/Wilmington, Del.
Died: July 9, 1929/Wilmington, Del.

Chamberlain, Elton P.
Born: November 5, 1867/Buffalo, N.Y.
Died: September 22, 1929/Baltimore, Md.

*Chapman, John Curtis
Born: May 8, 1842/Brooklyn, N.Y.
Died: June 10, 1916/Brooklyn, N.Y.

Childers, William
Born: Date unknown/St. Louis, Mo.
Died: Date and location unknown

Clark, Robert H.
Born: May 18, 1863/Covington, Ky.
Died: August 21, 1919/Covington, Ky.

Clark, William Winfield
Born: April 11, 1875/Circleville, Ohio
Died: April 15, 1959/Los Angeles, Calif.

*Clarke, Fred Clifford
Born: October 3, 1872/Winterset, Iowa
Died: August 14, 1960/Winfield, Kansas

Paul Cook (*University of Louisville Photographic Archives*)

Clarke, Joshua Baldwin
Born: March 8, 1879/Winfield, Kansas
Died: July 2, 1962/Ventura, Calif.

Clarke, William H.
Born: January 7, 1865/Oswego, N.Y.
Died: June 3, 1911/Lorian, Ohio

Clausen, Frederick William
Born: April 26, 1869/New York, N.Y.
Died: February 11, 1960/Memphis, Tenn.

Cline, John P.
Born: March 3, 1858/Louisville, Ky.
Died: September 23, 1916/Louisville, Ky.

Clingman, William Frederick
Born: November 21, 1869/Cincinnati, Ohio
Died: May 14, 1958/Cincinnati, Ohio

Clinton, James Lawrence
Born: August 10, 1850/New York, N.Y.
Died: September 3, 1921/Brooklyn, N.Y.

Collins, Daniel Thomas
Born: July 12, 1854/St. Louis, Mo.
Died: September 21, 1883/New Orleans, La.

Collins, George Hubbert
Born: April 15, 1864/Louisville, Ky.
Died: May 21, 1892/Brooklyn, N.Y.

Collins, James Joseph
Born: January 16, 1870/Buffalo, N.Y.
Died: March 6, 1943/Buffalo, N.Y.

Connor, John
Born: August, 1854/Scotland
Died: October 13, 1932/Boston, Mass.

Cook, Paul
Born: May 5, 1863/Caledonia, N.Y.
Died: May 25, 1905/Rochester, N.Y.

Cote, Henry Joseph
Born: February 19, 1864/Troy, N.Y.
Died: April 28, 1940/Troy, N.Y.

Craver, William H.
Born: 1844/Troy, N.Y.
Died: June 17, 1901/Troy, N.Y.

Croft, Henry T.
Born: August 1, 1875/Chicago, Ill.
Died: December 11, 1933/Oak Park, Ill.

Crooks, John Charles
Born: November 9, 1866/St. Paul, Minn.
Died: January 29, 1918/St. Louis, Mo.

Cross, Amos C.
Born: 1861/Austro–Hungary
Died: July 16, 1888/Cleveland, Ohio

Cross, Lafayette Napoleon
Born: May 12, 1866/Milwaukee, Wisc.
Died: September 6, 1927/Toledo, Ohio

Crotty, Joseph P.
Born: December 24, 1860/Cincinnati, Ohio
Died: June 22, 1926/Minneapolis, Minn.

Crowell, William Theodore
Born: November 6, 1865/Cincinnati, Ohio
Died: July 24, 1935/Ft. Worth, Texas

Crowley, William Michael
Born: April 8, 1857/Philadelphia, Penn.
Died: July 14, 1891/Gloucester, N.J.

Cunningham, Ellsworth Elmer
Born: November 25, 1865/Wilmington, Del.
Died: May 14, 1952/Cragmere, Del.

Daily, Edward M.
Born: September 7, 1862/Providence, R.I.
Died: October 21, 1891/Washington, D.C.

Darragh, James S.
Born: July 17, 1866/Edensburg, Penn.
Died: August 12, 1939/Rochester, Penn.

#Davidson, Mordecai H.
Born: November 30, 1846/Port Washington, Ohio
Died: September 6, 1940/Louisville, Ky.

Davis, Harry H.
Born: July 19, 1873/Philadelphia, Penn.
Died: August 11, 1947/Philadelphia, Penn.

Deagle, Lorenzo Burroughs
Born: June 26, 1858/New York, N.Y.
Died: December 24, 1936/Kansas City, Mo.

Decker, George A.
Born: June 1, 1869/York, Penn.
Died: June 9, 1909/Compton, Calif.

Delahanty, Thomas James
Born: March 9, 1872/Cleveland, Ohio
Died: January 10, 1951/Sanford, Fla.

Denny, Jeremiah Dennis (born Jeremiah Dennis Eldridge)
Born: March 16, 1859/New York, N.Y.
Died: August 16, 1927/Houston, Texas

Devlin, James Alexander
Born: 1849/Philadelphia, Penn.
Died: October 10, 1883/Philadelphia, Penn.

Dexter, Charles Dana
Born: June 15, 1876/Evansville, Ind.
Died: June 9, 1934/Cedar Rapids, Iowa

Dickerson, Louis Pessano
Born: October 11, 1858/Tyaskin, Md.
Died: July 23, 1920/Baltimore, Md.

Dolan, Joseph
Born: February 24, 1873/Baltimore, Md.
Died: March 24, 1938/Omaha, Neb.

Donovan, Patrick Joseph
Born: March 16, 1865/Queenstown, Ireland
Died: December 25, 1953/Lawrence, Mass.

Dooms, Henry E.
Born: January 30, 1867/St. Louis, Mo.
Died: December 14, 1899/St. Louis, Mo.

Doran, John F.
Born: 1869/New Jersey
Died: Date and location unknown

Dowling, Henry Peter
Born: Date unknown/St. Louis, Mo.
Died: June 30, 1905/Hot Lake, Ore.

Dowse, Thomas Joseph
Born: August 12, 1866/Ireland
Died: December 14, 1946/Riverside, Calif.

Driscoll, John F.
Born: November 19, 1855/Lowell, Mass.
Died: July 11, 1886/Lowell, Mass.

Patsy Donovan
(National Baseball Library and Archive, Cooperstown, NY)

Dungan, Samuel Morrison
Born: January 29, 1866/Ferndale, Calif.
Died: March 16, 1939/Santa Ana, Calif.

Dyler, John F.
Born: June, 1852/Louisville, Ky.
Died: (Unknown)

Earle, William Moffat
Born: November 10, 1867/Philadelphia, Penn.
Died: May 30, 1946/Omaha, Neb.

Easterday, Henry P.
Born: September 16, 1864/Philadelphia, Penn.
Died: March 30, 1895/Philadelphia, Penn.

Ehret, Philip Sydney
Born: August 31, 1868/Louisville, Ky.
Died: July 28, 1940/Cincinnati, Ohio

Ely, Frederick William
Born: June 7, 1863/North Girard, Penn.
Died: January 10, 1952/Imola, Calif.

Emig, Charles H.
Born: April 5, 1875/Cincinnati, Ohio
Died: October, 1975/Oklahoma City, Okla.

*Esterbrook, Thomas John (known as Dude Esterbrook)
Born: June 9, 1857/Staten Island, N.Y.
Died: April 30, 1901/Middletown, N.Y.

Eustace, Frank John
Born: November 7, 1873/New York, N.Y.
Died: October 20, 1932/Pottsville, Penn.

Evans, Roy
Born: March 19, 1874/Knoxville, Tenn.
Died: August 15, 1915/Galveston, Texas

Ewing, John
Born: June 1, 1863/Cincinnati, Ohio
Died: April 23, 1895/Denver, Colo.

Fauver, Clayton King
Born: August 1, 1872/North Eaton, Ohio
Died: March 3, 1942/Chatsworth, Ga.

Fisher, Charles
Born: Date unknown/Baltimore, Md.
Died: Date and location unknown

Fitzgerald, John T.
Born: Date unknown/Leadville, Colo.
Died: Date and location unknown)

Flaherty, Patrick Henry
Born: January 31, 1876/St. Louis, Mo.
Died: January 28, 1946/Chicago, Ill.

Flaherty, Patrick Joseph
Born: June 29, 1876/Mansfield, Penn.
Died: January 23, 1969/Alexandria, La.

Flanagan, Edward J.
Born: September 15, 1861/Lowell, Mass.
Died: November 10, 1926/Lowell, Mass.

Fox, George B.
Born: December 1, 1869/Pottstown, Penn.
Died: May 8, 1914/Philadelphia, Penn.

Fraser, Charles Carrolton
Born: March 17, 1871/Chicago, Ill.
Died: May 8, 1940/Wendell, Idaho

Friend, Frank B.
Born: Date unknown/Washington, D.C.
Died: September 8, 1897/Atlantic City, N.J.

Fulmer, Charles John
Born: February 12, 1851/Philadelphia, Penn.
Died: February 15, 1940/Philadelphia, Penn.

Fusselbach, Edward L.
Born: July 4, 1858/Philadelphia, Penn.
Died: April 14, 1926/Philadelphia, Penn.

Galligan, John T.
Born: 1868/Easton, Penn.
Died: July 17, 1906/New York, N.Y.

Gaule, Michael John
Born: August 4, 1869/Baltimore, Md.
Died: January 24, 1918/Baltimore, Md.

Geer, William Henry Harrison (born George Harrison Geer)
Born: August 13, 1849/Syracuse, N.Y.
Died: January 5, 1922/Syracuse, N.Y.

*Gerhardt, John Joseph
Born: February 14, 1855/Washington, D.C.
Died: March 11, 1922/Middletown, N.Y.

Gettinger, Lewis Thomas Leyton
Born: December 11, 1868/Frederick, Md.
Died: July 26, 1943/Pensacola, Fla.

Gilbert, Peter
Born: September 6, 1867/Baltic, Ct.
Died: January 1, 1912/Springfield, Mass.

Joe Gerhardt (University of Louisville Photographic Archives)

Glasscock, John Wesley
Born: July 22, 1859/Wheeling, W.Va.
Died: February 24, 1947/Wheeling, W.Va.

Gleason, John Day
Born: July 14, 1854/St. Louis, Mo.
Died: September 4, 1944/St. Louis, Mo.

Gleason, William G.
Born: November 12, 1859/St. Louis, Mo.
Died: July 21, 1932/St. Louis, Mo.

Goodall, Herbert Frank
Born: March 10, 1870/Mansfield, Penn.
Died: January 20, 1938/Mansfield, Penn.

Grim, John Helm
Born: August 9, 1867/Lebanon, Ky.
Died: July 28, 1961/Indianapolis, Ind.

Gumbert, William Skeen
Born: August 8, 1865/Pittsburgh, Penn.
Died: April 13, 1946/Pittsburgh, Penn.

Hach, Irvin William
Born: June 6, 1873/Louisville, Ky.
Died: August 13, 1936/Louisville, Ky.

Hague, William L. (born William L. Haug)
Born: 1852/Philadelphia, Penn.
Died: Date and location unknown

Haldeman, John Avery
Born: December 2, 1855/Pee Wee Valley, Ky.
Died: September 17, 1899/Louisville, Ky.

Hall, George William
Born: March 29, 1849/Stepney, England
Died: June 11, 1923/Ridgewood, N.Y.

Hamburg, Charles H. (known as Charles H. Hambrick)
Born: November 22, 1863/Louisville, Ky.
Died: May 18, 1931/Union, N.J.

Harrington, Jeremiah Peter
Born: August 12, 1869/Keokuk, Iowa
Died: April 16, 1913/Keokuk, Iowa

#Hart, James Aristotle
Born: July 10, 1855/Fairview, Penn.
Died: July 18, 1919/Chicago, Ill.

Hartsel, Tully Frederick
Born: June 26, 1874/Polk, Ohio
Died: October 14, 1944/Toledo, Ohio

Hassamaer, William Louis
Born: July 26, 1864/St. Louis, Mo.
Died: May 29, 1910/St. Louis, Mo.

Hastings, Winfield Scott
Born: August 10, 1846/Hillsboro, Ohio
Died: August 14, 1907/Sawtelle, Calif.

Hatfield, Gilbert
Born: January 27, 1855/Hoboken, N.J.
Died: May 27, 1921/Hoboken, N.J.

Healy, John J.
Born: October 27, 1866/Cairo, Ill.
Died: March 16, 1899/St. Louis, Mo.

Hecker, Guy Jackson
Born: April 3, 1856/Youngsville, Ohio
Died: December 3, 1938/Wooster, Ohio

Heinzman, John Peter
Born: September 27, 1863/New Albany, Ind.
Died: November 10, 1914/Louisville, Ky.

Hemming, George Earl
Born: December 15, 1868/Carrollton, Ohio
Died: June 3, 1930/Springfield, Mass.

Hemp, William H.
Born: December 27, 1867/St. Louis, Mo.
Died: March 6, 1923/St. Louis, Mo.

Herman, Arthur
Born: May 11, 1871/Louisville, Ky.
Died: September 20, 1955/Los Angeles, Calif.

Hill, William Cicero
Born: August 2, 1874/Chattanooga, Tenn.
Died: January 28, 1938/Cincinnati, Ohio

Holbert, William H.
Born: March 14, 1855/Baltimore, Md.
Died: March 1, 1935/Laurel, Md.

Holmes, James William
Born: January 28, 1869/Des Moines, Iowa
Died: August 6, 1932/Truro, Iowa

Hoy, William Ellsworth
Born: May 23, 1862/Houckstown, Ohio
Died: December 15, 1961/Cincinnati, Ohio

Hulswitt, Rudolph Edward
Born: February 23, 1877/Newport, Ky.
Died: January 16, 1950/Louisville, Ky.

Hunter, William Robert
Born: Date unknown/St. Thomas, Ontario, Canada
Died: Date and location unknown

Inks, Albert Preston (born Albert Preston Inkstein)
Born: January 27, 1871/Ligonier, Ind.
Died: October 3, 1941/Ligonier, Ind.

Irwin, John
Born: July 21, 1861/Toronto, Ontario, Canada
Died: February 28, 1934/Boston, Mass

Jennings, Hugh Ambrose
Born: April 2, 1869/Pittston, Penn.
Died: February 1, 1928/Scranton, Penn.

Johnson, Albert J.
Born: July 26, 1872/Sweden
Died: May 2, 1924/Oak Forest, Ill.

Jones, Alexander H.
Born: December 25, 1869/Bradford, Penn.
Died: April 4, 1941/Woodville, Penn.

Jones, James Tilford
Born: December 25, 1876/London, Ky.
Died: May 6, 1953/London, Ky.

Jones, Michael
Born: Date unknown/Hamilton, Ontario, Canada
Died: March 24, 1894/Hamilton, Ontario, Canada

Hughie Jennings
(National Baseball Library and Archive, Cooperstown, NY)

Jones, Ryerson L.
Born: Date unknown/Cincinnati, Ohio
Died: Date and location unknown

Kelley, Michael Joseph
Born: December 2, 1875/Templeton, Mass.
Died: June 6, 1955/Minneapolis, Minn.

#Kelly, John O.
Born: October 31, 1856/New York, N.Y.
Died: March 27, 1926/Malba, N.Y.

Kemmer, William Edward (born William E. Kemmerer)
Born: November 15, 1873/Pennsylvania
Died: June 8, 1945/Washington, D.C.

Kennedy, Theodore A.
Born: February, 1865/Henry, Ill.
Died: October 31, 1907/St. Louis, Mo.

*Kerins, John Nelson
Born: July 15, 1858/Indianapolis, Ind.
Died: September 8, 1919/Louisville, Ky.

Ketcham, Frederick L.
Born: July 27, 1875/Elmira, N.Y.
Died: March 12, 1908/Cortland, N.Y.

Kilroy, Matthew Aloysius
Born: June 21, 1866/Philadelphia, Penn.
Died: March 2, 1940/Philadelphia, Penn.

Kinslow, Thomas F.
Born: January 12, 1866/Washington, D.C.
Died: February 22, 1901/Washington, D.C.

Kittridge, Malachi Jeddidah
Born: October 12, 1869/Clinton, Mass.
Died: June 23, 1928/Gary, Ind.

Kling, William
Born: January 14, 1867/Kansas City, Mo.
Died: August 26, 1934/Kansas City, Mo.

Knell, Philip H.
Born: March 2, 1865/Mill Valley, Calif.
Died: June 5, 1944/Santa Monica, Calif.

Kostal, Joseph William
Born: March 17, 1876/Chicago, Ill.
Died: October 10, 1933/Guelph, Ontario, Canada

Krehmeyer, Charles L.
Born: July 5, 1863/St. Louis, Mo.
Died: February 10, 1926/St. Louis, Mo.

Kuehne, William J.
Born: October 24, 1858/Leipzig, Germany
Died: October 27, 1921/Sulphur Springs, Ohio

Lafferty, Frank Bernard
Born: May 4, 1854/Scranton, Penn.
Died: February 8, 1910/Wilmington, Del.

Lake, Frederick Lovett
Born: October 16, 1866/Nova Scotia
Died: November 24, 1931/Boston, Mass.

Langsford, Robert William (b. Robert Hugo Lankswert)
Born: August 5, 1865/Louisville, Ky.
Died: January 10, 1907/Louisville, Ky.

LaRoque, Samuel H.J.
Born: February 26, 1864/St. Mathias, Quebec, Canada
Died: Date and location unknown

Latham, George Warren
Born: September 6, 1852/Utica, N.Y.
Died: May 26, 1914/Utica, N.Y.

Latimer, Clifford Wesley
Born: November 30, 1877/Loveland, Ohio
Died: April 24, 1936/Loveland, Ohio

Leach, Thomas William
Born: November 4, 1877/French Creek, N.Y.
Died: September 29, 1969/Haines City, Fla.

Leary, John J.
Born: 1858/New Haven, Ct.
Died: Date and location unknown

Little, Harry A.
Born: St. Louis, Mo.
Died: Date and location unknown

Long, Daniel W.
Born: August 27, 1867/Boston, Mass.
Died: April 30, 1929/Sausalito, Calif.

Matty Kilroy
(National Baseball Library and Archive, Cooperstown, NY)

Long, James M.
Born: November 15, 1862/Louisville, Ky.
Died: December 12, 1932/Louisville, Ky.

Luby, John Perkins
Born: 1868/Charleston, S.C.
Died: April 24, 1899/Charleston, S.C.

Lucid, Cornelius Cecil
Born: February 24, 1874/Dublin, Ireland
Died: June 25, 1931/Houston, Texas

Luff, Henry T.
Born: September 14, 1856/Philadelphia, Penn.
Died: October 11, 1916/Philadelphia, Penn.

Lutenberg, Charles William
Born: October 4, 1864/Quincy, Ill.
Died: December 24, 1938/Quincy, Ill.

*Mack, Dennis Joseph (born Dennis Joseph McGee)
Born: 1851/Easton Penn.
Died: April 10, 1889/Wilkes–Barre, Penn.

Mack, Joseph ("Reddy Mack"; born Joseph McNamara)
Born: May 2, 1866/Ireland
Died: December 30, 1916/Newport, Ky.

Magee, William J.
Born: 1875/Canada
Died: Date and location unknown

Mahaffey, Louis Wood
Born: January 3, 1874/Madison, Wisc.
Died: October 24, 1949/Torrance, Calif.

Martin, Frank
Born: February 28, 1879/Chicago, Ill.
Died: September 30, 1924/Chicago, Ill.

Maskrey, Harry H.
Born: December 21, 1861/Mercer, Penn.
Died: August 17, 1930/Mercer, Penn.

Maskrey, Samuel Leech
Born: February 11, 1854/Mercer, Penn.
Died: April 1, 1922/Mercer, Penn.

Mays, Albert C.
Born: May 17, 1865/Canal Dover, Ohio
Died: May 17, 1905/Parkersburg, W.Va.

McCaffrey, Harry Charles
Born: November 25, 1858/St. Louis, Mo.
Died: April 29, 1928/St. Louis, Mo.

#McCloskey, John James
Born: April 4, 1862/Louisville, Ky.
Died: November 17, 1940/Louisville, Ky.

McCormick, William J.
Born: December 25, 1874/Maysville, Ky.
Died: January 28, 1956/Cincinnati, Ohio

McCreery, Thomas Livingston
Born: October 19, 1874/Beaver, Penn.
Died: July 3, 1941/Beaver, Penn.

McDermott, Michael Joseph
Born: September 7, 1862/St. Louis, Mo.
Died: June 30, 1943/St. Louis, Mo.

McFarlan, Alexander Shepard
Born: October 11, 1869/St. Louis, Mo.
Died: March 2, 1939/Pee Wee Valley, Ky.

McFarlan, Anderson Daniel
Born: November 26, 1874/Gainesville, Texas
Died: September 24, 1924/Louisville, Ky.

McFarland, Hermas William
Born: March 11, 1870/Des Moines, Iowa
Died: September 21, 1935/Richmond, Va.

McGann, Ambrose
Born: Date unknown/Baltimore, Md.
Died: Date and location unknown

#McGunnigle, William Henry
Born: January 1, 1855/Boston, Mass.
Died: March 9, 1899/Brockton, Mass.

McLaughlin, Thomas
Born: March 28, 1860/Louisville, Ky.
Died: July 21, 1921/Louisville, Ky.

Meakim, George Clinton
Born: July 11, 1865/Brooklyn, N.Y.
Died: February 17, 1923/Queens, N.Y.

Meekin, Jouett
Born: February 21, 1867/New Albany, Ind.
Died: December 14, 1944/New Albany, Ind.

Menefee, John
Born: January 15, 1868/West Virginia
Died: March 11, 1953/Belle Vernon, Penn.

Merrill, Edward M.
Born: May 1860/Kentucky
Died: Date and location unknown

Merritt, William Henry
Born: July 30, 1870/Lowell, Mass.
Died: November 17, 1937/Lowell, Mass.

Messitt, Thomas John
Born: July 27, 1874/Frankfort, Penn.
Died: September 22, 1934/Chicago, Ill.

Miller, Burt
Born: Date unknown/Kalamazoo, Mich.
Died: Date and location unknown

Miller, George Frederick
Born: August 15, 1864/Brooklyn, N.Y.
Died: April 6, 1909/Brooklyn, N.Y.

Miller, Joseph A.
Born: February 17, 1861/Baltimore, Md.
Died: April 23, 1923/Wheeling, W.Va.

Minnehan, Daniel Joseph
Born: November 28, 1865/Troy, N.Y.
Died: August 8, 1929/Troy, N.Y.

Morrison, Thomas J.
Born: 1875/St. Louis, Mo.
Died: Date and location unknown

Mullane, Anthony John
Born: January 30, 1859/Cork, Ireland
Died: April 25, 1944/Chicago, Ill.

Murphy, Clarence
Born: Date and location unknown
Died: Date and location unknown

Murray, Jeremiah J.
Born: January 1, 1865/Boston, Mass.
Died: January 1, 1922/Boston, Mass.

Nance, William G. (born William G. Cooper)
Born: August 2, 1876/Fort Worth, Texas
Died: May 28, 1958/Fort Worth, Texas

Neale, Joseph Hunt
Born: May 7, 1866/Wadsworth, Ohio
Died: December 30, 1913/Akron, Ohio

Nichols, Albert H.
Born: Date unknown/Brooklyn, N.Y.
Died: Date and location unknown

Nicol, George Edward
Born: October 17, 1870/Barry, Ill.
Died: August 10, 1924/Milwaukee, Wisc.

O'Brien, John J.
Born: July 14, 1870/St. John, New Brunswick, Canada
Died: May 13, 1913/Lewiston, Maine

O'Connor, Daniel Cornelius
Born: August, 1868/Guelph, Ontario, Canada
Died: March 3, 1942/Guelph, Ontario, Canada

O'Rourke, Timothy Patrick
Born: May 18, 1864/Chicago, Ill.
Died: April 20, 1939/Seattle, Wash.

Pearce, Franklin Johnson
Born: March 30, 1860/Jefferson County, Ky.
Died: November 13, 1926/Louisville, Ky.

Peppers, Harrison
Born: September 1866/Kentucky
Died: November 5, 1903/Webb City, Mo.

Pettee, Patrick E.
Born: January 10, 1863/Natick, Mass.
Died: October 9, 1934/Natick, Mass.

*Pfeffer, Nathaniel Frederick
Born: March 17, 1860/Louisville, Ky.
Died: April 10, 1932/Chicago, Ill.

Phelan, Daniel T.
Born: July, 1865/Thomaston, Ct.
Died: December 7, 1945/West Haven, Ct.

Phillippe, Charles Louis
Born: May 23, 1872/Rural Retreat, Va.
Died: March 30, 1952/Avalon, Penn.

Pickering, Oliver Daniel
Born: April 9, 1870/Olney, Ill.
Died: January 20, 1952/Vincennes, Ind.

Pierce, Grayson S.
Born: Date unknown/New York, N.Y.
Died: August 29, 1894/New York, N.Y.

Pinckney, George Burton
Born: January 11, 1862/Orange Prairie, Ill.
Died: November 10, 1926/Peoria, Ill.

Powers. Michael Riley
Born: September 22, 1870/Pittsfield, Penn.
Died: April 26, 1909/Philadelphia, Penn.

Preston, Walter B.
Born: 1870/Richmond, Va.
Died: Date and location unknown

Prince, Walter Farr
Born: May 9, 1861/Amherst, N.H.
Died: March 2, 1938/Bristol, N.H.

Ramsey, Thomas A.
Born: August 8, 1864/Indianapolis, Ind.
Died: March 27, 1906/Indianapolis, Ind.

Raymond, Harry H.
Born: February 20, 1862/Utica, N.Y.
Died: March 21, 1925/San Diego, Calif.

Reccius, John
Born: October 29, 1859/Louisville, Ky.
Died: September 1, 1930/Louisville, Ky.

Reccius, Philip
Born: June 7, 1862/Louisville, Ky.
Died: February 15, 1903/Louisville, Ky.

Reeder. Nicholas (born Nicholas Herchenroeder)
Born: March 22, 1867/Louisville, Ky.
Died: September 26, 1894/Louisville, Ky.

Rhines, William Pearl
Born: March 14, 1869/Ridgeway, Penn.
Died: January 30, 1922/Ridgeway, Penn.

Rhodes, William Clarence
Born: Date unknown/Pottstown, Penn.
Died: Date and location unknown

Richardson, Daniel
Born: January 25, 1863/Elmira, N.Y.
Died: September 12, 1926/New York, N.Y.

Richter, John M.
Born: February 8, 1873/Louisville, Ky.
Died: October 4, 1927/Louisville, Ky.

Ritchey, Claude Cassius
Born: October 5, 1873/Emlenton, Penn.
Died: November 8, 1951/Emlenton, Penn.

Robinson, William (born William Anderson)
Born: Date unknown/Taylorsville, Ky.
Died: Date and location unknown

*Rogers, James F.
Born: April 9, 1872/Hartford, Ct.
Died: January 21, 1900/Bridgeport, Ct.

Roseman, James John
Born: July 4, 1856/Brooklyn, N.Y.
Died: July 4, 1938/Brooklyn, N.Y.

Ryan, John Bernard
Born: November 12, 1869/Haverhill, Mass.
Died: August 21, 1952/Boston, Mass.

Ryan, John Joseph
Born: October, 1853/Philadelphia, Penn.
Died: March 22, 1902/Philadelphia, Penn.

Sanders, Alexander Bennett
Born: February 16, 1865/Catharpen, Va.
Died: August 29, 1930/Memphis, Tenn.

Say, James I.
Born: 1862/Baltimore, Md.
Died: June 23, 1894/Baltimore, Md.

Schellhase, Albert Herman
Born: September 13, 1864/Evansville, Ind.
Died: January 3, 1919/Evansville, Ind.

Schenck, William G.
Born: Date unknown/Brooklyn, N.Y.
Died: Date and location unknown

Scherer, Harry
Born: Date unknown/Baltimore, Md.
Died: Date and location unknown

Schreckengost, Ossee Freeman
Born: April 11, 1875/New Bethlehem, Penn.
Died: July 9, 1914/Philadelphia, Penn.

Seery, John Emmett
Born: February 13, 1861/Princeville, Ill.
Died: Date and location unknown

Shaffer, George
Born: 1852/Philadelphia, Penn.
Died: Date and location unknown

*Shannon, Daniel W.
Born: March 23, 1865/Bridgeport, Ct.
Died: October 25, 1913/Bridgeport, Ct.

Shannon, John Francis
Born: December 3, 1873/San Francisco, Calif.
Died: February 27, 1934/Boston, Mass.

Shinnick, Timothy James
Born: November 6, 1867/Exeter, N.H.
Died: May 18, 1944/Exeter, N.H.

Shugart, Frank Harry (born Frank Harry Shugarts)
Born: December 10, 1866/Luthersburg, Penn.
Died: September 9, 1944/Clearfield, Penn.

Smith, Charles Marvin
Born: October 12, 1856/Digby, Nova Scotia, Canada
Died: April 18, 1927/Boston, Mass.

Smith, George Henry
Born: October 24, 1871/Pittsburgh, Penn.
Died: June 25, 1939/Buffalo, N.Y.

Smith, Harry W.
Born: February 5, 1856/North Vernon, Ind.
Died: June 4, 1898/North Vernon, Ind.

Smith, Oliver H.
Born: 1868/Mt. Vernon, Ohio
Died: Date and location unknown

Smith, Samuel J.
Born: March 19, 1869/Baltimore, Md.
Died: April 26, 1916/St. Louis, Mo.

Smith, Thomas E.
Born: December 5, 1871/Boston, Mass.
Died: March 2, 1929/Dorchester, Mass.

Snyder, Charles N.
Born: October 6, 1854/Washington, D.C.
Died: October 29, 1924/Washington, D.C.

Snyder, Frank C.
Born: Date unknown/Toronto, Ontario, Canada
Died: March 9, 1917/Toronto, Ontario, Canada

Somerville, Edward
Born: March 1, 1853/Philadelphia, Penn.
Died: October 1, 1877/London, Ontario, Canada

Spies, Henry
Born: June 12, 1866/New Orleans, La.
Died: July 8, 1942/Los Angeles, Calif.

Springer, Edward H.
Born: February 9, 1861/California
Died: April 24, 1926/Los Angeles, Calif.

Stafford, James Joseph
Born: July 9, 1868/Webster, Mass.
Died: September 11, 1923/Webster, Mass.

Steelman, Morris James
Born: June 29, 1875/Millville, N.J.
Died: September 16, 1944/Merchantville, N.J.

Stockwell, Leonard Clark
Born: August 25, 1859/Cordova, Ill.
Died: January 28, 1905/Niles, Calif.

Stouch, Thomas Carl
Born: December 2, 1870/Perryville, Ohio
Died: October 7, 1956/Lancaster, Penn.

Strang, Samuel Nicklin (born Samuel Strang Nicklin)
Born: December 16, 1876/Chattanooga, Tenn.
Died: March 13, 1932/Chattanooga, Tenn.

Stratton, C. Scott
Born: October 2, 1869/Campbellsburg, Ky.
Died: March 8, 1939/Louisville, Ky.

Strauss, Joseph (born Joseph Strasser)
Born: November 16, 1858/Cincinnati, Ohio
Died: June 24, 1906/Cincinnati, Ohio

Strick, John Quincy Adams
Born: Date unknown/Louisville, Ky.
Died: Date and location unknown

Sullivan, Daniel C.
Born: May 9, 1857/Providence, R.I.
Died: October 26, 1893/Providence, R.I.

Sullivan, Thomas
Born: March 1, 1860/New York, N.Y.
Died: April 12, 1947/Cincinnati, Ohio

Sullivan, Thomas Jefferson
Born: Date unknown/St. Louis, Mo.
Died: September 25, 1899/Camden, N.J.

Sweeney, Daniel J.
Born: January 28, 1868/Philadelphia, Penn.
Died: July 13, 1913/Louisville, Ky,

Sweeney, Peter Jay
Born: December 31, 1863/California
Died: August 22, 1901/San Francisco, Calif

Sylvester, Louis J.
Born: February 14, 1855/Springfield, Ill.
Died: Date and location unknown

Taylor, Harry Leonard
Born: April 4, 1866/Halsey Valley, N.Y.
Died: July 12, 1955/Buffalo, N.Y.

Taylor, William H.
Born: 1872/Pittsburgh, Penn.
Died: September 12, 1905/Cincinnati, Ohio

Terrell, John Thomas
Born: June 29, 1867/Louisville, Ky.
Died: July 9, 1893/Louisville, Ky.

Todd, George Franklin
Born: October 18, 1869/Aberdeen, Md.
Died: August 11, 1919/Havre de Grace, Md.

Tomney, Philip H.
Born: June 17, 1863/Reading, Penn.
Died: March 18, 1892/Reading, Penn.

Traffley, John
Born: 1862/Chicago, Ill.
Died: July 17, 1900/Baltimore, Md.

Treadway, George B.
Born: November 11, 1866/Greenup County, Ky.
Died: Date and location unknown

Philip Tomney (University of Louisville Photographic Archives)

Trost, Michael J.
Born: 1866/Philadelphia, Penn.
Died: March 24, 1901/Philadelphia, Penn.

Twitchell, Lawrence Grant
Born: February 18, 1864/Cleveland, Ohio
Died: April 23, 1930/Cleveland, Ohio

Vaughn, Henry Francis
Born: March 1, 1864/Rural Dale, Ohio
Died: February 21, 1914/Cincinnati, Ohio

Veach, William Walter
Born: June 15, 1862/Indianapolis, Ind.
Died: November 12, 1937/Indianapolis, Ind.

Viau, Leon A.
Born: July 5, 1866/Corinth, Vt.
Died: December 17, 1947/Hopewell, N.J.

Waddell, George Edward
Born: October 13, 1876/Bradford, Penn.
Died: April 1, 1914/San Antonio, Texas

Wadsworth, John L.
Born: December 17, 1867/Wellington, Ohio
Died: July 8, 1941/Elyria, Ohio

Wagner, John Peter
Born: February 24, 1874/Mansfield, Penn.
Died: December 6, 1955/Carnegie, Penn.

#Walsh, Michael John
Born: April 29, 1850/Ireland
Died: February 2, 1929/Louisville, Ky.

Warner, John Joseph
Born: August 15, 1872/New York, N.Y.
Died: December 21, 1943/Queens, N.Y.

Weaver, Samuel H.
Born: July 10, 1855/Philadelphia, Penn.
Died: February 1, 1914/Philadelphia, Penn.

Weaver, William B.
Born: March 23, 1865/Parkersburg, W.Va.
Died: January 25, 1943/Akron, Ohio

Weckbecker, Pete
Born: August 30, 1864/Butler, Penn.
Died: May 16, 1935/Hampton, Va.

Welch, Curtis Benton
Born: February 11, 1862/East Liverpool, Ohio
Died: August 29, 1896/East Liverpool, Ohio

Welsh, James J.
Born: July 3, 1866/St. Louis, Mo.
Died: Date and location unknown

Wentz, John George (born John George Wernz)
Born: March 4, 1863/Louisville, Ky.
Died: September 14, 1907/Louisville, Ky.

Werden, Percival Wheritt
Born: July 21, 1865/St. Louis, Mo.
Died: January 9, 1934/Minneapolis, Minn.

Werrick, Joseph Abraham
Born: October 25, 1861/St. Paul, Minn.
Died: May 10, 1943/St. Peter, Minn.

Weyhing, August
Born: September 29, 1866/Louisville, Ky.
Died: September 4, 1955/Louisville, Ky.

Whistler, Lewis (born Lewis Wissler)
Born: March 10, 1868/St. Louis, Mo.
Died: December 30, 1959/St. Louis, Mo.

White, William Dighton
Born: May 1, 1860/Bridgeport, Ohio
Died: December 29, 1924/Bellaire, Ohio

Whiting, Edward C.
Born: 1860/Philadelphia, Penn.
Died: Date and location unknown

Whitrock, William Franklin
Born: March 4, 1870/Cincinnati, Ohio
Died: July 26, 1935/Derby, Ct.

Wilhelm, Harry Lester
Born: April 7, 1874/Uniontown, Penn.
Died: February 20, 1944/Republic, Penn.

Wills, Davis Bowles
Born: January 26, 1877/Charlottesville, Va.
Died: October 12, 1959/Washington, D.C.

Wilson, William G.
Born: October 28, 1867/Hannibal, Mo.
Died: May 9, 1924/St. Paul, Minn.

Winkelman, George Edward
Born: June 14, 1861/Philadelphia, Penn.
Died: May 19, 1960/Washington, D.C.

*Wolf, William Van Winkle
Born: May 12, 1862/Louisville, Ky.
Died: May 16, 1903/Louisville, Ky.

Woods, Walter Sydney
Born: April 28, 1875/Rye, N.H.
Died: October 30, 1951/Portsmouth, N.H.

Wright, Joseph
Born: 1873/Pittsburgh, Penn.
Died: Date and location unknown

Zahner, Frederick Joseph
Born: June 5, 1870/Louisville, Ky.
Died: July 24, 1900/Louisville, Ky.

Zimmer, Charles Louis
Born: November 23, 1860/Marietta, Ohio
Died: August 22, 1949/Cleveland, Ohio

* Player/Manager   # Manager
All others are players only.
Total: 312 (Players, Managers and Player/Managers)

LOUISVILLE'S SEASONAL MAJOR-LEAGUE ROSTERS
(1876-1877 & 1882-1899)

LOUISVILLE NATIONAL LEAGUE 1876

Allison, Arthur Algernon
Bechtel, George A.
Carbine, John C.
Chapman, John Curtis
Clinton, James Lawrence
Collins, Daniel Thomas
Devlin, James Alexander
Fulmer, Charles John
Gerhardt, John Joseph
Hague, William L.
Hastings, Winfield Scott
Holbert, William H.
Pearce, Frank
Ryan, John Joseph
Snyder, Charles N.
Somerville, Edward

LOUISVILLE NATIONAL LEAGUE 1877

Craver, William H.
Crowley, William Michael
Devlin, James Alexander
Gerhardt, John Joseph
Hague, William L.
Haldeman, John Avery
Hall, George William
Lafferty, Frank Bernard
Latham, George Warren
Little, Harry A.
Nichols, Albert H.
Shaffer, George
Snyder, Charles N.

LOUISVILLE AMERCIAN ASSOCIATION 1882

Bohn, Charles
Booth, Amos Smith
Browning, Louis Rogers

Crotty, Joseph P.
Dyler, John F.
Hecker, Guy Jackson
Mack, Dennis Joseph
Maskrey, Harry H.
Maskrey, Samuel Leech
McCaffrey, Harry Charles
Mullane, Anthony John
Pierce, Grayson S.
Reccius, John
Reccius, Philip
Say, James I.
Schenk, William G.
Smith, Charles Marvin
Strick, John
Sullivan, Daniel C.
Wolf, William Van Winkle

LOUISVILLE AMERICAN ASSOCIATION 1883

Brown, Lewis J.
Browning, Louis Rogers
Gerhardt, John Joseph
Gleason, John Day
Hecker, Guy Jackson
Jones, Ryerson L.
Latham, George Warren
Leary, John J.
Luff, Henry T.
Maskrey, Samuel L.
McLaughlin, Thomas
Prince, Walter Farr
Reccius, John
Reccius, Philip
Sullivan, Daniel C.
Sullivan, Thomas Jefferson
Weaver, Samuel H.
Whiting. Edward C.
Winkelman, George Edward
Wolf, William Van Winkle

Louisville American Association 1884

Andrews, William Walter
Browning. Louis Rogers
Cline, John P.
Deagle, Lorenzo Burroughs
Dickerson, Louis Pessano
Driscoll, John F.
Gerhardt, John Joseph
Hecker, Guy Jackson
Hunter, William Robert
Latham, George Warren
Maskrey, Samuel Leech
McLaughlin, Thomas
Reccius, Philip
Stockwell, Leonard Clark
Sullivan, Daniel C.
Whiting, Edward C.
Wolf, William Van Winkle

Louisville American Association 1885

Baker, Norman Leslie
Browning, Louis Rogers
Cline, John F.
Connor, John
Cross, Amos C.
Crotty, Joseph P.
Geer, William Henry Harrison
Hecker, Guy Jackson
Kerins, John Nelson
Krehmeyer, Charles L.
Mack, Joseph
Maskrey, Samuel Leech
Mays, Albert C.
McLaughlin, Thomas
Miller, Joseph A.
Murray, Jeremiah J.
Ramsey, Thomas A.
Reccius, Philip
Strauss, Joseph
Sullivan, Daniel C.
Wolf, William Van Winkle

Louisville American Association 1886

Browning, Louis Rogers
Chamberlain, Elton P.
Collins, George Hubbert
Cook, Paul
Cross, Amos C.
Ely, Frederick William
Hecker, Guy Jackson
Heinzman, John Peter
Kennedy, Theodore H.
Kerins, John Nelson
Mack, Joseph
Maskrey, Samuel Leech
Murphy, Clarence
Neale, John Hunt
Ramsey, Thomas A.
Reccius, Philip
Strauss, Joseph
Sullivan, Thomas
Sylvester, Louis J.
Terrell, John Thomas
Werrick, Joseph Abraham
White, William Dighton
Wolf, William Van Winkle

Louisville American Association 1887

Browning, Louis Rogers
Chamberlain, Elton P.
Collins, George Hubbert
Cook, Paul
Cross, Amos C.
Cross, Lafayette Napoleon
Hecker, Guy Jackson
Hemp, William H.
Kerins, John Nelson
Mack, Joseph
Neale, Joseph Hunt
Ramsey, Thomas A.
Reccius, Philip
Veach, William Walter
Werrick, Joseph Abraham

White, William Dighton
Wolf, William Van Winkle

LOUISVILLE AMERICAN ASSOCIATION 1888

Andrews, William Walter
Browning, Louis Rogers
Burnett, Hercules H.
Chamberlain, Elton P.
Collins, George Hubbert
Cook, Paul
Cross, Napoleon Lafayette
Crowell, William Theodore
Esterbrook, Thomas John
Ewing, John
Fusselbach, Edward L.
Hecker, Guy Jackson
Kerins, John Nelson
Long, Daniel W.
Mack, Joseph
Ramsey, Thomas A.
Raymond, Harry H.
Reccius, Philip
Smith, Samuel J.
Stratton, C. Scott
Tomney, Philip H.
Vaughn, Henry Francis
Weaver, William B.
Werrick, Joseph Abraham
White, William Dighton
Wolf, William Van Winkle

LOUISVILLE AMERICAN ASSOCIATION 1889

Browning, Louis Rogers
Carl, Frederick E.
Cook, Paul
Ehret, Philip Sydney
Esterbrook, Thomas John
Ewing, John
Fisher, Charles
Flanagan, Edward J.
Galligan, John T.

Gaule, Michael John
Gleason, William G.
Hecker, Guy Jackson
Kerins, John Nelson
McDermott, Michael Joseph
Ramsey, Thomas A.
Raymond, Harry H.
Robinson, William
Ryan, John Bennett
Scherer, Harry
Shannon, Daniel W.
Smith, Harry W.
Springer, Edward H.
Stratton, C. Scott
Tomney, Philip H.
Traffley, John
Vaughn, Henry Francis
Weaver, William B.
Wolf, William Van Winkle

LOUISVILLE AMERICAN ASSOCIATION 1890

Bligh, Edwin Forrest
Daily, Edward M.
Easterday, Henry P.
Ehret, Philip Sydney
Goodall, Herbert Frank
Hamburg, Charles H.
Jones, Michael
Meakin, George Clinton
O'Connor, Daniel Cornelius
Phelan, Daniel T.
Raymond, Harry H.
Roseman, James John
Ryan, John Bennett
Shinnick, Timothy James
Stratton, C. Scott
Sweeney, Peter Jay
Taylor, Harry Leonard
Tomney, Philip H.
Weaver, William B.
Weckbecker, Peter
Wolf, William Van Winkle

LOUISVILLE AMERICAN ASSOCIATION 1891

Beard, Oliver Perry
Bell, Charles C.
Boone, George Morris
Briggs, Grant
Cahill, Thomas H.
Cline, John P.
Cook, Paul
Daily, Edward M.
Darragh, James S.
Donovan, Patrick Joseph
Doran, John F.
Ehret, Philip Sydney
Fitzgerald, John T.
Fox, George B.
Gerhardt, John Joseph
Irwin, John
Jennings, Hugh Ambrose
Kuehne, William J.
LaRoque, Samuel H.J.
Long, James M.
Meekin, Jouett
Pattee, Patrick E.
Raymond, Harry H.
Reeder, Nicholas
Ryan, John Bennett
Schellhase, Albert Herman
Shinnick, Timothy James
Stratton, C. Scott
Taylor, Harry Leonard
Weaver, William B.
Wentz, John George
Wolf, William Van Winkle

LOUISVILLE NATIONAL LEAGUE 1892

Bassett, Charles Edwin
Brown, Thomas T.
Browning, Louis Rogers
Clausen, Frederick William
Dooms, Henry E.
Dowse, Thomas Joseph

Fitzgerald, John T.
Grim, John Helm
Healy, John J.
Hemming, George Earl
Jennings, Hugh Ambrose
Jones, Alexander H.
Kuehne, William J.
McFarlan, Alexander Shepard
Meekin, Jouett
Merritt, William Henry
Pfeffer, Nathaniel Frederick
Sanders, Alexander Bennett
Seery, John Emmett
Stratton, C. Scott
Taylor, Harry Leonard
Viau, Leon A.
Weaver, William B.
Whistler, Lewis

LOUISVILLE NATIONAL LEAGUE 1893

Brown, Thomas T.
Brown, Willard
Browning, Louis Rogers
Clark, Robert H.
Clausen, Frederick William
Denny, Jeremiah Dennis
Grim, John Helm
Gumbert, William Skeen
Harrington, Jeremiah Peter
Hemming, George Earl
Jennings, Hugh Ambrose
Kilroy, Matthew Aloysius
Lucid, Cornelius Cecil
Menefee, John
O'Rourke, Timothy Patrick
Pfeffer, Nathaniel Frederick
Pinckney, George Burton
Rhines, William Pearl
Rhodes, William Clarence
Stratton, C. Scott
Twitchell, Lawrence Grant
Weaver, William B.

Welch, Curtis Benton
Whistler, Lewis
Whitrock, William Franklin

LOUISVILLE NATIONAL LEAGUE 1894

Brown, Thomas T.
Brown, Willard
Clarke, Fred Clifford
Cote, Henry Joseph
Denny, Jeremiah Dennis
Dungan, Samuel Morrison
Earle, William Moffatt
Flaherty, Patrick Henry
Gilbert, Peter
Grim, John Helm
Hemming, George Earl
Inks, Albert Preston
Kilroy, Matthew Aloysius
Knell, Philip H.
Lake, Frederick Lovett
Lutenberg, Charles William
Menefee, John
Nicol, George Edward
O'Rourke, Timothy Patrick
Peppers, Harrison
Pfeffer, Nathaniel Frederick
Richardson, Daniel
Smith, Oliver H.
Stratton, C. Scott
Twitchell, Lawrence Grant
Wadsworth, John L.
Weaver, William B.
Whitrock, William Franklin
Zahner, Frederick Joseph

Clarke, Fred Clifford
Collins, James Joseph
Cote, Henry Joseph
Cunningham, Ellsworth Elmer
Gettinger, Thomas L.
Glasscock, John Wesley
Hassamaer, William Louis
Hatfield, Gilbert
Holmes, James William
Inks, Albert Preston
Kemmer, William E.
Kling, William
Knell, Philip H.
Luby, John Perkins
McCormick, William J.
McCreery, Thomas Livingston
McDermott, Michael Joseph
McFarlan, Anderson Daniel
McGann, Ambrose
Meakim, George Clinton
Minnehan, Daniel Joseph
Morrison, Thomas J.
O'Brien, John J.
Pfeffer, Nathaniel Frederick
Preston, Walter B.
Shugart, Frank Harry
Spies, Henry
Sweeney, Daniel J.
Trost, Michael J.
Wadsworth, John L.
Warner, John Joseph
Welsh, James J.
Weyhing, August
Wright, Joseph
Zahner, Frederick Joseph

LOUISVILLE NATIONAL LEAGUE 1895

Borchers, George Bernard
Briggs, Grant
Brouthers, Dennis Joseph
Burnett, Hercules H.
Childers, William

LOUISVILLE NATIONAL LEAGUE 1896

Boyle, Edward J.
Cassidy, Peter Francis
Clarke, Fred Clifford
Clausen, Frederick William
Clingman, William Frederick

Crooks, John Charles
Cunningham, Ellsworth Elmer
Dexter, Charles Dana
Dolan, Joseph
Emig, Charles H.
Eustace, Frank John
Fraser, Charles Carrolton
Friend, Frank B.
Hassamaer, William Louis
Herman, Arthur
Hill, William Cicero
Holmes, James William
Johnson, Albert J.
Kinslow, Thomas F.
Kostal, Joseph William
McCreery, Thomas Livingston
McDermott, Michael Joseph
McFarland, Herman Walter
Miller, George Frederick
Morrison, Thomas J.
O'Brien, John J.
Pickering, Oliver Daniel
Rogers, James F.
Shannon, John Francis
Smith, Thomas E.
Strang, Samuel Nicklin
Treadway, George B.
Warner, John Joseph
Weyhing, August
Wright, Joseph

LOUISVILLE NATIONAL LEAGUE 1897

Butler, Richard H.
Clark, William Winfield
Clarke, Fred Clifford
Clarke, William H.
Clingman, William Frederick
Cunningham, Ellsworth Elmer
Delahanty, Thomas James
Dexter, Charles Dana
Dolan, Joseph
Dowling, Henry Peter

Evans, Roy
Fraser, Charles Carrolton
Hach, Irving William
Hemming, George Earl
Herman, Arthur
Hill, William Cicero
Holmes, James William
Johnson, Albert J.
Jones, James Tilford
Magee, William J.
Martin, Frank
McCreery, Thomas Livingston
Miller, Burt
Nance, William G.
Pickering, Oliver Daniel
Rogers, James F.
Schreckengost, Ossee Freeman
Smith, George Henry
Stafford, James Joseph
Waddell, George Edward
Wagner, John Peter
Werden, Percival Wherritt
Wilson, William G.

LOUISVILLE NATIONAL LEAGUE 1898

Altrock, Nicholas
Carey, George C.
Clarke, Fred Clifford
Clarke, James Baldwin
Clarke, William H.
Clingman, William Frederick
Cunningham, Ellsworth Elmer
Davis, Harry H.
Decker, George A.
Dexter, Charles Dana
Dowling, Henry Peter
Ehret, Philip Sydney
Fraser, Charles Carrolton
Hartsel, Tully Frederick
Hoy, William Ellsworth
Kittridge, Malachi Jeddidah
Leach, Thomas William

Magee, William J.
Mahaffey, Louis Wood
Nance, William G.
Powers, Michael Riley
Richter, John M.
Ritchey, Claude Cassius
Smith, George Henry
Snyder, Frank C.
Stafford, James Joseph
Stouch, Thomas Carl
Taylor, William H.
Todd, George Franklin
Wagner, John Peter
Wilson, William G.

LOUISVILLE NATIONAL LEAGUE 1899

Brashear, Roy Parks
Byers, Burley
Clarke, Fred Clifford
Clingman, William Frederick
Croft, Henry T.
Cunningham, Ellsworth Elmer
Decker, George A.
Dexter, Charles Dana

Dowling, Henry Peter
Fauver, Clayton King
Flaherty, Patrick Joseph
Hartsel, Tully Frederick
Hoy, William Ellsworth
Hulswitt, Rudolph Edward
Kelley, Michael Joseph
Ketcham, Frederick L.
Kittridge, Malachi Jeddidah
Langsford, Robert William
Latimer, Clifford Wesley
Leach, Thomas William
Magee, William J.
Messitt, Thomas John
Phillippe, Charles Louis
Powers, Michael Riley
Ritchey, Claude Cassius
Steelman, Morris James
Waddell, George Edward
Wagner, John Peter
Wilhelm, Harry Lester
Wills, Davis Bowles
Woods, Walter Sydney
Zimmer, Charles Louis

CHAPTER NINE
LOUISVILLE'S BIG SHOW NUMBERS:
LOUISVILLE'S PRINCIPAL MAJOR-LEAGUE STATISTICS
ANNUAL FRANCHISE STANDINGS & MAJOR-LEAGUE TOTALS (1876-1899)

NATIONAL LEAGUE I

	Games	Won	Lost	Ties	N-D	Pct.	Finish
1876	69	30	36	3	0	.455	5–8
1877	61	35	25	1	0	.583	2–6
	130	**65**	**61**	**4**	**0**	**.516**	

AMERICAN ASSOCIATION

	Games	Won	Lost	Ties	N–D	Pct.	Finish
1882	80	42	38	0	0	.525	3–6
1883	98	52	45	1	0	.536	5–8
1884	110	68	40	2	0	.630	3–13
1885#	112	53	59	0	0	.473	5–8
1886	138	66	70	2	0	.485	4–8
1887	139	76	60	3	0	.559	4–8
1888	139	48	87	4	0	.356	7–8
1889	140	27	111	2	0	.196	8–8
1890	136	88	44	4	0	.667	1–9
1891	139	54	83	2	0	.394	7–9
	1231	**574**	**637**	**20**	**0**	**.474**	

NATIONAL LEAGUE II

	Games	Won	Lost	Ties	N–D	Pct.	Finish
1892*	154	63	89	2	0	.414	9–12
1893	126	50	75	1	0	.400	11–12
1894	131	36	94	0	1	.277	12–12
1895	133	35	96	2	0	.267	12–12
1896	134	38	93	3	0	.290	12–12
1897	136	52	78	4	2	.400	11–12
1898	154	70	81	3	0	.464	9–12
1899	156	75	77	3	1	.493	9–12
	1124	**419**	**683**	**18**	**4**	**.380**	

PROFESSIONAL WON/LOST TOTALS BY LEAGUE AFFILIATION

National League I & II: 1,228 Games   484–744   .394
American Association: 1,211 Games   574–637   .474

MAJOR–LEAGUE WON/LOST TOTALS

2,439 Games   1058–1381   .434

In 20 years of major–league play, Louisville had six winning campaigns and 14 losing seasons. Broken down by league affiliation, they were 1–9 in 10 years of National League play (1–1 in their first stint and 0–8 in their second tenure), and 5–5 in 10 years of American Association membership.

During that time, they played a grand total of 2,485 games, that figure including 42 ties and four no–decisions (N–D) — incomplete games never replayed.

Percentage based on wins and losses only.

"Finish" category composed of Louisville's placing and number of teams in circuit that year respectively. Thus, in 1876, its first professional season, Louisville finished fifth in an eight–club circuit (5–8).

In 1885 (#), it tied for fifth place. In 1892 (*), the season was split. Figures given for 1892 season are cumulative totals of first half (30–47/11th place in 12–team league) and second half (33–42/ninth place in 12–team league).

Early 1890s Louisville Major-League action shot.
(University of Louisville Photographic Archives)

LOUISVILLE MANAGERS AND RECORDS

Year	Manager	Games	Won	Loss	Ties	N-D	Pct.	Finish	
1876	Chapman	69	30	36	3	0	.455	5–8	
1877	Chapman	61	35	25	1	0	.583	2–6	
1882	Mack	80	42	38	0	0	.525	3–6	
1883	Gerhardt	98	52	45	1	0	.536	5–8	
1884	Walsh	110	68	40	2	0	.630	3–13	
1885	Hart	112	53	59	0	0	.473	#5–8	
1886	Hart	138	66	70	2	0	.485	4–8	
1887	Kelly	139	76	60	3	0	.559	4–8	
1888	Kelly	39	10	29	0	0	.256	8–8	
	Davidson	3	1	2	0	0	.333	8–8	
	Kerins	7	3	4	0	0	.429	8–8	
	Davidson	90	34	52	4	0	.395	7–8	
1889	Esterbrook	10	2	8	0	0	.200	8–8	
	Wolf	65	14	51	0	0	.215	8–8	
	Shannon	58	10	46	2	0	.179	8–8	
	Chapman	7	1	6	0	0	.143	8–8	
1890	Chapman	136	88	44	4	0	.667	1–9	
1891	Chapman	139	54	83	2	0	.394	7–9	
1892	Chapman	54	21	33	0	0	.389	10–12	(FH)
	Pfeffer	23	9	14	0	0	.391	11–12	(FH)
	Pfeffer	77	33	42	2	0	.440	9–12	(SH)
1893	Barnie	126	50	75	1	0	.400	11–12	
1894	Barnie	131	36	94	0	1	.277	12–12	
1895	McCloskey	133	35	96	2	0	.267	12–12	
1896	McCloskey	19	2	17	0	0	.105	12–12	
	McGunnigle	115	36	76	3	0	.321	12–12	
1897	Rogers	44	17	24	2	1	.415	9–12	
	Clarke	92	35	54	2	1	.393	11–12	
1898	Clarke	154	70	81	3	0	.464	9–12	
1899	Clarke	156	75	77	3	1	.493	9–12	

\# - Tie

FH - first half

SH - second half

SEASONAL TEAM PITCHING AND BATTING LEADERS

1876 Jimmy Devlin (30–35)
Jimmy Devlin (.315)

1877 Jimmy Devlin (35–25)
George Hall (.323)

1882 Tony Mullane (30–24)
Pete Browning (**.378 league champion**)

1883 Guy Hecker (28–25)
Pete Browning (.338)

1884 Guy Hecker (**52–20 league champion**)
Pete Browning (.336)

1885 Guy Hecker (30–23)
Pete Browning (**.362 league champion**)

1886 Toad Ramsey (38–27)
Guy Hecker (**.341 league champion**)

1887 Toad Ramsey (37–27)
Pete Browning (.402)

1888 Icebox Chamberlain (14–9)
Pete Browning (.313)

1889 Red Ehret (10–29)
Chicken Wolf, Farmer Weaver (both .291)

1890 Scott Stratton (34–14)
Chicken Wolf (**.363 league champion**)

1891 John Fitzgerald (14–18)
Patsy Donovan (.321)

1892 Scott Stratton (21–19)
Harry Taylor (.260)

1893 George Hemming (18–17)
Willard Brown (.304)

1894 George Hemming (13–19)
Fred Pfeffer (.308)

1895 Bert Cunningham (11–16)
Fred Clarke (.347)

1896 Chick Fraser (12–27)
Tom McCreery (.351)

1897 Chick Fraser (15–19)
Fred Clarke (.390)

1898 Bert Cunningham (28–15)
Fred Clarke (.307)

1899 Deacon Phillippe (21–17)
Fred Clarke (.342)

OPENING AND CLOSING DAY RESULTS

Day/Date	Pitcher	Result	Opponent	Site/Att.
TU/4–25–76*	J. Devlin	Lost 4–0	Chicago	H/6,000
TH/10–5–76	J. Clinton	Lost 11–2	Hartford	H/(NA)

*First shutout in National League history

Day/Date	Pitcher	Result	Opponent	Site/Att.
TH/5–10–77	J. Devlin	Lost 15–9	Cincinnati	H/(NA)
SA/10–6–77	J. Devlin	Lost 4–0	Chicago	A/(NA)
TU/5–2–82	T. Mullane	Lost 9–7	St. Louis	A/(NA)
TU/10–1–82	T. Mullane	Won 5–1	St. Louis	A/(NA)
TU/5–1–83	G. Hecker	Won 6–5	Columbus	A/1,500
SU/9–30–83	G. Hecker	Won 10–5	Philadelphia	H/(NA)
TH/5–1–84	G. Hecker	Won 5–1	Toledo	H/(NA)
WE/10–15–84	G. Hecker	Won 9–3	Pittsburgh	A/(NA)
SU/4–19–85	G. Hecker	Lost 4–1	Cincinnati	H/10,000
TH/10–1–85	*(3 pitchers)	Lost 13–8	Baltimore	A/(NA)

*(G. Hecker, C. Wolf and P. Reccius; Hecker — losing pitcher;
called after six innings on account of darkness)

Day/Date	Pitcher	Result	Opponent	Site/Att.
SA/4–17–86	G. Hecker	Won 5–1	Cincinnati	A/5,000
SU/10–10–86	G. Hecker	Lost 8–6	Philadelphia	H/1,500
SA/4–16–87	T. Ramsey	Won 8–3	St. Louis	H/3,000
SU/10–7–87	T. Ramsey	Lost 2–0	Cincinnati	H/5,000
WE/4–18–88	T. Ramsey	Lost 8–0	St. Louis	A/5,000
SU/10–14–88	T. Ramsey	Won 2–1	Kansas City	H/(*)
	S. Stratton	Won 9–1	Kansas City	H/(*)

*(Doubleheader; total attendance for both games listed as 3,000)

Day/Date	Pitcher	Result	Opponent	Site/Att.
WE/4–17–89	J. Ewing	Lost 7–4	Kansas City	H/2,500
MO/10–14–89	J. Ewing	Lost 7–5	Kansas City	H/(NA)
FR/4–18–90	S. Stratton	Lost 11–8	St. Louis	H/5,523
TU/10–14–90	R. Ehret	Won 13–1	St. Louis	H/(NA)

Day/Date	Pitcher	Result	Opponent	Site/Att.
WE/4–8–91	E. Daily	Won 7–6	Columbus	H/5,000
SU/10–4–91	J. Meekin*	Lost 8–0	St. Louis	A/(**)
	J Fitzgerald	Won 4-3	St. Louis	A(/**)

*(Lost to rookie Ted Breitenstein, who pitched no–hitter in first major–league start)

**(Doubleheader; total attendance for both games listed as 5,000)

Day/Date	Pitcher	Result	Opponent	Site/Att.
TU/4–12–92	J. Meekin	Won 5–2	Cleveland	H/5,993
SA/10–15–92	F. Clausen	Lost 11–2	Cleveland	A/300
TH/4–27–93	S. Stratton	Lost 4–2	St. Louis	A/12,000
FR/9–29–93*	M. Kilroy	Won 6–0	Baltimore	H/(NA)

*(Called after five innings on account of darkness)

Day/Date	Pitcher	Result	Opponent	Site/Att.
FR/4–20–94	J. Menefee	Won 10–3	Cleveland	H/4,000
SU/9–30–94*	J. Wadsworth	Won 10–8	Brooklyn	H/(NA)
	B. Inks	Lost 12–4	Brooklyn	H/(NA)

*(Doubleheader; second game called after five innings on account of darkness)

Day/Date	Pitcher	Result	Opponent	Site/Att.
TH/4–18–95	B. Inks	Won 11–2	Pittsburgh	H/8,000
SU/9–29–95*	T. McCreery	Won 13–8	Cleveland	H/(NA)

*(Called after eight innings on account of darkness)

Day/Date	Pitcher	Result	Opponent	Site/Att.
TH/4–16–96	C. Fraser	Lost 4–2	Chicago	H/10,000
SA/9–26–96	A. Herman	Lost 3–2	Cleveland	A/4,000
TH/4–22–97	C. Fraser	Won 3–1	Cleveland	H/12,000
SU/10–3–97	C. Fraser	Lost 9–7	Cincinnati	H/5,000
FR/4–15–98	B. Cunningham	Won 10–3	Pittsburgh	H/10,000
SA/10–15–98	B. Magee	Won 5–4	Cleveland	H/(NA)
FR/4–14–99	B. Cunningham	Lost 15–1	Chicago	H/10,000
SU/10–15–99	D. Phillippe	Won 9–5	Chicago	A/(NA)

Totals: 10–10 in openers,
10–10 in closers

CLUB PRESIDENTS

1876–1877	(NL)	Walter N. Haldeman
1882–1883	(AA)	J.H. Plank
1884	(AA)	William L. Jackson, Jr.
1885–1887	(AA)	Zack Phelps
1888	(AA)	W.L. Lyons
1889	(AA)	Mordecai H. Davidson
1890	(AA)	Lawrence S. Parsons
1891	(AA)	Julian B. Hart
1892	(NL)	Dr. T. Hunt Stuckey
1893–1896	(NL)	Fred Drexler
1897–1899	(NL)	Harry C. Pulliam
1899	(NL)	Barney Dreyfuss

Note: *Presidents usually controlled the majority of stock.*

APPENDIXES
EXTRA INNINGS:
LOST STARS, LINGO, KENTUCKY IN THE MAJORS, KENTUCKY BASEBALL TRAVEL SITES, LOUISVILLE & KENTUCKY MINOR-LEAGUE HIGHLIGHTS

Pete Browning (University of Louisville Photographic Archives)

LOST STARS:
THE HALL-OF-FAME CASE FOR THE AMERICAN ASSOCIATION'S PREMIER STARS

AUTHOR'S NOTE: "Lost Stars" originally appeared in the July, 1992 edition of *Oldtyme Baseball News*. The abridged version is included here because three of the nine "lost" stars — Pete Browning, Tony Mullane and Gus Weyhing — have direct or indirect connections with Louisville.

*W*hen the storied American Association collapsed after the 1891 season due to financial difficulties, it marked the end to a colorful and progressive major-league circuit which had been founded 10 years earlier in a Pittsburgh saloon hall.

Given little hope of survival by its National League detractors, the league was quickly tagged "The Beer And Whiskey League". The derisive moniker referred to the league owners, many of whom were engaged in the liquor industry, and also to the the American Association's plan to sell beer at all its ballparks.

Nonetheless, the American Association proved to be the senior circuit's most formidable opponent during the game's pre-modern era (1876-1900), giving the National League (whom it called "The Rich Men's League") all it could handle... and then some.

Charging admission prices that were half that of the National League (25 cents as opposed to 50 cents, a huge sum at the time), it opened up the game to the working masses, who were further aided by the American Association's policy of Sunday baseball (most convenient since most working people at that time worked a standard six-day week).

The American Association also boldly re-opened such fertile western baseball strongholds as Cincinnati, St. Louis and Louisville (all formerly National League cities).

Fiercely competitive, the American Association lasted only a brief decade from 1882 through 1891. Yet, despite its short duration, this alleged "inferior" league — not the National League or the American League — gave baseball a host of innovations and historic firsts. Integral to the success of the American Association, many of them still endure today.

Those pioneering ways included Sunday baseball;

the sale of beer at the ballpark; the development of "Ladies Day" as a standard baseball promotion; league control of umpires; the percentage system of determining pennant winners; standardized contractural procedures; participation in the first World Series (an abbreviated affair in 1882); and the first black ballplayer in the history of the major leagues — Moses Fleetwood Walker (1884).

The American Association's greatest legacy today, though, remains its premier stars, a set of nine top–line players who unquestionably merit membership in baseball's pantheon — Cooperstown.

Yet, more than a century after its demise, the American Association is not represented in Cooperstown by one single player who spent the bulk of his career in that circuit.

Who were these men and why aren't they in Cooperstown where they belong?

PETE BROWNING

Unquestionably the player most synonymous with the epic American Association, this legendary Louisville batsman during a 13-year career (1882–1894) compiled a lifetime .341 batting average, 12th highest in the annals of the game and fifth–best among the sport's right–handed stickmen.

A three-time batting champion, Browning took two titles for Louisville in the American Association (.378 in 1882 and .362 in 1885) and another in the Players' League for Cleveland (.373 in 1890).

His personal best was a .402 mark in 1887.

Off the field, Browning — a star in three different major league circuits during his career (the American Asociation, the Players' League and the National League) — also made substantial history.

In the spring of 1884, the story has it, Browning allowed a young apprentice woodworker named John A. "Bud" Hillerich to make him the first custom-crafted, barrel-shaped baseball bat. The historicial incident birthed both the famed Louisville Slugger bat and this country's most famed batmaker, Hillerich & Bradsby.

Nicknamed "The Gladiator" by the lively sporting press of the day for his battles with them, flyballs and liquor, Browning was a constant source of news — and entertainment — his entire career.

One of the game's most colorful figures, Browning died prematurely at age 44 in 1905 and was subsequently buried in Louisville's historic Cave Hill Cemetery,

In September of 1984, the firm of Hillerich & Bradsby — as part of their centennial celebration — joined with the city of Louisville (via then–Mayor Harvey I. Sloane) to erect a new four-and-a-half-foot-tall marker over Browning's gravesite.

The headstone, which fully detailed Browning's fabulous baseball achievments and correctly spelled his name, replaced the weathered gravestone that had marked Browning's final resting place for more than three-quarters of a century.

Note: See Chapter III for extensive profile of Browning.

Tony Mullane
(National Baseball Library and Archive, Cooperstown, NY)

TONY MULLANE

A lifetime 285-220 hurler off five 30-win seasons and three 20-victory campaigns over a 13-year career (1881-1894), Irish–born Tony Mullane has the most lifetime victories by a pre–modern era (pre–1900) pitcher *not* in the Hall of Fame.

He might well have finished with 300 lifetime wins, a figure considered automatic for Cooperstown, had he not been suspended during the 1885 season.

Handsome as well as talented, the ambidextrous Mullane was known as "The Count" and "The Apollo Of The Box" because of his classic countenance. Those good looks literally led to the popularization of "Ladies Day" as a standard baseball promotion in the late 1880s when Mullane was pitching for the Cincinnati American Association club.

Noticing that women flocked to the park whenever Mullane pitched, owner Aaron Stern shrewdly capitalized on that phenomenon by scheduling him regularly against poor-drawing clubs and billing those contests as "Ladies Day" events. The result was the conversion of an experimental idea into a basic baseball marketing tool that endures to this day.

Like another American Association star, Bob Caruthers, Mullane — who became a Chicago policeman after he retired from the game — is buried in an unmarked grave in the Chicago area.

Note: See extended Mullane profile in Chapter IV.

GUS WEYHING

Considered by historians to be the first hurler to win 100 games in two different historically and statistically–recognized major–league circuits (115 wins in the American Association, 119 victories in the National League), Gus Weyhing racked up a 264-235 lifetime record between 1887 and 1901, the bulk of it for also-rans.

That work included four 30-win seasons and three 20-win campaigns. The large numbers were a vivid contrast to the slender hurler (5'10", 145 pounds), who never suffered the grievous arm trouble that ended the careers of many pre-modern era slingers prematurely.

A native of Louisville (like fellow American Association standout Pete Browning), Weyhing attributed his longevity and success to keeping his arm in hot water and out of the hands of trainers.

Weyhing enjoyed much of his success with Phila-delphia clubs in both the American Association and the National League. One of the biggest of those teams was the 1894 National League aggregation, which included three Hall-of-Famers — Ed Delahanty, Sam Thompson and Billy Hamilton. (It could be effectively argued that Weyhing was the "Robin Roberts" of his time.)

Note: Long-text profile of Weyhing appears in Chapter VI.

BID MCPHEE

Considered by many to be the finest second-baseman of the pre-modern era (pre-1900), John Alexander "Bid" McPhee was proof paramount that the American Association produced glovemen, too.

During an 18-year career (1882-1899), all of it with Cincinnati in first the American Association and then the National League, McPhee was a defensive wizard.

Gus Weyhing (third from left, middle row) and teammates of the 1888 Philadelphia Athletics American Assocation team.
(National Baseball Library and Archive, Cooperstown, NY)

Nine times he led his circuit's second-basemen in fielding average; eight times in putouts; assists six times; double plays 11 times; and total chances per game six times.

A member of the American Association's first pennant winner (Cincinnati in 1882), McPhee mixed his golden glovework with a career .272 batting average that included 2,260 hits. A native of Massena, N.Y., McPhee died in San Diego, Calif. on January 3, 1943 at the age of 83.

BOB CARUTHERS

A giant from yesteryear who flashed across the skies like a meteor in the late 19th century, Robert Lee "Bob" Caruthers compiled a spectacular 218-97 win/loss record as a pitcher.

The bulk of that premier work — a pair of 40-win seasons, one 30-win year and three 20-win campaigns — came during a six-year span, when he starred for five pennant winners, three of them World champions or co-world champions.

Unquestionably, the biggest of Caruthers' numbers was his phenomenal career .692 win percentage, still the all-time major-league record for pitchers.

In retropsect, the figures become almost larger than life when the length of his pitching career is factored in.

Pencil-thin in size, the 5-7, 140-pound hurler racked them up in just nine seasons of play before a blown out arm — dating back to his first full major-league season in 1885, when he worked a staggering 482.1 innings — caught up with him.

A 10-year veteran (1884-1893) who also doubled as an outfielder, Caruthers was equally skilled at the plate, where he posted a solid .282 career batting average. In addition, the Memphis, Tenn., native — whose family moved to Chicago when he was a teenager — was considered a fine fielder and baserunner as well.

Bid McPhee (far right, back row) and Will White (middle row with glasses) in a pose with other members of the 1882 Cincinnati American Assocation pennant-winning team, that circuit's inaugural flagwinner. White is profiled on page 136. (National Baseball Library and Archive, Cooperstown, NY)

Virtually the only Brown who contributed anything of consequence in the World Series against the etroit Wolverines, Caruthers took four of his team's ve victories in an astonishing 15-game post-season owdown that toured ten different cities.

Traded to Brooklyn along with Foutz after the 87 season, Caruthers was scarely done with the orld Series. In 1889, he pitched the American Asso- ation squad to a pennant (in a close fight with his rmer team, St. Louis) with a 40-11 mark that also cluded a league-topping .784 win percentage.

Though Brooklyn switched its allegiance to the ational League in 1890, it made no difference, as aruthers posted a 23-11 mark that helped send them to the World Series against Louisville.

A rarity who threw right, but batted left-handed, aruthers was nicknamed "Parisian Bob" because of s dandefied dressing habits (a reference to Paris, then garded as the center of the fashion world).

Like a number of players from the pre–modern a, Caruthers died young, at age 47 in August 1911 in Peoria, Ill., hospital.

aruthers' final resting place has a ve Memphis to it, at least in name. Located just blocks away from Chicago's venerable Wrigley Field, Graceland Cemetery is the home to a number of the city's and state's politicians, business- men, industrialists and sports figures.

Along with Dave Foutz, Caruthers was part of a powerful one-two punch for the St. Louis Browns, one of the game's earliest dynasties who copped four successive American Association pennants (1885-1888). The first three flags were directly attributable to the sensational tandem, who combined for nearly 200 victories in those three flag-winning years.

The 1886 World Series, against the Chicago White Stockings of Cap Anson, was Caruthers' magnus opus in the fall classic. Caruthers won two games — includ-ing the finale — and batted nearly .300 in a repeat match between the two squads, which unlike the pre-vious year's contest, saw a clear-cut winner — the St. Louis Browns.

A close second to his 1886 World Series work was his 1887 World Series performance. Despite an attack of malaria that year, Caruthers was in fine form, though in a losing cause.

WILL WHITE

The brother of National League star Deacon White, right-hander Will White ran off a 229-166 total during his brief 10-year career (1877-1886) that included three 40-win seasons and two 30-win campaigns.

A member of several flag-winning teams, one of them the 1882 Cincinnati American Association squad (which also included Bid McPhee), White was — according to some historians — the first major-leaguer to wear glasses on the diamond.

There was nothing meek, though, about the Caton, N.Y. native, who died in Port Carling, Ontario, Canada, at age 56 in 1911.

On the contrary, he was a fierce competitor wh personally necessitated a change in the rules regardin hit batsmen. Enamored of driving hitters away fror the plate by hitting them, his actions led the America Association to adopt a rule in 1884 that hit batsme would automatically get first base, a rule later adopte by the National League in 1887.

SILVER KING

Yet another member of the American Association' 200-career-victory club, right-hander Silver King — whose real name was Charles Frederick Koenig — put u a fine 207-152 career record over a brief 10-year perio (1886-1897). His work included one 40-win season, a tri of 30-win campaigns and one 20-win year.

Incredibly, in his first full season of play, he led St. Louis staff that included Bob Caruthers and Dav Foutz with 34 wins. The next year, even with Caruther and Foutz gone, St. Louis took their fourth straigh American Association flag as King posted a career best 45-21 mark that included league leadership i victories, ERA, games, games started, complete game and innings pitched.

A colorful player and part of a team photograph o page 18, this St. Louis native was well-remembered by his hometown press when he died at age 70 in 1938.

HARRY STOVEY

A member of several flag-winning teams and generally regarded as the first man in professional baseball to use sliding pads, Harry Stovey — born Harold Duffield Stowe — was a multi-dimensional hitter whose abilities to hit for average and with power were thoroughly complemented by his fine speed.

During a 14-year career, the best of which easily were seven years with Philadelphia in the American Association and another season with Boston in the Players' League, Stovey reeled off a lifetime .288 batting average that included 1,769 hits.

His career batwork included league crowns in slugging, doubles, triples, home runs (he hit home runs in a

Harry Stovey
(National Baseball Library and Archive, Cooperstown, NY)

record 56 different ballparks and was the first player to hit 100 career home runs), RBIs, runs scored and stolen bases. Overall, one-third of Stovey's hits (339 doubles, 177 triples and 121 home runs) were for extra bases.

Born in Philadelphia five days before Christmas in 1856, Stovey died at age 80 in New Bedford, Mass., in September of 1937.

DAVE FOUTZ

A championship right-handed pitcher who switched to first base and the outfield because of arm trouble, Dave Foutz posted an extraordinary set of numbers during his mercurial 13-year career (1884-1896).

His 147-66 career mound record included one 40-win, one 30-win and one 20-win season. It also produced a mammoth .690 lifetime winning percentage, second on the all-time list (just behind the .692 mark of Bob Caruthers, his teammate on five pennant-winning clubs) and just a tick ahead of Hall-of-Famer Whitey Ford.

Nicknamed "Scissors" because of his lean six-two frame which carried only 160 pounds, Foutz also left the game with a solid .277 batting average and 1,254 career hits. Like McPhee, Caruthers, White and Stovey, he managed for a time in the big leagues.

A native of Carroll County, Md., Foutz — like a number of players from the pre-modern era, notably American Association standouts Pete Browning and Bob Caruthers — died young.

Barely six months after his final professional season, he passed away at age 40 in early March of 1897 in Waverly, Md., a victim of asthma.

∾⧓∽

With the exception of Charlie Comiskey, no American Association player to date has made it into the Hall of Fame. And Comiskey was elected not as a player, but rather via the Pioneer/Executive category.

The absence of American Association players from Cooperstown has long rested primarily on the "inferior league" argument, an unviable position best addressed by the peerless David Nemec.

In the classic baseball work, *The Ultimate Baseball Book*, Nemec traced the exclusion of American Association stars from Cooperstown "to a lingering grudge inherited from old National Leaguers, who privately could not accept the Association as a true major league even after technically recognizing it as such."

Nemec then followed with a sound example of the parity of these two circuits. That was the 1890 season, the only year that American Association stars and National League stars ever played under the same flag — the Players' League (the "outlaw" circuit drew stars from both the American Association and the National League).

Interestingly enough, the top two batsmen that year were not National League standouts, but Pete Browning and Davey Orr — both American Association luminaries.

But, that was only the tip of the proverbial iceberg.

The stolen-base king (79 steals) in the Players'

Dave Foutz
(National Baseball Library and Archive, Cooperstown, NY)

League that year was another great from the rolls of the American Association — Harry Stovey.

And, to top it all off, the winningest pitcher in the Players' League that season was yet another American Association standout, Silver King, who led the circuit with 32 victories.

Backing up the Players' League statistics are the statistics of post–season play between the American Association and the National League.

The American Association operated for a decade (1882–1891). During that timeframe, the American Association and the National League met regularly in World Series action. In addition, the two loops regularly engaged in pre- and post-season exhibitions as well.

In neither instance — the World Series nor the exhibitions — did either league truly display an overwhelming superiority.

The "inferior league" argument has also been severely compromised in two other major ways.

In 1968, the Special Baseball Records Committee

– 138 –

Davey Orr
(National Baseball Library and Archive, Cooperstown, NY)

carried the seasonal statistics of the American Association and the career figures of its players.

The fate of the American Association stars — a major case to be sure — rests in the hands of the Veterans' Committee, a body whose many duties include acting as a kind of "court of last resort" for just such old–time greats. Does the rectification of the American Association "Lost Stars" dilemma really make a difference?

Absolutely.

Baseball is in grave danger of losing one of the most valuable parts of the first quarter-century of its history, foundation pieces that shaped the game we know and avidly follow today. The danger of that possible, egregious loss cannot be overstated. And the Veterans' Committee is the only organziation that can reverse that horrific trend.

Consider this passage from a *Sports Illustrated* article years ago by B.L. Gilbert.

An appreciation of history is a fundamental human obligation, one which peoples in all times have accepted and discharged. By caring about and being moved by the deeds of our ancestors, we give assurance — and are assured — of a sort of immortality. Very shortly our times will be historical ones, our possessions antiques and ourselves ancestors. Soon and forever, we will be at the mercy of generations unborn. Nobody has ever remembered himself.

Baseball would do well to heed those words, for as long as the anti-American Association elitism flourishes, the rich legacy that the American Association left to the game so long ago — prime among them its nine major stars — will remain unclaimed.

And, baseball will be all the poorer for it.

recognized six circuits as having "major-league" status: the American Association (1882–1891); the American League (1901–present); the Federal League (1914–1915); the National League (1876–present); the Players' League (1890); and the Union Association (1884).

And, to date, every edition of *The Baseball Encyclopedia*, the standard reference book of the game which is published by the Macmillan Company, has

LINGO: THE LANGUAGE OF BASEBALL

*I*f there is one thing more colorful than the game of baseball, this country's oldest organized sport, it is the language of baseball. In its century-plus existence, the game has utilized a variety of sources including famous people, racing slang, mechanical and military apparatuses, railroad and nautical terms, food, medicine, animals, insects, geography, anatomy, and even mythology to produce a body of language unmatched by any other American sport.

Yet, few followers of the game today fully understand or appreciate this rich heritage of colorful words and phrases they use on a daily basis, beginning ironically enough with the lifeblood of the game — fan.

That word came into popular usage roughly a century ago, according to many sources, when Chris von der Ahe, the eccentric owner of the world champion St. Louis Browns, repeatedly mispronounced the word "fanatic" in describing a patron who attended every home game without fail. Because of his thick German accent, von der Ahe emphasized the first syllable of the word, a version subsequently picked up by the media.

International wordsmiths, however, claim that the word has an even earlier origin than that and in a different country, coming from the 19th-century British phrase for patrons of boxing events, who were labelled "The Fancy".

Among others, this is strongly backed up by Joseph McBride, the author of *High and Inside: The Complete Guide to Baseball Slang*. Still, the word's origin, according to him, has been subject to more dispute than any other in the game, except possibly "charley horse". As proof of that, McBride offers Connie Mack's theory that spectators were called "fans" because they fanned themselves during hot weather. McBride's listing on the word also includes two verbal forms, one meaning to strike out (whiffing the air with a bat), the other meaning to talk about baseball (shooting the breeze).

Another baseball word with a multiple origin is ace, which refers to the star pitcher of a team's pitching staff. Card players have long insisted that the word came from their game in which the ace is often the highest or best card in the deck. Baseball historians prefer their own version, which dates to the undefeated 1869 Red Stockings, baseball's first professional team who were led by star hurler Asa Brainard.

Baseball purists such as McBride, however, point out that the word is older than that, though it has changed its meaning. Originally, it was a term taken from the British game of rounders, one of the predecessors of the national pastime. Along with the word count, it was used interchangeably to mean a run. As baseball evolved, however, the British terms were abandoned and ace took on a whole new meaning.

Perhaps the most famous person to contribute to baseball's vocabulary was the legendary Annie Oakley, the lady sharpshooter who displayed her skills with Buffalo Bill's famed Wild West shows during the late 19th century. Her stunts included a special trick where she threw a playing card into the air, then shot holes in it as it fell.

In time, complimentary baseball tickets became known as "Annie Oakleys", because the free tickets were punched full of holes so that they would not be included as paid admissions when all the ticket stubs were tallied at the ballpark's business office. The phrase (long out of use) was later adapted to describe a walk, or base on balls, which is a "free pass" or "free ticket" to first base.

Famous places, as well as famous people, have secured a niche in baseball's lexicon. A type of weak fly that barely falls beyond the infield for a hit, "Texas Leaguer" was coined to describe the type of hits that enabled one-time Texas League star Arthur Sunday to compile a fat .398 batting average with Toledo of the International League in 1890. (Today, it still goes by that name as well as several others, including "parachutes", "quail shots", and "wounded ducks" according to Mike Whiteford's *How To Talk Baseball*.)

An "around-the-horn" double play (from third to second to first) was created by an anonymous sportswriter, who adapted an old nautical term to describe the longest way to make a double play. Also used to describe the ritual of throwing the ball around the infield, the phrase referred to the time when a voyage between the Pacific and the Atlantic Oceans — before the Panama Canal's completion in 1914 — required a long trip around South America's Cape Horn.

Several other geographically-related terms include bleachers and southpaw.

Bleacher seats, the cheapest seating available at ballparks, refers to a section of stands in the outfield unprotected by a roof and thus directly exposed to the sun, thereby "bleaching" the fans who sit there. Southpaw denotes a left-handed pitcher, based on the standard layout of a diamond, which usually has the hurler facing west while the batter faces east, with the sun at his back and not in his eyes. When the pitcher throws from the left-hand side, or the first-base side of the field, his arm is facing south.

Transportation, both on land and at sea, has been crucial in the development of baseball's unique language.

Before the airlines became popular in the 1950s, railroads were the sunshine game's main method of traveling between cities. From railroads, baseball has gotten the terms "bunt" and "doubleheader".

A bunt in baseball is a pitch that is lightly tapped, and is taken from the railroad term describing the shoving of a car onto a short siding. (Some sources, including McBride, attribute it to the 1870s when it was called "butting" and eventually corrupted to "bunting".) A doubleheader means the most to the fans for their money: two games for the price of one. Railroaders use the term to describe a situation where two locomotives are used to pull one train.

And though baseball is a "landlubber's" sport, several other nautical terms besides around-the-horn have crept into the game's dictionary: "on deck" and "in the hole."

These terms date to 1872 when Boston played an exhibition game in Belfast, Maine, a town where practically every male was a seafarer. As a result, the official scorekeeper referred to the next two batters up as if they were on a ship, the first being "on deck", the second being "in the hold", the latter phrase long ago corrupted to "in the hole."

Even the most basic form of transportation in the twentieth century, the automobile, has added its two cents worth with "clutch" and "battery".

On a car, a clutch is a vital mechanism that when engaged, will cause it to move; any malfunction by that part will result in failure. Likewise in baseball, clutch refers to a vital situation that demands immediate and successful action, the lack of which will result in failure and defeat.

In baseball, a battery is the pitcher-catcher combination, to many named after the car's energy device, which has both a sending and receiving pole. According to McBride's book, however, the origin of battery is much older and different from that. McBride traces the word, in use by the late 1860s, to a military term denoting two pieces of artillery acting as a unit. According to him, the word originally referred to the hurler, ostensibly the biggest weapon in a club's arsenal.

Long called "The Sport Of Kings", because of its exclusivity that several centuries ago saw royalty and nobility as its only participants, Thoroughbred racing — known today as The King Of Sports"—has enriched the game with one, possibly two terms: shutout and charley horse.

When a pitcher "shuts out" a team, a phrase dating to the late 1870s according to McBride, he prevents them from scoring a run, much like the racefan who fails to pick even one winner during a day at the track. (The racetrack version also refers to a bettor whose attempt to place a last-minute wager fails.)

Charley horse, which describes a muscle strain, may have the most interesting historical background of any word or phrase in baseball's vocabulary.

Most historians (McBride included) and etymologists attribute the phrase to a mid-17th century English

King, Charles I, who habitually palmed off his aging guard horses, or "Charleys", onto the London police force. In time, broken-down horses picked up the tag of "old Charleys". The monicker was later taken over by baseball, whose ballparks once utilized the services of old horses. If a ballplayer was seen limping around, he was likened to the old horses and said to have a "charley horse."

Some historians say that the phrase came into popular usage courtesy of Billy Sunday, a late 19th-century ballplayer who later became a nationally-known evangelist. Sunday supposedly coined the phrase in 1886 following a trip to a local racetrack where he and his band of teammates bet on a horse named Charley, who went lame during the race and finished last.

The next day, teammate George Gore was denied an easy inside-the-park home run after pulling a muscle rounding second. As Gore limped into third, Sunday cried, "Here comes that Charley horse!"

McBride, however, credits the popularization of this enigmatic term not to Sunday, but to another Chicago player of that same time — Joe Quest, an apprentice in a machine shop co-owned by his father before he entered the majors. Quest, as did his teammates, suffered a tightness of the legs occasionally. Because no one had a name for it, Quest called it a "charley horse" after his father's horse, "Charley", who had suffered leg injuries from constantly pulling heavy loads. (This is alluded to in a June 30, 1889 Louisville Courier-Journal article on Pete Browning.)

A precisely designed game drawn along strong geometric lines, baseball has even absorbed mathematics, economics and architecture into its lingo.

Although the field is a square, a basic geometric pattern, it is often called "the diamond," because when viewed from virtually any angle, that's what it looks like. Cycle is a general economic term used to describe a series of events that on their completion form a single unit of action. In baseball parlance, a player who "hits for the cycle" gets every type of hit possible (single, double, triple and home run) in one game. Keystone is an architectural term that refers to the centralpiece in the highest point of an arch. In baseball, "the keystone bag" is second base, which when viewed from home plate, is the highest point of an imaginary arch formed by the base paths from first base to third base.

Baseball also has a host of less complicated terms that are obvious in meaning.

"Cellar", the bottom of a building, refers to a last-place club. "Cleanup" is the fourth spot in the batting order, in which ideally the first three men will get on base, with the fourth batter then "cleaning up the

Billy Sunday
(National Baseball Library and Archive, Cooperstown, NY)

bases" with an extra-base hit, the greatest of which is a home run. The "hot corner" refers to third base, a phrase created in 1889 by writer Ren Mulford, who watched Cincinnati third-baseman Hick Carpenter field seven line drives in a game that nearly tore him apart.

"Homer" is either baseball supreme's hit or an umpire who favors the home team so as not to incur the wrath of its supporters. A home run is also called a "gopher ball" by pitchers, a derogatory pun for a baseball hit so hard and far it will surely "go for" all the bases possible. Its companion is the "o-for" (as in 0-for-3) and "the collar" (the shape of a zero), both signifying that a batter went hitless in a game.

Often, a hitter receives a retaliation for a long hit, particularly a home run, in the form of a "brushback" (an inside pitch designed to move him away from the plate) or a "duster" (an even tighter inside pitch, also known as "the knockdown" for obvious reasons, which literally forces the batter to hit the dust). The most serious retaliatory pitch is the "beanball", so named because it is aimed at a hitter's "bean", or his head.

If revenge is sweet, it is also two-sided, and often the batter exacts hits with a "cripple", a pitch that follows a count of 3-0 or 3-1. Because the pitcher is so careful, especially in a tight situation or close game, to get the ball over the plate and avoid a walk, he literally cripples his pitch by sacrificing power for accuracy.

Certainly one of baseball's most familiar terms today is bullpen, the area where relief pitchers warm up.

This term dates to the game's earliest professional years (in the mid-1870s) when some teams had roped-in areas near the outfield. Those seats were substantially cheaper than the grandstand seats, priced at 50 cents. Because the patrons and later the relievers, says McBride in his book, were herded into it like animals, sportswiters took to calling it the the "bull pen", as well as "the pen" and "the corral".

A popular misconception is that the word originated in the early 1900s from the Bull Durham tobacco advertisements that adorned those area in many ballparks. Those advertisements popularized the term, however, and nothing more.

Easily the best-known animal in baseball today is the "goat", a derisive term used to describe a player blamed for a defeat because of a crucial failure either in the field or at the plate. The word originates with mythological rites and beliefs, which held that animal to be the symbol of bad luck and misfortune.

Baseball's vocabulary, however, is not hopelessly linked to history, ancient or otherwise. Modern times have forced baseball to expand its terminology, either because of changes in the game, or because of the sport's desire to remain "hip" and current, a reflection of the society it inhabits.

A classic example of the former was the introduction of artificial playing surfaces. Known today as "rugs" and "carpets", those speedy surfaces have given us "worm-burners" (fast groundballs that don't bounce) and "bug on the rug" (a sharply-hit ball that bounces between outfielders).

Natural causes (the times), though, have produced almost all of baseball's new words and phrases, most of them self-explanatory and many of them listed in Mike Whiteford's book.

That flock includes four colorful aliases for hard-hit line drives. Once called "blue darters", today they are known as "ropes", "frozen ropes", "clothes lines" and "screaming meemies".

Some performers have "guns" (powerful throwing arms) or "good wheels" (great speed); others excel at "picking it" (fielding groundballs, particularly difficult ones).

A team with "good arms" has a great pitching staff, and since pitching is 90 percent of the game, that team is considered a strong contender for its divisional title, a league pennant and a World Series championship.

When a pitcher "brings it", or throws with great "velocity" (speed), that is called "putting the mustard on it." Such a fastball may also be called a "heater", "gas" or "smoke".

An extraordinary fastball (in the high nineties and definitely in triple figures on the radar gun) will earn the ultimate compliment. It is called an "aspirin tablet" because it looks that small to the hitter by the time it reaches the plate. In all likelihood, such a pitch will result in a strikeout, denoted by the latter "k" (the last letter in the word struck) and not the letter "s", the long-standing baseball symbol for a sacrifice.

Let a pitcher make a mistake, though, and hitters will rack up a pile of "ribbies" (RBIs). The worst damage can be done in the "power alleys" (the "gaps" in left center and right center) and "over the wall" (over the fence for a home run).

Home runs and the act of hitting them have as extensive a lingo as do pitchers and fastballs.

Though pitchers loathe home runs ("gopher balls"), hitters love "dingers" or "taters" (two slang words for home runs picked from the glorious old Negro Leagues). They are frequently the product of a pitcher letting a pitch get into a batter's "wheelhouse" (the prime part of his strike zone). When that happens, the chances increase for a "tape-measure shot" (an exceptionally long home run).

Drilling a home run has an exquisite array of terms including "jerking it out", "juicing one", "juicing one out", "jacking it out", "taking him (the pitcher) deep", "taking him (the hurler) downtown", and "dialing a pitcher long distance."

Without question, no word or phrase more personifies baseball's new lexicon than "flake". Introduced in the 1960s, it gained instant acceptance and popular usage.

Replacing such antiquated terms as "bonehead" and "screwball", it has been joined in recent times by a synonymous brother — "space cadet".

Used to describe an eccentric player, the word "flake" and its brotherly phrase "space cadet" prove how well baseball terminology has stayed in touch with the sport and its times, even if some of its participants have not.

Clearly, baseball lingo, despite its advanced age, is never at a loss for words.

KENTUCKY IN THE MAJORS

ROSTER OF KENTUCKY-BORN MAJOR-LEAGUE PLAYERS, 1876-1995

Allison, Mack Pendleton
Born: January 23, 1887/Owensboro, Ky.
Died: March 13, 1964/St. Joseph, Mo.
Major–League Debut: September 13, 1911

Anderson, David Carter
Born: August 1, 1960/Louisville, Ky.
Major-League Debut: May 8, 1983

Arnold, Scott Gentry
Born: August 18, 1962/Lexington, Ky.
Major-League Debut: April 7, 1988

Bacon, Edgar Suter
Born: April 8, 1895/Franklin County, Ky.
Died: October 2, 1963/Frankfort, Ky.
Major-League Debut: August 13, 1917

Baldwin, Clarence Geoghan
Born: November 1, 1864/Newport, Ky.
Died: July 12, 1897/Cincinnati, Ohio
Major-League Debut: July 27, 1884

Ball, Arthur
Born: April, 1876/Kentucky
Died: December 26, 1915/Chicago, Ill.
Major-League Debut: August 1, 1894

Ballou, Noble Winfield
Born: November 30, 1897/Mt. Morgan, Ky.
Died: January 30, 1963/San Francisco, Calif.
Major-League Debut: August 24, 1925

Barger, Eros Bolivar
Born: May 18, 1885/Jamestown, Ky.
Died: September 23, 1964/Columbia, Ky.
Major-League Debut: August 30, 1906

Barker, Leonard Harold
Born: July 27, 1955/Ft. Knox, Ky.
Major-League Debut: September 14, 1976

Beard, Oliver Perry
Born: May 2, 1862/Lexington, Ky.
Died: May 28, 1929/Cincinnati, Ohio
Major-League Debut: April 17, 1889

Bell, David Russell
Born: November 15, 1928/Louisville, Ky.
Died: May 7, 1995/Montgomery, Ohio
Major-League Debut: May 30, 1950

Bell, Herman S.
Born: July 16, 1897/Mt. Sherman, Ky.
Died: June 7, 1949/Glendale, Calif.
Major-League Debut: April 16, 1924

Bellman, John Hutchins
Born: March 4, 1864/Louisville, Ky.
Died: December 8, 1931/Louisville, Ky.
Major-League Debut: April 23, 1889

Benton, Stanley W.
Born: September 29, 1901/Cannel City, Ky.
Died: June 7, 1984/Mesquite, Texas
Major-League Debut: September 13, 1922

Benzinger, Todd Eric
Born: February 11, 1963/Dayton, Ky.
Major-League Debut: June 21, 1987

Berte, Harry Thomas
Born: May 10, 1872/Covington, Ky.
Died: May 6, 1952/Los Angeles, California
Major-League Debut: September 17, 1903

Bickford, Vernon Edgell
Born: August 17, 1920/Hellier, Ky.
Died: May 6, 1960/Concord, Va.
Major-League Debut: April 24, 1948

Black, John Falconer (born John Falconer Haddow)
Born: February 23, 1890/Covington, Ky.
Died: March 20, 1962/Rutherford, N.J.
Major–League Debut: June 20, 1911

Blackburn, James Ray
Born: June 19, 1924/Warsaw, Ky.
Died: October 26, 1969/Cincinnati, Ohio
Major–League Debut: July 24, 1948

Blackwell, Frederick William
Born: September 7, 1891/Bowling Green, Ky.
Died: December 8, 1975/Morgantown, Ky.
Major–League Debut: September 25, 1917

Blair, William Allen
Born: December 18, 1965/Painstville, Ky.
Major–League Debut: April 11, 1990

Boone, George Morris
Born; March 1, 1871/Louisville, Ky.
Died: September 24, 1910/Louisville, Ky.
Major–League Debut: April 23, 1891

Bouldin, Carl Edward
Born: September 17, 1939/Germantown, Ky.
Major–League Debut: September 2, 1961

Bradley, Mark Allen
Born: December 3, 1956/Elizabethtown, Ky.
Major–League Debut: September 3, 1981

Brady, Cornelius Joseph
Born: March 4, 1897/Covington, Ky.
Died: June 19, 1947/Ft. Mitchell, Ky.
Major–League Debut: September 25, 1915

Browne, Earl James
Born: March 5, 1911/Louisville, Ky.
Died: January 12, 1993/Whittier, Calif.
Major–League Debut: September 12, 1935

Browning, Frank
Born: October 29, 1882/Falmouth, Ky.
Died: May 19, 1948/San Antonio, Texas
Major-League Debut: April 16, 1910

Browning, Louis Rogers
Born: June 17, 1861/Louisville, Ky.
Died: September 10, 1905/Louisville, Ky.
Major–League Debut: May 2, 1882

Bruner, Walter Roy
Born: February 10, 1917/Cecilia, Ky.
Died: November 30, 1986/St. Matthews, Ky.
Major–League Debut: September 14, 1939

Bryant, Derek Roszell
Born: October 9, 1951/Lexington, Ky.
Major–League Debut: April 24, 1979

Buhner, Jay Campbell
Born: August 13, 1964/Louisville, Ky.
Major–League Debut: September 11, 1987

Bunning, James Paul David
Born: October 23, 1931/Southgate, Ky.
Major–League Debut: July 20, 1955

Burnett, Hercules H.
Born: August 13, 1869/Louisville, Ky.
Died: October 4, 1936/Louisville, Ky.
Major–League Debut: June 26, 1888

Burpo, George Harvie
Born: June 19, 1922/Jenkins, Ky.
Major–League Debut: June 9, 1946

Byers, Burley (born Christopher A. Bayer)
Born: December 19, 1875/Louisville, Ky.
Died: May 30, 1933/Louisville, Ky.
Major–League Debut: June 17, 1899

Byrd, Paul Gregory
Born: December 3, 1970/Louisville, Ky.
Major–League Debut: July 28, 1995

Camnitz, Henry Richardson
Born: October 26, 1884/McKinney, Ky.
Died: January 6, 1951/Louisville, Ky.
Major–League Debut: April 14, 1909

Camnitz, Samuel Howard
Born: August 22, 1881/Covington, Ky.
Died: March 2, 1960/Louisville, Ky.
Major–League Debut: April 22, 1904

Campbell, Joseph Earl
Born: March 10, 1944/Louisville, Ky.
Major–League Debut: May 3, 1967

Carroll, Dorsey Lee
Born: May 9, 1891/Paducah, Ky.
Died: October 13, 1984/Jacksonville, Fla.
Major–League Debut: September 12, 1919

Center, Marvin Earl
Born: April 22, 1912/Hazel Green, Ky.
Major–League Debut: September 11, 1942

Chapman, Raymond Johnson
Born: January 15, 1891/Beaver Dam, Ky.
Died: August 17, 1920/New York, N.Y.
Major–League Debut: August 30, 1912

Clark, Robert H.
Born: May 18, 1863/Covington, Ky.
Died: August 21, 1919/Covington, Ky.
Major–League Debut: April 17, 1886

Cline, John P.
Born: March 3, 1858/Louisville, Ky.
Died: September 23, 1916/Louisville, Ky.
Major–League Debut: July 4, 1882

Collins, Hubert B.
Born: April 15, 1864/Louisville, Ky.
Died: May 21, 1892/Brooklyn, N.Y.
Major–League Debut: September 4, 1886

Combs, Earle Bryan
Born: May 14, 1899/Pebworth, Ky.
Died: July 21, 1976/Richmond, Ky.
Major–League Debut: April 16, 1924

Conley, Robert Burns
Born: February 1, 1934/Mousie, Ky.
Major–League Debut: September 11, 1958

Conover, Theodore
Born: March 10, 1868/Lexington, Ky.
Died: July 27, 1910/Paris, Ky.
Major–League Debut: May 26, 1889

Cowley, Joseph Alan
Born: August 15, 1958/Lexington, Ky.
Major–League Debut: April 13, 1982

Crutcher, Richard Louis
Born: November 25, 1889/Frankfort, Ky.
Died: June 19, 1952/Frankfort, Ky.
Major–League Debut: April 14, 1914

Derringer, Samuel Paul
Born: October 17, 1906/Springfield, Ky.
Died: November 17, 1987/Sarasota, Fla.
Major–League Debut: April 16, 1931

Dolan, John
Born: September 12, 1867/Newport, Ky.
Died: May 8, 1948/Springfield, Ohio
Major–League Debut: September 5, 1890

Doyle, Brian Reed
Born: January 26, 1955/Glasgow, Ky.
Major–League Debut: April 30, 1978

Doyle, Robert Dennis
Born: January 17, 1944/Glasgow, Ky.
Major–League Debut: April 7, 1970

Drahman, Brian Stacy
Born: November 7, 1966/Kenton, Ky.
Major–League Debut: April 16, 1991

Durham, Donald Gary
Born: March 21, 1949/Yosemite, Ky.
Major–League Debut: July 16, 1972

Durning, Richard Knott
Born: October 10, 1892/Louisville, Ky.
Died: September 23, 1948/Castle Point, N.Y.
Major–League Debut: April 16, 1917

Dyler, John F.
Born: June, 1852/Louisville, Ky.
Died: Date and location unknown
Major–League Debut: July 22, 1882

Eden, Charles M.
Born: January 18, 1855/Lexington, Ky.
Died: September 17, 1920/Cincinnati, Ohio
Major–League Debut: August 17, 1877

Edmundson, Robert E.
Born: April 30, 1879/Paris, Ky.
Died: August 14, 1931/Lawrence, Kansas
Major–League Debut: July 30, 1908

Ehret, Philip Sydney
Born: August 31, 1868/Louisville, Ky.
Died: July 28, 1940/Cincinnati, Ohio
Major–League Debut: July 7, 1888

Elder, George Rezin
Born: March 10, 1921/Lebanon, Ky.
Major–League Debut: July 22, 1949

Engle, Richard Douglas
Born: April 7, 1957/Corbin, Ky.
Major–League Debut: September 2, 1981

Fannin, Clifford Bryson
Born: May 13, 1924/Louisa, Ky.
Died: December 11, 1966/Sanduskey, Ohio
Major–League Debut: September 2, 1945

Farrell, John Sebastian
Born: December 4, 1876/Covington, Ky.
Died: May 14, 1921/Kansas City, Mo.
Major–League Debut: April 26, 1901

Finley, Steven Allen
Born: March 12, 1965/Paducah, Ky.
Major–League Debut: April 3, 1989

Flynn, Robert Douglas
Born: April 18, 1951/Lexington, Ky.
Major–League Debut: April 9, 1975

Foley, Marvis Edwin
Born: August 29, 1953/Stanford, Ky.
Major–League Debut: September 11, 1978

Foster, Leonard Norris
Born: February 2, 1951/Covington, Ky.
Major–League Debut: July 9, 1971

Frank, Frederick
Born: March 11, 1874/Louisa, Ky.
Died: March 27, 1950/Ashland, Ky.
Major–League Debut: July 9, 1971

Fryman, David Travis
Born: March 25, 1969/Lexington, Ky.
Major–League Debut: July 7, 1990

Fryman, Woodrow Thompson
Born: April 15, 1940/Ewing, Ky.
Major–League Debut: April 15, 1966

Gastright, Henry Carl
Born: March 29, 1865/Covington, Ky.
Died: October 9, 1937/Cold Springs, Ky.
Major–League Debut: April 19, 1889

Grace, Robert Earl
Born: February 24, 1907/Barlow, Ky.
Died: December 22, 1980/Phoenix, Ariz.
Major–League Debut: April 23, 1929

Graham, William Albert

Born: January 21, 1937/Flemingsburg, Ky.

Major–League Debut: October 2, 1966

Gray, Milton Marshall

Born: February 21, 1914/Louisville, Ky.

Died: June 30, 1969/Quincy, Fla.

Major–League Debut: May 27, 1937

Greenfield, Kent

Born: July 1, 1902/Guthrie, Ky.

Died: March 14, 1978/Guthrie, Ky.

Major–League Debut: September 28, 1924

Greenwell, Michael Lewis

Born: July 18, 1963/Louisville, Ky.

Major–League Debut: September 5, 1985

Grigsby, Denver Clarence

Born: March 25, 1901/Jackson, Ky.

Died: November 10, 1973/Sapulpa, Okla.

Major–League Debut: September 1, 1903

Grim, John Helm

Born: August 9, 1867/Lebanon, Ky.

Died: July 28, 1961/Indianapolis, Ind.

Major–League Debut: September 29, 1888

Grubbs, Thomas Dillard

Born: February 22, 1894/Mt. Sterling, Ky.

Died: January 28, 1986/Mt. Sterling, Ky.

Major–League Debut: October 3, 1920

Gullett, Donald Edward

Born: January 6, 1951/Lynn, Ky.

Major–League Debut: April 10, 1970

Haas, George Edwin

Born: May 26, 1935/Paducah, Ky.

Major–League Debut: September 8, 1957

Hach, Irvin William

Born: June 6, 1873/Louisville, Ky.

Died: August 13, 1936/Louisville, Ky.

Major–League Debut: July 1, 1897

Haldeman, John Avery

Born: December 2, 1855/Pewee Valley, Ky.

Died: September 17, 1899/Louisville, Ky.

Major–League Debut: July 3, 1877

Hall, Andrew Clark

Born: March 27, 1963/Louisville, Ky.

Major–League Debut: September 14, 1986

Hall, Joseph Geroy

Born: March 6, 1966/Paducah, Ky.

Major–League Debut: April 5, 1994

Hall, Robert Russell

Born: September 29, 1871/Shelbyville, Ky.

Died: July 1, 1937/Los Angeles, Calif.

Major–League Debut: April 15, 1898

Hamburg, Charles H. (also known as Charles H. Hambrick)

Born: November 22, 1863/Louisville, Ky.

Died: May 18, 1931/Union, N.J.

Major–League Debut; April 18, 1890

Hamilton, Steven Absher

Born: November 30, 1935/Columbia, Ky.

Major–League Debut: April 23, 1961

Harper, George Washington

Born: June 24, 1892/Arlington, Ky.

Died: August 18, 1978/Magnolia, Ark.

Major–League Debut: April 15, 1916

Hart, William Franklin

Born: July 19, 1865/Louisville, Ky.

Died: September 19, 1936/Cincinnati, Ohio

Major–League Debut: July 26, 1886

Hatter, Clyde Melno

Born: August 7, 1908/Poplar, Ky.

Died: October 16, 1937/Yosemite, Ky.

Major–League Debut: April 23, 1935

Henderson, Rodney Wood
Born: March 11, 1971/Greensburg, Ky.
Major–League Debut: April 19, 1994

Herman, Arthur
Born: May 11, 1871/Louisville, Ky.
Died: September 20, 1955/Los Angeles, Calif.
Major–League Debut: June 29, 1896

Heving, John Aloysius
Born: April 29, 1896/Covington, Ky.
Died: December 24, 1968/Salisbury, N.C.
Major–League Debut: September 24, 1920

Heving, Joseph William
Born: September 2, 1900/Covington, Ky.
Died: April 11, 1970/Covington, Ky.
Major–League Debut: April 29, 1930

Higbee, Mahlon Jesse
Born: August 16, 1901/Louisville, Ky.
Died: April 7, 1968/DePauw, Ind.
Major–League Debut: September 27, 1922

Hobbs, William Lee
Born: May 7, 1893/Grant's Lick, Ky.
Died: January 5, 1945/Hamilton, Ohio
Major–League Debut: August 9, 1913

Hohnhorst, Edward Hicks
Born: January 31, 1885/Kentucky
Died: March 28, 1916/Covington, Ky.
Major–League Debut: September 10, 1910

Holley, Edward Edgar
Born: July 23, 1899/Benton, Ky.
Died: Ocober 26, 1986/Paducah, Ky.
Major–League Debut: May 24, 1928

Holmes, James Scott
Born: August 2, 1882/Lawrenceburg, Ky.
Died: March 10, 1960/Jacksonville, Fla.
Major–League Debut: September 8, 1906

Howell, Homer Elliott
Born: April 24, 1920/Louisville, Ky.
Died: October 5, 1990/Binghampton, N.Y.
Major–League Debut: May 6, 1947

Howell, Millard
Born: January 7, 1920/Bowman, Ky.
Died: March 18, 1960/Hollywood, Fla.
Major–League Debut: September 14, 1940

Hulswitt, Rudolph Edward
Born: February 23, 1877/Newport, Ky.
Died: January 16, 1950/Louisville, Ky.
Major–League Debut: June 16, 1899

Hunter, Edison Franklin
Born: February 6, 1905/Bellevue, Ky.
Died: March 14, 1967/Colerain, Ohio
Major–League Debut: August 5, 1933

Hurst, Frank O'Donnell
Born: August 12, 1905/Maysville, Ky.
Died: December 6, 1952/Los Angeles Calif.
Major–League Debut: May 13, 1928

Jacobs, Morris Elmore
Born: December, 1877/Louisville, Ky.
Died: March 21, 1949/Louisville, Ky.
Major–League Debut: August 16, 1902

Jarvis, Kevin Thomas
Born: August 1, 1969/Lexington, Ky.
Major–League Debut: April 6, 1994

Jeffries, Irvine Franklin
Born: September 10, 1905/Louisville, Ky.
Died: June 8, 1982/Louisville, Ky.
Major–League Debut: April 30, 1930

Jennings, Alfred Gorden
Born: November 30, 1850/Newport, Ky.
Died: November 2, 1894/Cincinnati, Ohio
Major–League Debut: August 15, 1878

Jessee, Daniel Edward
Born: February 22, 1901/Olive Hill, Ky.
Died: April 30, 1970/Venice, Fla.
Major–League Debut: August 14, 1929

Johnson, Edwin Cyril
Born: March 31, 1899/Morganfield, Ky.
Died: July 3, 1975/Morganfield, Ky.
Major-League Debut: 1920

Johnson, Louis Brown
Born: September 22, 1934/Lexington, Ky.
Major–League Debut: April 17, 1960

Jones, James Tilford
Born: December 25, 1876/London, Ky.
Died: May 6, 1953/London, Ky.
Major–League Debut: June 29, 1897

Keenan, Harry Leon
Born: 1875/Louisville, Ky.
Died: June 11, 1903/Covington, Ky.
Major–League Debut: August 11, 1891

Kennedy, William Edward
Born: April 5, 1861/Bellevue, Ky.
Died: December 22, 1912/Cheyenne, Wyo.
Major–League Debut: May 17, 1884

Kilgus, Paul Nelson
Born: February 2, 1962/Bowling Green, Ky.
Major–League Debut: June 7, 1987

Kinzie, Walter Harris
Born: March 16, 1857/Kentucky
Died: November 5, 1909/Chicago, Ill.
Major–League Debut: June 17, 1882

Kissinger, William Francis
Born: April 15, 1871/Dayton, Ky.
Died: August 20, 1929/Cincinnati, Ohio
Major–League Debut: May 30, 1895

Koster, Frederick Charles
Born: December 21, 1905/Louisville, Ky.
Died: April 24, 1979/St. Matthews, Ky.
Major–League Debut: April 27, 1931

Kuhn, Kenneth Harold
Born: March 20, 1937/Louisville, Ky.
Major–League Debut: July 7, 1955

Land, Grover Cleveland
Born: September 22, 1884/Frankfort, Ky.
Died: July 22, 1958/Phoenix, Ariz.
Major–League Debut: September 2, 1908

Langsford, Robert William (born Robert Hugo Lankswert)
Born: August 5, 1865/Louisville, Ky.
Died: January 10, 1907/Louisville, Ky.
Major–League Debut: June 18, 1899

Littrell, Jack Napier
Born: January 22, 1929/Louisville, Ky.
Major–League Debut: April 19, 1952

Long, James M.
Born: November 15, 1862/Louisville, Ky.
Died: December 12, 1932/Louisville, Ky.
Major–League Debut: August 9, 1891

Long, Jeoffrey Keith
Born: October 9, 1941/Covington, Ky.
Major–League Debut: July 31, 1963

Ludwig, William Lawrence
Born: May 27, 1882/Louisville, Ky.
Died: September 25, 1947/Louisville, Ky.
Major–League Debut: April 16, 1908

Mack, Tony Lynn
Born: April 30, 1961/Lexington, Ky.
Major–League Debut: July 27, 1985

Marcum, John Alfred
Born: September 9, 1909/Campbellsburg, Ky.
Died: September 10, 1984/Louisville, Ky.
Major–League Debut: September 7, 1933

Mays, Carl William
Born: November 12, 1891/Liberty, Ky.
Died: April 4, 1971/El Cajon, Calif.
Major–League Debut: April 15, 1915

McClellan, Harvey McDowell
Born: December 22, 1894/Cynthiana, Ky.
Died: November 6, 1925/Cynthiana, Ky.
Major–League Debut: May 31, 1919

McCloskey, John James
Born: April 4, 1862/Louisville, Ky.
Died: November 17, 1940/Louisville, Ky.
Major–League Debut: April 18, 1895

McCormick, William J.
Born: December 25, 1874/Maysville, Ky.
Died: January 28, 1956/Cincinnati, Ohio
Major–League Debut: September 5, 1895

McGann, Dennis Lawrence
Born: July 15, 1871/Shelbyville, Ky.
Died: December 13, 1910/Louisvile, Ky.
Major–League Debut: August 8, 1896

McKeon, Joel Jacob
Born: February 25, 1963/Covington, Ky.
Major–League Debut: May 6, 1986

McLaughlin, Thomas
Born: March 28, 1860/Louisville, Ky.
Died: July 21, 1921/Louisville, Ky.
Major–League Debut: July 17, 1883

McQuery, William Thomas
Born: June 28, 1861/Garrard County, Ky.
Died: June 12, 1900/Covington, Ky.
Major–League Debut: August 20, 1884

Merrill, Edward Mason
Born: May, 1860/Maysville, Ky.
Died: Date and place unknown
Major–League Debut: June 20, 1882

Miller, George C.
Born: February 19, 1853/Newport, Ky.
Died: July 24, 1929/Norwood, Ohio
Major–League Debut: September 6, 1877

Milton, Samuel Lawrence
Born: May 4, 1879/Owensboro, Ky.
Died: May 16, 1942/Tulsa, Okla.
Major–League Debut: May 7, 1903

Minshall, James Edward
Born: July 4, 1947/Covington, Ky.
Major–League Debut: September 14, 1974

Moford, Herbert
Born: August 6, 1928/Brooksville, Ky.
Major–League Debut: April 12, 1955

Monroe, Edward Oliver
Born: February 22, 1895/Louisville, Ky.
Died: April 29, 1969/Louisville, Ky.
Major–League Debut: May 29, 1917

Moore, Graham Edward
Born: January 18, 1899/Barlow, Ky.
Died: February 10, 1976/Ft. Myers, Fla.
Major–League Debut: September 25, 1923

Morris, Danny Walker
Born: June 11, 1946/Greenville, Ky.
Major–League Debut: September 10, 1968

Morrison, John Dewey
Born: October 22, 1895/Pelleville, Ky.
Died: March 20, 1966/Louisville, Ky.
Major–League Debut: September 28, 1920

Niehaus, Richard J.
Born: October 24, 1892/Covington, Ky.
Died: March 12, 1957/Atlanta, Ga.
Major–League Debut: September 9, 1913

Niles, William E.
Born: January 11, 1867/Covington, Ky.
Died: July 3, 1936/Springfield, Ohio
Major–League Debut: May 13, 1895

O'Bradovich, James Thomas
Born: September 13, 1949/Ft. Campbell, Ky.
Major–League Debut: September 12, 1978

O'Neal, Randall Jeffrey
Born: August 30, 1960/Ashland, Ky.
Major–League Debut: September 12, 1984

O'Neil, John Francis
Born: April 19, 1920/Shelbiana, Ky.
Major–League Debut; April 16, 1946

Osburn, Larry Patrick
Born: May 4, 1949/Murray, Ky.
Major–League Debut: April 13, 1974

Park, James
Born: November 10, 1892/Richmond, Ky.
Died: December 17, 1970/Lexington, Ky.
Major–League Debut: September 7, 1915

Payne, George Washington
Born: May 23, 1890/Mt. Vernon, Ky.
Died: January 24, 1959/Bellflower, Calif.
Major–League Debut: May 8, 1920

Pearce, Franklin Johnson
Born: March 30, 1860/Jefferson County, Ky.
Died: November 13, 1926/Louisville, Ky.
Major–League Debut: October 4, 1876

Pearce, Franklin Thomas
Born: August 31, 1905/Middletown, Ky.
Died: September 3, 1950/Van Buren, N.Y.
Major–League Debut: April 20, 1933

Pears, Frank H.
Born: August 30, 1866/Kentucky
Died: November 29, 1923/St. Louis, Mo.
Major–League Debut: October 6, 1889

Peppers, Harrison
Born: September, 1866/Kentucky
Died: November 5, 1903/Webb City, Mo.
Major–League Debut: June 30, 1894

Pfeffer, Nathaniel Frederick
Born: March 17, 1860/Louisville, Ky.
Died: April 10, 1932/Chicago, Ill.
Major–League Debut: May 1, 1882

Poland, Hugh Reid
Born: January 19, 1913/Tompkinsville, Ky.
Died: March 30, 1984/Guthrie, Ky.
Major–League Debut: April 22, 1943

Potter, Maryland Dykes
Born: September 7, 1910/Ashland, Ky.
Major–League Debut: April 26, 1938

Potter, Squire
Born: March 18, 1902/Flatwoods, Ky.
Died: January 27, 1983/Ashland, Ky.
Major–League Debut: August 7, 1923

Powers, Ellis Foree
Born: March 2, 1906/Crestwood, Ky.
Died: December 2, 1983/Louisville, Ky.
Major–League Debut: August 19, 1932

Reccius, John
Born: October 29, 1859/Louisville, Ky.
Died: September 1, 1930/Louisville, Ky.
Major–League Debut: May 2, 1882

Reccius, Philip
Born: June 7, 1862/Louisville, Ky.
Died: February 15, 1903/Louisville, Ky.
Major–League Debut: September 25, 1882

Reeder, Nicholas (born Nicholas Herchenroeder)
Born: March 22, 1867/Louisville, Ky.
Died: September 26, 1894/Louisville, Ky.
Major–League Debut: April 11, 1891

Rees, Stanley Milton
Born: February 25, 1899/Cynthiana, Ky.
Died: August 30, 1937/Lexington, Ky.
Major–League Debut: June 12, 1918

Reese, Harold Henry
Born: July 23, 1918/Ekron, Ky.
Major–League Debut: April 23, 1940

Reis, Thomas Edward
Born: August 6, 1914/Newport, Ky.
Major–League Debut: April 27, 1938

Richter, John M.
Born: February 8, 1873/Louisville, Ky.
Died: October 4, 1927/Louisville, Ky.
Major–League Debut: October 6, 1898

Roberts, Dale
Born: April, 12, 1942/Owenton, Ky.
Major–League Debut: September 9, 1967

Robinson, Don Allen
Born: June 8, 1957/Ashland, Ky.
Major–League Debut: April 10, 1978

Robinson, William (born William Anderson)
Born: Date unknown/Taylorsville, Ky.
Died: Date and location unknown
Major–League Debut: August 12, 1889

Roof, Eugene Lawrence
Born: January 13, 1958/Paducah, Ky.
Major–League Debut: September 3, 1981

Roof, Phillip Anthony
Born: March 5, 1941/Paducah, Ky.
Major–League Debut: April 29, 1961

Ross, Chester Franklin
Born: March 11, 1903/Kuttawa, Ky.
Died: April 24, 1982/Mayfield, Ky.
Major–League Debut: June 15, 1924

Savage, John Joseph
Born: April 22, 1964/Louisville, Ky.
Major–League Debut: September 14, 1987

Schultz, Robert Duffy
Born: November 27, 1923/Louisville, Ky.
Died: March 31, 1979/Nashville, Tenn.
Major–League Debut; April 20, 1951

Schupp, Ferdinand Maurice
Born: January 16, 1891/Louisville, Ky.
Died: December 16, 1971/Los Angeles, Calif.
Major–League Debut: April 19, 1913

Schwartz, William August
Born: April 3, 1864/Jamestown, Ky.
Died: December 22, 1940/Newport, Ky.
Major–League Debut: May 3, 1883

Schwenck, Rudolph Christian
Born: April 6, 1884/Louisville, Ky.
Died: November 27, 1941/Anchorage, Ky.
Major–League Debut: September 23, 1909

Sechrist, Theodore O'Hara
Born: February 10, 1876/Williamstown, Ky.
Died: April 2, 1950/Louisville, Ky.
Major–League Debut: April 28, 1899

Shaw, Benjamin Nathaniel
Born: June 18, 1893/La Center, Ky.
Died: March 16, 1959/Aurora, Ohio
Major–League Debut: April 11, 1917

Shelby, John T.
Born: February 23, 1958/Lexington, Ky.
Major–League Debut: September 15, 1981

Shreve, Leven Lawrence
Born: January 14, 1869/Louisville, Ky.
Died: October 18, 1942/Detroit, Mich.
Major–League Debut: May 2, 1887

Shumpert, Terrance Darnell
Born: August 16, 1966/Paducah Ky.
Major–League Debut: May 1, 1990

Slayback, Elbert
Born: October 3, 1901/Paducah, Ky.
Died: November 30, 1979/Cincinnati, Ohio
Major–League Debut: September 26, 1926

Smith, George Shelby
Born: October 27, 1901/Louisville, Ky.
Died: May 26, 1981/Richmond, Va.
Major–League Debut: April 21, 1926

Smith, Jack Hatfield
Born: November 15, 1935/Pikeville, Ky.
Major–League Debut: September 10, 1962

Smith, John William (born Jan Smadt)
Born: December 2, 1892/Dayton, Ky.
Died: October 11, 1935/Dayton, Ky.
Major–League Debut: April 12, 1913

Smith, Rex (born Henry W. Schmidt)
Born: 1864/Louisville, Ky.
Died: July 21, 1895/Louisville, Ky.
Major–League Debut: July 11, 1886

Snopek, Christopher Charles
Born: September 20, 1970/Cynthiana, Ky.
Major–League Debut: July 31, 1995

Sommer, Joseph John
Born: November 20, 1858/Covington, Ky.
Died: January 16, 1938/Cincinnati, Ohio
Major–League Debut: July 8, 1880

Sorrell, William
Born: October 14, 1940/Morehead, Ky.
Major–League Debut: September 2, 1965

Sowders, John
Born: December 10, 1866/Louisville, Ky.
Died: July 29, 1908/Indianapolis, Ind.
Major–League Debut: June 28, 1887

Sowders, Leonard
Born: June 29, 1861/Louisville, Ky.
Died: November 19, 1888/Indianapolis, Ind.
Major–League Debut: September 10, 1886

Sowders, William Jefferson
Born: November 29, 1864/Louisville, Ky.
Died: February 2, 1951/Indianapolis, Ind.
Major–League Debut: April 24, 1888

Spence, Stanley Orville
Born: March 20, 1915/South Portsmouth, Ky.
Died: January 9, 1983/Kinston, N.C.
Major–League Debut: June 8, 1940

Stephenson, John Herman
Born: April 13, 1941/South Portsmouth, Ky.
Major–League Debut: April 14, 1964

Stratton, C. Scott
Born: October 2, 1869/Campbellsburg, Ky.
Died: March 8, 1939/Louisville, Ky.
Major–League Debut: April 21, 1888

Strick, John Quincy Adams
Born: Date unknown/Louisville, Ky.
Died: Date and location unknown
Major–League Debut: May 18, 1882

Stultz, George Irvin
Born: June 30, 1873/Louisville, Ky.
Died: March 19, 1955/Louisville, Ky.
Major–League Debut: September 22, 1894

Sweeney, William John
Born: March 6, 1886/Covington, Ky.
Died: May 26, 1948/Cambridge, Mass.
Major–League Debut: June 14, 1907

Tannehill, Jesse Niles
Born: July 14, 1874/Dayton, Ky.
Died: September 22, 1956/Dayton, Ky.
Major–League Debut: June 17, 1894

Tannehill, Lee Ford
Born: October 26, 1880/Dayton, Ky.
Died: February 16, 1938/Live Oak, Fla.
Major–League Debut: April 22, 1903

Terrell, John Thomas
Born: June 29, 1867/Louisville, Ky.
Died: July 9, 1893/Louisville, Ky.
Major–League Debut: October 5, 1886

Textor, George Bernhardt
Born: December 27, 1888/Newport, Ky.
Died: March 10, 1954/Massillon, Ohio
Major–League Debut: April 19, 1914

Thacker, Morris Benton
Born: May 21, 1934/Louisville, Ky.
Major–League Debut: April 20, 1958

Thobe, John Joseph
Born: November 19, 1970/Covington, Ky.
Major–League Debut: September 18, 1995

Thobe, Thomas Neal
Born: September 3, 1969/Covington, Ky.
Major–League Debut: September 12, 1995

Thompson, Mark Radford
Born: April 7, 1971
Major–League Debut: July 26, 1994

Thoney, John
Born: December 8, 1879/Ft. Thomas, Ky.
Died: October 24, 1948/Covington, Ky.
Major–League Debut: April 26, 1902

Tinsley, Lee Owen
Born: March 4, 1969/Shelbyville, Ky.
Major–League Debut: April 6, 1993

Tomlin, David Allen
Born: June 22, 1949/Maysville, Ky.
Major–League Debut: September 2, 1972

Toth, Paul Louis
Born: June 30, 1935/McRoberts, Ky.
Major–League Debut: April 22, 1962

Treadway, George B.
Born: November 11, 1866/Greenup County, Ky.
Died: Date and location unknown
Major–League Debut: April 27, 1893

Turner, Christopher Wan
Born: March 23, 1969/Bowling Green, Ky.
Major–League Debut: August 27, 1993

Turner, Theodore Holhot
Born: May 4, 1892/Lawrenceburg, Ky.
Died: February 4, 1958/Lexington, Ky.
Major–League Debut: April 20, 1920

Turner, William Matthew
Born: February 18, 1967/Lexington, Ky.
Major–League Debut: April 23, 1993

Veach, Robert Hayes
Born: June 29, 1888/Island, Ky.
Died: August 7, 1945/Detroit, Mich.
Major–League Debut: August 6, 1912

Watkins, David Roger
Born: March 15, 1944/Owensboro, Ky.
Major–League Debut: April 9, 1969

Weaver, Orville Forest
Born: June 4, 1886/Newport, Ky.
Died: November 28, 1970/New Orleans, La.
Major–League Debut: September 14, 1910

Wentz, John George (born John George Wernz)
Born: March 4, 1863/Louisville, Ky.
Died: September 14, 1907/Louisville, Ky.
Major–League Debut: April 15, 1891

West, Richard Thomas
Born: November 24, 1915/Louisville, Ky.
Major–League Debut: September 28, 1938

Weyhing, August
Born: September 29, 1866/Louisville, Ky.
Died: September 4, 1955/Louisville, Ky.
Major–League Debut: May 2, 1887

Weyhing, John
Born: June 24, 1869/Louisville, Ky.
Died: June 20, 1890/Louisville, Ky.
Major–League Debut: July 13, 1888

Wheeler, Floyd Clark
Born: March 2, 1898/Marion, Ky.
Died: September 18, 1968/Marion, Ky.
Major–League Debut: September 30, 1921

Williams, Elisha Alphonso
Born: October 6, 1855/Ludlow, Ky.
Died: October 22, 1939/Covington, Ky.
Major–League Debut: August 12, 1876

Wilson, Finis Elbert
Born: December 9, 1889/East Fork, Ky.
Died: March 9, 1959/Coral Gables, Fla.
Major–League Debut: September 26, 1914

Wise, Hugh Edward
Born: March 9, 1906/Campbellsville, Ky.
Died: July 21, 1987/Plantation, Fla.
Major–League Debut: September 26, 1930

Wolf, William Van Winkle
Born: May 12, 1862/Louisville, Ky.
Died: May 16, 1903/Louisville, Ky.
Major–League Debut: May 2, 1882

Yantz, George Webb
Born: July 27, 1886/Louisville, Ky.
Died: February 26, 1967/Louisville, Ky.
Major–League Debut: September 30, 1912

Zahner, Frederick Joseph
Born: June 5, 1870/Louisville, Ky.
Died: July 24, 1900/Louisville, Ky.
Major–League Debut: July 23, 1894

TOTAL: 234 Kentucky–Born Major–Leaguers (1876–1995)

KENTUCKY BASEBALL TRAVEL SITES

BEAVER DAM

Birthplace of Cleveland Indians shortstop Ray Chapman, a fatal victim of a pitch by Yankee pitcher Carl Mays in 1920 (to date, the only on–the–field fatality in major–league baseball history). Ironically enough, both players were Kentucky natives. (Beaver Dam is midway between Owensboro and Bowling Green on US 231 in the western end of the state)

CORYDON

Birthplace of Hall–of–Fame Baseball Commissioner A.B. "Happy" Chandler. NOTE: See "Versailles" listing also. (Corydon is due west of Owensboro, southeast of Henderson)

DAYTON

Birthplace of Pirate and Red Sox pitching great Jesse Tannehill (197–116/1894–1911). Dayton is located northeast of Covington in northern Kentucky on the Ohio River.

EKRON

Birthplace of Dodger Hall–of–Fame shortstop Harold "Pee Wee" Reese, who has resided in nearby Louisville for most of his life. (Ekron is located southwest of Louisville)

FRANKFORT
(KENTUCKY STATE CAPITAL)

Site of old state penitentiary ballpark (corner of Holmes and Regan, between State Office Building and Frankfort Scrap Metal Company).

Worth a look because of the necessary security logistics of the park (double fencing, barbed wire, bars over windows, etc.). Grandstand made of stone. (Frankfort is a 45–minute drive from Lexington, off I–64, the principal east–west corridor between the state's two largest cities — Lexington and Louisville.)

GLASGOW

Birthplace of second basemen/brothers Brian and Denny Doyle. (Glasgow is located east of Bowling Green)

ISLAND

Birthplace of outfielder Bobby Veach, a career .310 hitter off play from 1912 through 1925. (Island is located near Owensboro)

LEXINGTON

Birthplace of Oriole/Dodger outfielder John Shelby. Also longtime home of Charles "Cotton" Nash, one of those rare athletes to have played both professional baseball and professsional basketball. In college, Nash was an All–American in basketball on that central Kentucky city's nationally–famous University of Kentucky Wildcat basketball team, and a Southeastern Conference baseball star (first base).

LIBERTY

Birthplace of Carl Mays, submarine–style hurler whose pitch killed fellow Kentuckian Ray Chapman (see entry under Beaver Dam) in 1920. (Liberty is southwest of Danville)

LOUISVILLE

To no one's surprise, the single biggest repository of notable baseball sites in the Bluegrass State. Birthplace of such stars as Pete Browning, John McCloskey,

brothers John and Philip Reccius, Gus Weyhing and Chicken Wolf (all detailed later in this listing).

Louisville is also the birthplace of Red Ehret (the pitching hero of the 1890 World Series); Bosox star Mike Greenwell; and Fred Pfeffer, one of two finest second-baseman of 19th century (Bid McPhee was the other).

Louisville is also the co–birthplace (December, 1875 at the old Louisville Hotel at Seventh and Main) of the National League, and was a charter member of the nation's oldest, continuously–active major–league circuit (1876).

Just a block west of that historic location, at Eighth and Main, are the new Hillerich & Bradsby headquarters, which consist of corporate offices, the bat factory and the bat museum (relocation accomplished in 1995 and 1996).

Other noteworthy baseball sites downtown include the corners of First and Market, site of the shop where John A. "Bud" Hillerich custom–made the first Louisville Slugger bat for the epic 19th–century batsman, Pete Browning. This act birthed the modern bat industry; its icon — the Louisville Slugger bat; and the world's most famous batmaker — Hillerich & Bradsby.

In addition, there is "Baseball Alley" and Green Street. The former, a remnant of Louisville's early minor–league years (it was a shortcut to the city's first minor–league ballpark, Eclipse Park, at Seventh and Kentucky) is located in the 900 block of Fourth.

Green Street, now called Liberty Street, was the site of Larry Gatto's saloon (another meeting place, so the story goes, of the 1875 Louisville/National League Western delegates).

Louisville's baseball park sites also offer a great deal of rich history.

The city's first two major–league clubs (the 1876

The peerless Ty Cobb selects a Louisville Slugger. (*University of Louisville Photographic Archives*)

and 1877 Louisville Grays) played on the present site of St. James Court.

A palatial mansion district since the 1890s, it is located just South of downtown Louisville.

Other major-league baseball park sites for the Louisville squads included the first Eclipse Park at 28th and Elliott and the second Eclipse Park (located across the street at 28th and Broadway). The former witnessed the bulk of the career success of three old-time Louisville major-league standouts–Pete Browning, Guy Hecker and Chicken Wolf.

It was also the site of the debut of a watershed ballplayer– Moses Walker, the sport's first black major-leaguer.

And, the first four games of the 1890 World Series (between Louisville and National League champion Brooklyn) were played at the first Eclipse Park.

The second Eclipse ballpark hosted the likes of such stars as Fred Clarke, Honus Wagner, Tommy Leach and Deacon Phillippe, the foundation of the great turn–of–the–century Pittsburgh Pirate teams.

Both ballparks were destroyed by fire. The first operated during the city's entire American Association tenure (1882–1891) and briefly at the start of its second National League tour. The second park operated for virtually all of Louisville's second membership in the National League (1892–1899).

Of particular interest also is the Falls City Park, which was at 16th and Magnolia (this intersection no longer exists). This was used by the Louisville Falls Citys of the National Colored Base Ball League. That was this country's second black major–league loop, which briefly did business in 1887.

The Falls Citys also played at the original Eclipse Park at 28th and Elliott. This team, by the way, was the forerunner of five Louisville entries in the old Negro Leagues (1930–31–32, 1949 and 1954).

Louisville currently is home to one of the sport's most succesful minor–league franchises — the Louisville Redbirds, a member of the American Association (AAA) whose parent club is the St. Louis Cardinals.

The first minor–league franchise to draw a million patrons in a season (1983), the Redbirds play at Cardinal Stadium (part of the Fairgrounds complex), just off the Watterson Expressway and five minutes away from the city's main airport — Standiford Field.

Another fascinating ballpark site is historic Parkway Field, near the University of Louisville.

Once the home of the Louisville Colonels, (the predecessor of the minor–league Redbirds), it also hosted some top–quality exhibition games over the years that featured marquee names in major–league baseball like Babe Ruth, Lou Gehrig, Grover Cleveland Alexander, Jackie Robinson, Pee Wee Reese (who began his career with the Colonels), Satchel Paige, Honus Wagner and Ted Williams.

The predecessor of Parkway Field was the aforementioned Eclipse Park at Kentucky and Seventh ("Baseball Alley"), which like its successor, provided top–line minor–league baseball during its stint as well as some crackerjack exhibition games that featured the likes of Ty Cobb, John McGraw, Walter Johnson, Connie Mack, Cy Young, "Shoeless" Joe Jackson, Christy Mathewson, Tris Speaker, Casey Stengel, Nap Lajoie, Dizzie Dean and the famed double–play trio of Joe Tinker, Johnny Evers and Frank Chance.

Distinguished burial sites include those of the legendary Pete Browning, Bud Hillerich, Chicken Wolf and Zack Phelps — all at famed Cave Hill Cemetery (701 Baxter) on the city's east side.

A three–time batting champion, career .341 stickman and afore–stated recipient of the first Louisville Slugger bat (1884), Louis Rogers "Pete" Browning is buried in Section A, Lot 549.

His final resting place is a must–see because of the elegant 4 1/2–foot tall marker which has adorned his grave since 1984 (the centennial of Hillerich & Bradsby).

Jointly financed by the city of Louisville and Hillerich & Bradsby, the marker replaced an old stone which incorrectly spelled Browning's first name and listed none of his fabled diamond achievments.

Hillerich, the other half of the historic bat–making tandem, is buried in a family plot in Section 26.

Wolf, a longtime teammate of Browning, is interred in Section 5, Lot 186. The 1890 batting champion of the American Association (.363), William V. "Chicken" Wolf led all Louisville batters in the 1890 World Series with a .360 batting average that included three doubles, one triple and eight RBIs (tops in that year's series).

Zack Phelps, Louisville American Association President (1885–1887) and twice President of the American Association (1890 and 1891), is buried near Browning (Section A, Lot 390).

Cave Hill is also the home to John and Philip Reccius, John Avery Haldeman, Hub Collins, and Harry C. Pullman.

The Reccius brothers, products of one of the great baseball families in Louisville, were members of the Louisville Eclipse entry in the American Association. John Reccius is buried in Section 24, south half of Lot 154; Philip Reccius is interred in Section 6, Range 197, Lot 8.

Haldeman was the son of Louisville Courier–Journal publisher and Louisville Grays President, Walter N. Haldeman. A member of the 1877 Louisville NL squad, the younger Haldeman was the reporter who broke the pennant–throwing scandal of Louisville's 1877 sellout, which allowed Boston to win a pennant they almost certainly never would have won otherwise. Haldeman is buried near Phelps and Browning (Section A, Lot 113).

Buried near Wolf is the brilliant and ill–fated Hub Collins (Section 5, Lot 152, NE 1/2), a Louisville native and high-class ballplayer who died at age 28 in 1892.

Harry C. Pulliam, President of the Louisville National League Club (1877-1899) and President of the National League (1903-1909), is buried in Section P, Lot 85.

Also on the east side of Louisville is Calvary Cemetery (1600 Newburg Road), which is home to Gus Weyhing and John McCloskey.

A legitimate Hall of Fame candidate like Pete Browning, Weyhing posted a 264–235 career mound record. He is buried in Section 23, Lot 64, Grave 1.

Within eyesight of Weyhing's gravesite is that of baseball pioneer John McCloskey, perhaps best–remembered today as the founder of the Texas League. His location (Section 24, Lot 81) is guarded by a handsome marker which has a moving accolade on one side, his lifedates on the other side.

Larry Gatto is buried in St. Louis Cemetery (Section C, Lot 5, Grave 3), which is near Calvary Cemetery. (Louisville is 1 1/2 hours west of Lexington on I–64, across the Ohio River from New Albany, Ind.)

LYNN

Birthplace of Reds/Yankees flamethrower Don Gullett. (Lynn is located due south of Portsmouth, Ohio)

PEBWORTH

Birthplace of Yankee Hall–of–Fame outfielder Earle Combs. His home at the time of his death in 1976 was Richmond, Ky., which is just south of Lexington. (Pebworth is southeast of Lexington)

SHELBYVILLE

Slugger "Dan" McGann, the first–baseman on several of John McGraw's turn–of–the–century New York Giant National League flagwinners, is buried in Grove Hill Cemetery (Section B, Lot 111).

Worth a mention because of the bizarre nature of McGann's death by his own hand around Christmastime of 1910. His death came some six months after another brother took his own life under almost similar circumstances (both shot themselves).

Dennis Lawrence "Dan" McGann is buried on a family plot which includes his Irish parents — Joseph McGann (1830–1896) and Kate McGann (1832–1888); a sister — Mary McGann (1856–1889); and brothers Timothy McGann (1857–1902), Daniel J. McGann (1864–1910) and Joseph D. McGann (1868–1940). (Shelbyville is located between Lexington and Louisville on I–64)

SOUTHGATE

Birthplace of pitcher Jim Bunning, author of two no–hitters (one a perfect game), winner of 100 games–plus in both the National and American Leagues, and a victor of 224 career games. (Southgate is located east of Covington in northern Kentucky.)

SPRINGIELD

Birthplace of pitcher Paul Derringer (223–212 career), who appeared in four World Series. His best post–season action came in the 1940 World Series, when he went 2–1 for the World Champion Cincinnati Reds. Posted four 20–win campaigns, including a 20–12 slate in 1940. (Springfield is southwest of Lexington)

TAYLORSVILLE

Record–setting champion pitcher Scott Stratton is buried in Valley Cemetery. Louisville's ace during its 1890 American Association flag–winning season, Stratton posted a 34–14 mark. That tabsheet included a recently–verified 16–game winning streak. (Taylorsville is located southwest of Shelbyville)

VERSAILLES

Hall–of–Fame Baseball Commissioner Albert Benjamin "Happy" Chandler, whose political career included two terms as Governor of Kentucky, resided there for years. He is buried at nearby Pisgah Presbyterian Church Cemetery. NOTE: See "Corydon" listing. (Versailles is due west of Lexington)

LOUISVILLE & KENTUCKY MINOR LEAGUE HIGHLIGHTS:

LOUISVILLE IN THE MINORS

*W*ith the exception of two timespans (1963–1967 and 1973–1981), Louisville has played minor-league baseball continuously since 1902. But for one five–year period (1968–1972), when the Louisville franchise was a member of the International League, all of that play has come in the American Association.

Louisville's minor–league history officially began in 1902 at Eclipse Park at Seventh and Kentucky. The team was called the Louisville Colonels. For the record, it should be noted that the American Association was initially considered an "outlaw league" for territorial transgressions by the National Asssociation of Professional Baseball Leagues (NAPBL), the governing body of minor–league baseball founded in September of 1901.

Besides some great minor–league play, the grand old park was also graced by the likes of such giant major–league names (via exhibition games) as Cobb,

Jackson, Johnson, Lajoie, Mack, Mathewson, McGraw, Speaker, Stengel, the celebrated double–play triad of Tinker, Evers and Chance, and Young.

Eclipse Park, not to be confused with the two major–league parks operated in the 1880s and 1890s on the city's west side, was destroyed by fire in late November of 1922. It was replaced by Parkway Field, which opened in early May of 1923.

This epic field, part of which still stands today (on the University of Louisville campus adjacent to Eastern Parkway), was the home of the Colonels from 1923 through 1956. And, like its predecessor, it also hosted both top–notch minor–league action and fabulous major–league stars (also via exhibition play) like Alexander, Dean, Gehrig, Pee Wee Reese (a Louisville Manual High School graduate who began his professional baseball career with the Colonels), Robinson, Paige, Ruth, Wagner (who, remarkably,

Eclipse Park, looking from the pressbox toward right field. (University of Louisville Photographic Archives)

Louisville Colonels Manager Jack Hayden cracks out a few during a 1914 practice session. Note the "Bull Durham" sign in the background (see page 143 regarding the term "bullpen"). The American Tobacco Company, manufacturers of Bull Durham, had these signs in numerous minor and major-league ball parks. If a player hit a ball against this sign in a regulation game, it was worth money (reportedly $25 at the time this photograph was taken). (University of Louisville Photographic Archivves)

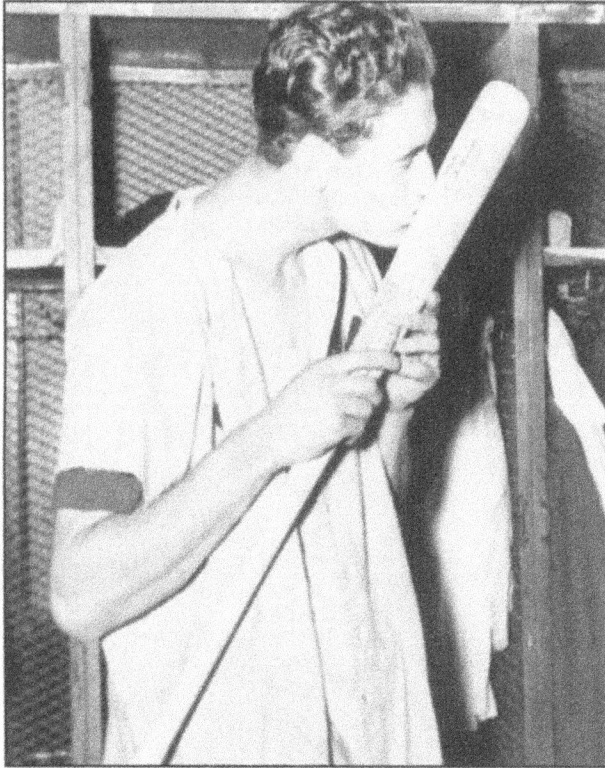

Hall-of-Famer Ted "The Splendid Splinter" Williams in company with another great baseball star — the world-famous Hillerich and Bradsby Louisville Slugger bat. (University of Louisville Photographic Archives)

had initiated his major–league career at Louisville in *another* century) and Williams.

Since 1957, the Louisville minor–league franchise has played at what is now known as Cardinal Stadium (formerly Fairgrounds Stadium) at the Fairgrounds complex near Standiford Field, the city's principal airport. Both the hiatuses in Louisville's minor–league baseball history, which were due to extraordinary conditions, have occurred during the club's stay there.

Its first leave of absence came when the American Association disbanded after the 1962 season, a set of events which left the city without a minor–league team from 1963 through 1967. The situation was finally remedied in 1968 when Louisville became a member of the International League, that membership running through 1972.

The second exit occurred after the 1972 season when the Fairgrounds Stadium (Cardinal Stadium) was expanded and redesigned primarily for football, and the Colonels were evicted.

There followed an even more extensive exile

A sell-out crowd at Cardinal Stadium (formerly Fairgrounds Stadium). (The Louisville Redbirds Baseball Club)

(1973–1981) for the Louisville minor–league franchise, which returned home to the baseball–starved city in 1982. The success was instantaneous as the franchise, under a new name — the Louisville Redbirds, set a single–season minor–league attendance record.

The next year (1983), the Redbirds turned into a wild success as they became the first minor–league franchise to draw a million patrons in a season. Clearly, the town's great baseball tradition had been resurrected.

The club is currently a Triple–A farm club for the Cardinals. Before that, the Louisville franchise served as a conduit for the Braves and the Red Sox.

Over the years, Louisville has sent a number of top–flight players to the majors. For the record, its roster of minor-league managers notably includes Hall-of-Famers Joe McCarthy, Burleigh Grimes and Max Carey, as well as Eddie Kasko, Darrell Johnson and Jim Fregosi.

The list of notable players to have worn a Louisville minor–league uniform is headlined by Cooperstown residents Earle Combs (speedy leadoff man/center fielder for the 1927 Yankees); second–sacker/hit–and–run artist Billy Herman, whose career included stints with the Cubs and Dodgers; and Dodger shortstop Pee Wee Reese, brilliant in the field and at the plate.

Other members of that group (including rehabs),

Parkway Field, 1942 (behind home plate, players facing the flag). (University of Louisville Photographic Archives)

many of whom made substantial marks in the big show, number Ted Abernathy, Merito Acosta, Jim Adduci, Luis Alicea, Allen Battle, Howie Bedell, Alan Benes, Juan Beniquez, Bruno Betzel, Dud Branom, Bunny Brief, Ozzie Canseco, Cris Carpenter, Chuck Carr, Mark Clark, Alex Cole, Vince Coleman, Cecil Cooper, Danny Cox, Tripp Cromer, Nick Cullop, Dave Danforth, Bert Daniels, Dixie Davis, Dwight Evans, Carlton Fisk, Curt Ford, Andres Galarraga, Babe Ganzel, Chico Genovese, Bernard Gilkey, Billy Goodman, Pedro Guerrero, Joe Guyon, Tex Hughson, Lance Johnson, Jay Kirke, Ray Lankford, Jim Lindeman, Jim Lonborg, Grover Cleveland Lowdermilk, Dolf Luque, John Mabry, Frank Malzone, Maurice McDermott, Willie McGee, Archie McKain, Phil Niekro, Jake Northrup, Don Nottebart, Ben Ogilvie, Freddy Olivo, Tom Pagnozzi, Terry Pendleton, Johnny Pesky, Jimmy Piersall, Juan Pizarro, Nick Polly, Ambrose Puttman, Gary Rajsich, Gene Roof, Stan Royer, Butch Simons, Jose Tartabull, Willie Tasby, Bob Tewksbury, Ben Tincup, Bob Uecker, Andy Van Slyke, Todd Worrell, Gerald Young and Todd Zeile.

Hall-of-Fame hurlers Satchel Paige (left) and Dizzy Dean during an exhibition game at Parkway Field. (University of Louisville Photographic Archives)

Hall-of-Famers Lou Gehrig (back row, in Larruping Lous uniform) and Babe Ruth (back row, Bustin' Babes uniform) pose for the camera at Parkway Field on October 24, 1928. The Yankee greats were part of a special game held for the Red Cross Florida Storm Relief. (University of Louisville Photographic Archives)

STARGAZER
Billy Herman
(National Baseball Library and Archive, Cooperstown, NY)

LAUGHING EARLE
Earle Combs
(University of Louisville Photographic Archives)

If it were a painting, this photograph could be well entitled: "Portrait of a Shortstop as a Young Man." Future Hall-of-Famer Harold "Pee Wee" Reese poses with Manual High School baseball coach Ralph Kimmel and three unidentified young ladies during his 1938 debut season with the Louisville Colonels. Despite his youth (age 19), Reese displays the lean and hungry look which would propel him to success in every facet of his career — as a Dodger, a broadcaster, Hillerich & Bradsby executive, and finally as a member of the Veterans Committee. Note the flourishing "L" on his uniform. (University of Louisville Photographic Archives)

ANNUAL STANDINGS OF LOUISVILLE MINOR-LEAGUE TEAMS: 1902-1995

1902	92–45	**1918**	41–36	**1934**	78–74	**1950**	82–71	**1971**	71–69
1903	87–54	**1919**	86–67	**1935**	52–97	**1951**	80–73	**1972**	81–63
1904	77–70	**1920**	88–79	**1936**	63–91	**1952**	77–77	**1982**	73–62
1905	76–75	**1921**	98–70	**1937**	62–91	**1953**	84–70	**1983**	78–57
1906	71–79	**1922**	77–91	**1938**	53–100	**1954**	85–68	**1984**	79–76
1907	77–77	**1923**	94–77	**1939**	75–78	**1955**	83–71	**1985**	74–68
1908	88–65	**1924**	90–75	**1940**	75–75	**1956**	60–93	**1986**	64–78
1909	93–75	**1925**	106–61	**1941**	87–66	**1957**	49–105	**1987**	78–62
1910	60–103	**1926**	105–62	**1942**	78–76	**1958**	56–95	**1988**	63–79
1911	67–101	**1927**	65–103	**1943**	70–81	**1959**	97–65	**1989**	71–74
1912	66–101	**1928**	62–106	**1944**	85–63	**1960**	85–68	**1990**	74–72
1913	94–72	**1929**	75–90	**1945**	84–70	**1961**	80–70	**1991**	51–92
1914	95–73	**1930**	93–60	**1946**	92–61	**1962**	71–75	**1992**	73–70
1915	78–72	**1931**	74–94	**1947**	85–68	**1968**	72–75	**1993**	68–76
1916	101–66	**1932**	67–101	**1948**	56–98	**1969**	77–63	**1994**	74–68
1917	88–66	**1933**	70–83	**1949**	70–83	**1970**	69–71	**1995**	74–70

1907 Louisville Colonels (University of Louisville Photographic Archives)

1909 Louisville Colonels, the city's first minor-league pennant winner. (University of Louisville Photographic Archives)

1909   Won American Association pennant

1916   Won American Association pennant

1921   Won American Association pennant, and won Little World Series

1925   Won American Association pennant, and lost Little World Series

1926   Won American Association pennant, and lost Little World Series

1930   Won American Association pennant, and lost Little World Series

1939   Won American Association playoffs, and won Junior World Series

1940   Won American Association playoffs, and lost Junior World Series

1941   Lost American Association playoff finals

1944   Won American Association playoffs, and lost Junior World Series

1945   Won American Association playoffs, and won Junior World Series

1946   Won American Association regular–season pennant and playoffs, lost Junior World Series

1947   Won American Association playoff openers, lost playoff finals

1951   Lost American Association playoff openers

1953   Lost American Association playoff openers

1954   Won American Association playoffs, and won Junior World Series

1955   Lost American Association playoff openers

1959   Won American Association Eastern Division crown, lost playoff openers

1960   Won American Association playoffs, and won Junior World Series

1961   Won American Association playoffs, and lost Junior World Series

1962   Won American Association playoffs, and lost Junior World Series

1969   Lost International League playoff openers

1972   Won International League pennant, and lost playoff finals

1983   Won American Association Eastern Division crown, lost playoff finals

1984   Won American Association playoffs

1985   Won American Association Eastern Division crown, won playoffs

1987   Lost American Association playoff openers

1994   Lost American Association playoff openers

1995   Won American Association playoffs

NOTES:

The Little World Series was renamed the Junior World Series in 1932. The Little World Series was held in 1904, 1906–1907, 1917, and 1920–1931. The Junior World Series was played in 1932–1934; 1936–62, 1970–1971, 1973, 1975, and was succeeded by the AAA Classic: 1988–1991. All three were "World Series" style competitions between the American Association and the International League.

The American Association has had three classifications during its history: Lone–A (A) loop (1902–1907); Double–A (AA) circuit (1908–1945); Triple–A (AAA) league (1946–present).

KENTUCKY IN THE MINORS

Ashland–Catlettsburg

Virginia Valley	1910	
Mountain States	1911–1912	1939–1942

Bowling Green

Kitty	1939–1942

Central City

Kitty	1954

Cynthiana

Blue Grass	1922–1924

Dawson Springs

Kitty	1916

Frankfort

Blue Grass	1908–1912
Ohio State	1915–1916

Fulton

Kitty	1911	1922–1924
	1936–1942	1946–1955

Harlan

Mountain States	1948–1954	
Appalachian	1961–1963	1965

Hazard

Mountain States	1948–1952

Henderson

Kitty	1903–1904	1910–1914
	1916	

Hopkinsville

Kitty	1903–1904	1910–1914
	1916	1922–1923
	1935–1942	1946–1954

Jenkins

Mountain States	1948–1951

Lawrence

Blue Grass	1908

Lexington

Blue Grass	1908–1912	1922–1923
Ohio State	1913–1916	
Kitty	1935–1938	
Mountain States	1954	

Louisville

American Association	1902–1962	1982–present
International League	1968–1972	

Madisonville

Kitty	1910, 1916, 1922, 1946–1955

Mayfield

Kitty	1922–1924	1936–1941
	1946–1955	

Maysville

Blue Grass	1910–1912	1922–1923
Ohio State	1913–1916	

Middlesboro

Appalachian	1913–1914	1961–1963
Mountain States	1949	

Mt. Sterling

Blue Grass	1912	1922–1923

Newport

Ohio State	1914

Nicholasville

Blue Grass	1912

Owensboro

Kitty	1913–1914	1916
	1936–1942	1946–1955

Paducah

Kitty	1903–1906	1910–1914
	1922–1923	1935–1941
	1951–1955	
Mississippi Ohio Valley	1949–1950	

Paintsville

Appalachian	1978–1984

Paris

Blue Grass	1909–1912	1922–1924
Ohio State	1914	

Pikeville

Appalachian	1982–1984

Pineville

Appalachian	1914

Princeton

Kitty	1905

Richmond

Blue Grass	1908–1912

Shelbyville

Blue Grass	1908–1910

Winchester

Blue Grass	1908–1912	1922–1924

Note: The "Kitty League" was a nickname for an old Class D circuit called the Kentucky–Illinois–Tennessee League. It operated over the parts of six decades: 1903–1906, 1910–1914, 1916, 1922–1924, 1935–1942 and 1946–1955. Source: *The Encyclopedia of Minor League Baseball.*

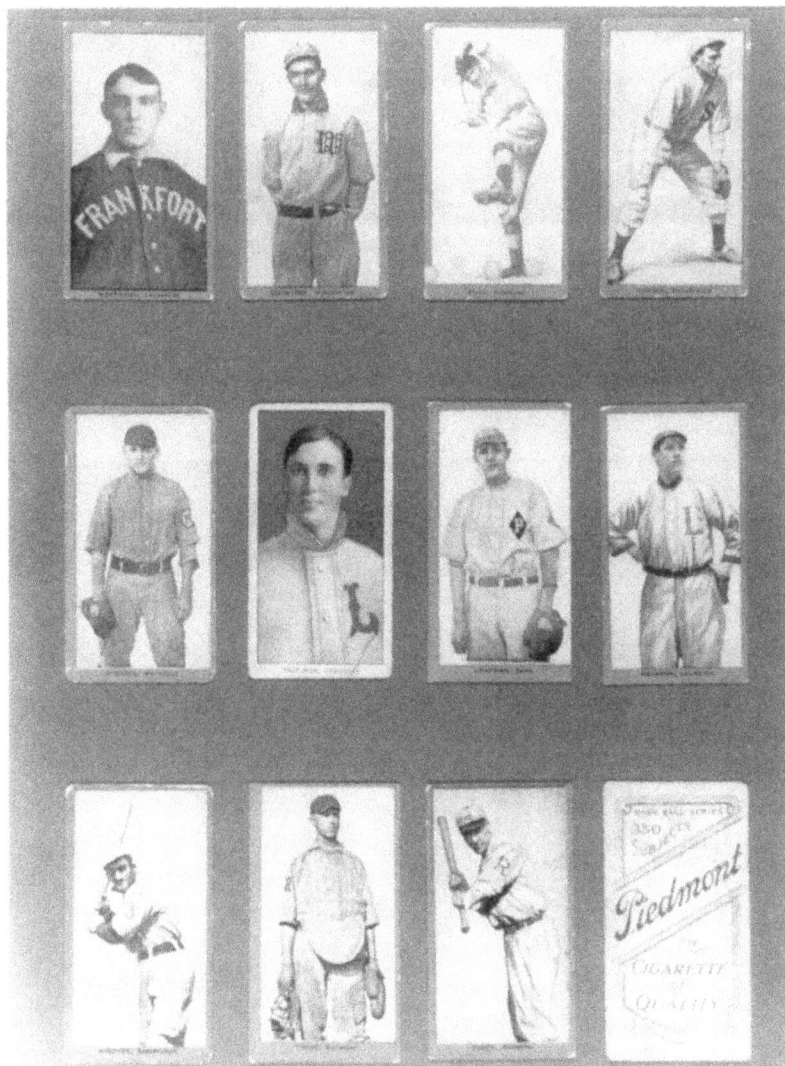

Circa 1910/1911 baseball card montage of players in the Blue Grass League (a central Kentucky minor-league loop). (University of Kentucky King Library, Special Collections and Archives)

1915 team. (University of Louisville Photographic Archives)

1919 Louisville Colonels pictured are (BACK ROW) Ben Tincup, pitcher; Jay Kirke, first base; Bob Bescher, outfield; Brad Kocher, catcher; Wolfe, utility; (MIDDLE ROW) Tim Hendryx, outfield; Joe McCarthy, manager/second base; Bill Knebelkamp, owner; Merito "Cubie" Acosta, outfield; Bruno Betzel, infield; Bill Meyer, catcher; (FRONT ROW) Emilo Palmero, pitcher; Chuck Wortman, shortstop; Tommy Long, pitcher; Dixie Davis, pitcher; and Bill "Shorty" Stewart, pitcher/outfield. *(University of Louisville Photographic Archives)*

1925 Louisville Colonels pictured are (FROM LEFT) Nick Cullop, pitcher; Maury Shannon, shortstop; Joe DeBerry, pitcher; Joe McCarthy, manager; Ben Tincup, pitcher; Ernie Koob, pitcher; Ed Holley, pitcher; Joe Guyon, outfield; Leo "Hooks" Cotter, first base; Joe Schepner, third base; Merito Acosta, outfield; and (back to camera) Ty Tyson, outfield. (University of Louisville Photographic Archives)

The 1939 Louisville Colonels pictured are (STANDING) Bill Burwell, manager; Jim Weaver, pitcher; (SEATED) Paul Campbell, first base; Harold "Pee Wee" Reese, shortstop; Junie Andres, infield; Bob Boken, utility; Tommy Irwin, infield; Charles Wagner, pitcher; (RECLINING) Wes Flowers, pitcher; and Vince Sherlock, second base. (University of Louisville Photographic Archives)

The 1944 Louisville Colonels (The Louisville Redbirds Baseball Club)

The 1946 Louisville Colonels *(University of Louisville Photographic Archives)*

Presented on RADIO APPRECIATION NIGHT— August 12, 1954
with the compliments
LOUISVILLE BASEBALL CLUB
RADIO STATION WINN
and
AETNA OIL CO.   EMMART PACKING CO.
LIBERTY NATIONAL BANK
Who Bring You the Louisville Colonels' Baseball Games
—broadcast play-by-play at time of play.

FRED E. GRIMM
President
Louisville Colonels

JOE BURKE
Secretary
Louisville Colonels

HARRY McTIGUE

JIM McINTYRE

Sportscasters

PEE WEE POWERS
Park Superintendent

Left to right—

THE LOUISVILLE COLONELS 1954

Back Row: Joe Mooney, Equipment Manager; Gene Stephens, Outfielder; Al Curtis, Pitcher; Bill Werle, Pitcher; Bill Kennedy, Pitcher; Norm Zauchin, First Base; Bennet Flowers, Pitcher; Tom Herrin, Pitcher; Herschel Freeman, Pitcher; George Susce, Pitcher; Al Van Alstyne, Outfielder; Win Green, Trainer

Middle Row: Frankie Malzone, Third Base; Don Buddin, Shortstop; Lew Damman, Second Base; Marty Keough, Outfielder; Pete Daley, Catcher; Pinky Higgins, Manager; Dave Ferris, Coach; Ivan DeLock, Pitcher; Ray Holton, Catcher; Connie Ryan, Second Base.

Front Row: Ivan Wittenbaum, Ball Boy; Herb Rossman, Infielder; Paul Foytack, Pitcher; Bob Smith, Pitcher; Bob Broome, Outfielder; Scott Duncan, Bat Boy; Jimmy Mahon, Bat Boy.

The 1954 Louisville Colonels (The Louisville Redbirds Baseball Club)

The 1960 Louisville Colonels on Opening Day that year. (The Louisville Redbirds Baseball Club)

The 1968 Louisville Colonels of the International League (*The Louisville Redbirds Baseball Club*)

The 1983 Louisville Redbirds, the first monor-league team to draw one million fans in one season. FOURTH ROW: Tom Nieto; Jeff Keener; Ken Reitz; Ralph Citarella; Kevin Hagen; Greg Guin; Rafael Santana; Jed Smith, bull pen catcher. THIRD ROW: Karl Dobronski, Traveling secretary; Mike Rhodes; Jeff Doyle; Gene Dotson; Ricky Oenbey; Ricky Horton; Jim Adduci; Andy Rincon; Eric Rasmussen; Gene Roof; Jerry McKune, trainer. SECOND ROW: Jose Gonzalez, Bombo Rivera; Kurt Kepshire; Gaylen Pitts, coach; Jim Fregosi, manager; Dyar Miller; Orlando Sanchez; Tito Landrum; Danny Cox. FIRST ROW: Bat boys- Billy Hite, Mike Heib, Pat Sohan, Doyle Harris, mascot; Bat boys-Chris Folden and Joe Mozzali. (The Louisville Redbirds Baseball Club)

Front (l-r): Mark O'Neal, trainer; T.J. Mathews; Aaron Holbert; Alan Benes; Coach Joe Cunningham;
(l-r): Jeff McNeely; Cris Carpenter; Tracy Woodson; Mike Raczka; Nate Minchey; Greg Cadaret; Dor
Marc Ronan; Allen Battle; Brian Deak; Tony Diggs; Terry Bradshaw; Trey Hyberger, Clubhouse Mgr.

ttini, Pitching Coach Dyar Miller; Francisco de la Rosa; Ramon Caraballo; Mark Petkovsek. Middle
Rich Batchelor; Brian Barber. Back (l-r): Jesse Thompson, Asst. Clubhouse Mgr.; Gary Buckels;
o Beltran; Cory Bailey; Joe Aversa; Darrel Deak; Ray Giannelli; Skeets Thomas; Howard Prager.

BIBLIOGRAPHY

Carter, Craig, ed. *The Complete Baseball Record Book*. St. Louis: The Sporting News, 1994.

Charlton, James, ed. *The Baseball Chronology*. New York: Macmillan, 1991.

Dewey, Donald and Acoccela, Nicholas. *Encyclopedia of Major League Baseball Teams*. New York: HarperCollins, 1993.

Gutman, Dan. *Baseball Babylon*. New York: Penguin, 1992.

Hoppel, Joe, ed. *Cooperstown: Baseball's Hall of Fame, Where the Legends Live Forever*. New York: Arlington House, 1986. (Text by Lowell Reidenbaugh).

Johnson, Lloyd and Wolff, Miles, eds. *The Encyclopedia of Minor League Baseball*. Durham, N.C.: Baseball America, 1993.

McBride, Joseph. *High and Inside: The Complete Guide to Baseball Slang*. New York: Warner Books, 1980.

Nemec, David. *The Beer and Whisky League*. New York: Lyons & Burford, 1994.

Okrent, Daniel and Wulf, Steve. *Baseball Anecdotes*. New York: HarperPerennial, 1989.

O'Neal, William. *The American Association: A Baseball History, 1902–1991*. Austin, TX: Eakin Press, 1991.

Seymour, Harold. *Baseball: The Early Years*. New York: Oxford University Press, 1960.

Smith, Robert. *Baseball in the Afternoon*. New York: Simon and Schuster, 1993.

Sullivan, Neil. *The Minors*. New York: St. Martin's Press. 1990.

Von Borries, Philip. *Legends of Louisville: Major-League Baseball in Louisville, 1876-1899*. West Bloomfield, MI: A & M Publishing Company, 1993.

Whiteford, Mike. *How to Talk Baseball*. New York. Dembner Books, 1987.

Wolff, Rick, ed. *The Baseball Encyclopedia*. New York: Macmillan, 1993.

Hall of Famer Joe McCarthy
(The Louisville Redbirds Baseball Club)

Louisville Redbirds manager Jim Fregosi
(The Louisville Redbirds Baseball Club)

*North Carolina native Frank Talmadge "Dixie"
Davis (1890-1944) pitched for the Louisville Colonels in 1917 and 1919. In the former campaign, he
tied for the American Association crown in victories
(25); in the latter season, he led the American
Association in strikeouts (165). Davis was 75-71
lifetime in the majors, principally in the 1920s with
the St. Louis Browns (where he was a teammate of
Hall-of-Famer George Sisler). Though he left the
majors in 1926, Davis continued to pitch for a
number of years afterward in the minors. That
twilight-career work included a protracted stint with
Kansas City (whose uniform he is wearing in this
1927 photograph. (Philip Von Borries Collection)*

INDEX

Editor's Note: This index does not include Chapter 8 nor Appendix: Kentucky in the Majors. The names listed in the above sections already appear in alphabetical order.

–A–

Abernathy, Ted   168
Acosta, Merito   168, 174, 175
Adduci, Jim   168, 179
Albert, Prince   65
Alexander, Grover Cleveland   161
Alicea, Luis   168
Allentown, Penn   57
Allison, Art   36
Amateurs   44, 45
Anderson, Sparky   6
Andres, Junie   175
Anson, Cap   12, 17, 89, 136
Arcaro, Eddie   26
Arny, C.   42
Arthur, Chester A.   14
Athletics   19
Atlanta Braves   70
Atlantic City   46

–B–

Baker, Norman   64
Baltimore   33, 56, 63, 67, 70, 74, 97, 128, 129
Baltimore Orioles   17, 20, 33
Banks, Ernie   6, 35, 99
Barleycorn, John   49
Barnes, Ross   12, 40
Barney, Mary   6
Barney, Walter   6
Battle, Allen   168
Bayless, George   95
Bechtel, George   12, 36
Bedell, Howie   168

Bench, Johnny   6
Benes, Alan   168
Beniquez, Juan   168
Bescher, Bob   174
Betzel, Bruno   168, 174
Bickel, H.W.   46
Blanco, Christoper   6
Bligh, Ned   81, 85, 87
Bodley, William S.   95
Boston   9, 10, 12, 28, 31, 34, 58, 77, 137
Boston Beaneaters   17
Boston Red Sox   74, 91
Boston Resolutes   25
Brainard, Asa   140
Branom, Dud   168
Breitenstein, Ted   129
Brief, Bunny   168
Brooklyn   63, 68, 71, 72, 74, 77, 79, 84, 90, 98, 129
Brooklyn Brotherhood   90
Brooklyns   31
Brouthers, Dan   34, 40, 54, 100
Brown, Ed   23, 26
Brown, Kent   6
Brown, Tom   31
Brown, Willard   33, 127
Browning, H.   45
Browning, Pete   6, 7, 18, 19, 21, 24, 25, 26, 27, 28, 29, 39, 40, 42, 43, 44, 45, 46, 47, 48, 50, 51, 53, 54, 55, 56, 57, 58, 59, 60, 61, 62, 64, 65, 68, 69, 70, 71, 72, 97, 98, 127, 131, 132, 134, 138, 158, 161, 162
Browning, Samuel   44
Browning, Tod   43
Bulkeley, Morgan   10
Bull Durham   143, 165
Bunning, Jim   163
Burnett, Hercules   59
Burns, Tommy   17, 68, 86, 87
Burwell, Bill   175
Bushong, Al   86, 87
Butler, Dick   92
Byrne, Charles H.   77

–C–

Caldwell, Mary 6

Caldwell, Standiford 6

Caldwell, Virginia 6

Calvary Cemetery 38, 162

Campbell, Paul 175

Canseco, Ozzie 168

Carbine, John 36

Cardinal Stadium 161, 166

Carew, Rod 35, 99

Carnighan, George 96

Carpenter, Cris 168

Carpenter, Hick 143

Carr, Chuck 168

Cartwright, Alexander 9

Caruthers 86

Caruthers, Bob 21, 26, 29, 87, 133, 135, 136, 137

Cassidy, Pete 99

Cassidy, Raymond 6

Cave Hill Cemetery 6, 28, 43, 59, 72, 133, 161

Chamberlain, Icebox 18, 25, 26, 62, 66, 68, 97, 127

Chance, Frank 161

Chandler, Albert Benjamin "Happy" 20, 21, 163

Chaney, Lon 43

Chapman, John 29, 36, 76, 77, 80, 81

Chapman, Ray 6, 99, 158

Chicago 9, 12, 14, 16, 17, 77, 96, 99, 128, 129, 142

Chicago Colts 55

Chicago White Sox 35, 91

Chicago White Stockings 21, 33, 62, 97

Cincinnati 9, 16, 18, 21, 37, 51, 52, 56, 70, 71, 75, 98, 128, 133, 134

Cincinnati Reds 9, 90, 163

Citarella, Ralph 179

City Hospital 59, 72

Clark, Mark 168

Clark, Robert 87

Clarke, Fred 18, 32, 33, 37, 88, 89, 92, 94, 98, 99, 127, 161

Clarke, William "Dad" 92

Clarkson, John 12, 17, 63, 98

Clausen, F. 129

Cleveland 31, 50, 54, 55, 129

Cleveland Indians 99

Cleveland, Presidents 48

Cline, Monk 64

Clingman, Bill 91, 92

Clinton, J. 128

Cobb, Ty 6, 93, 160, 161

Cole, Alex 168

Coleman, Prest 95

Coleman, Vince 168

Collins 86

Collins, Hub 67, 68, 87, 162

Collins, Jimmy 32, 34, 37, 94

Columbus 19, 46, 70, 77, 128, 129

Combs, Earle 162, 167, 169

Comiskey, Charlie 29, 56, 138

Connor, Roger 54

Cook, Paul 68, 69, 102

Cooper, Cecil 168

Cooperstown 132, 133, 138, 167

Corcoran, Larry 12, 17, 62, 66, 97

Corkhill, John 87

Cotter, Leo "Hooks" 175

Cox, Danny 168, 179

Craver, Bill 13, 96

Cromer, Tripp 168

Cross, Amos 64

Cross, Lafayette Napoleon "Lave" 25

Cross, Lave 67

Crotty, Joe 64

Crowley, Bill 13, 44

Cullop, Nick 168, 175

Cunningham, Bert 35, 92, 127, 129

Curry, Wesley 77, 84

–D–

Daily, Ed 79, 85, 87, 129

Daily, T. 45

Dalrymple, Abner 17

Daly, Tom   86, 87
Danforth, Dave   168
Daniels, Bert   168
Davidson, Mordecai   18, 50, 53, 65, 67, 130
Davis, Dixie   6, 168, 174, 183
Davis, Harry   34
Dean, Dizzy   161, 168
DeBerry, Joe   175
Delahanty, Ed   91, 134
Denny, Jerry   33, 34
Derringer, Paul   163
Detroit Tigers   29, 74
Detroit Wolverines   26, 136
Devlin, Jimmy   13, 14, 36, 37, 44, 96, 127, 128
Dexter, Charlie   92
Dobronski, Karl   179
Donovan, Patsy   18, 29, 79, 86, 87, 104
Dotson, Gene   179
Doubleday, Abner   9
Dowse, T.J.   98
Doyle, Denny   158
Doyle, Jeff   179
Drexler, Fred   130
Dreyfuss, Barney   35, 130
Duffy, Hugh   31, 41

–E–

Eclipse Park   15, 25, 160, 161, 164
Ehret, Red   27, 37, 69, 71, 72, 75, 78, 79, 80, 81, 85, 87, 127, 128, 160
Ely, Fred   57
Emig, Charles   34
Esterbrook, Dude   70
Evans, Dwight   168
Evans, Roy   92
Evers, Johnny   161
Ewing, Buck   27
Ewing, John   27, 29, 67, 69, 71, 128

–F–

Fairgrounds Stadium   166

Falls City Park   15, 25
Field, Al G.   27
Fisk, Carlton   168
Fitzgerald, John   127, 129
Flanagan, Ed   69
Flowers, Wes   175
Folden, Chris   179
Fontana, Joseph   96
Ford, Curt   168
Ford, Whitey   138
Foutz, Dave   21, 26, 29, 48, 79, 86, 87, 136, 137, 138
Fraser, Chick   92, 127, 129
Fregosi, Jim   167, 179, 182
Fuller, Harry   96
Fulmer, Chick   36

–G–

Galarraga, Andres   168
Galligan, John   69
Galt House   10, 89
Ganzel, Babe   168
Garfield, President   42, 45
Gatto, Larry   11, 27, 54, 160, 162
Gehrig, Lou   161, 168
General Hospital   59
Genovese, Chico   168
Gerhardt, Joe   36, 44, 106
Gilbert, B.L.   139
Gilkey, Bernard   168
Glasscock, Jack   34
Goebbel, William   28
Gonzalez, Jose   179
Goodall, Herb   80, 81
Goodman, Billy   168
Gore, George   12, 17, 142
Graceland Cemetery   136
Greenwell, Mike   160
Griffith, D.W.   43
Grimes, Burleigh   167
Grove, Lefty   6, 74, 98
Guerrero, Pedro   168

Guin, Greg 179
Gullett, Don 162
Gutman, Dan 6
Guyon, Joe 168, 175

–H–

Hagen, Kevin 179
Hague, Bill 36, 37
Haldeman, John Avery 13, 37, 45, 96, 162
Haldeman, Walter N. 13, 97, 130
Hall, George 13, 44, 96, 127
Hamburg, Charlie 80, 81, 85, 87
Hamilton, Billy 34, 91, 134
Hamilton County Home 75
Hanlon, Ned 33
Harris, Doyle 179
Harris, Greg 62, 97
Hart, Jim 64
Hart, Julian B. 130
Hartford 9
Hartford Ball Club Grounds 14
Hartsel, Topsy 33, 35, 94
Hastings, Scott 36
Hawley, Rick 58
Hayden, Jack 165
Hecker Baseball SupplyCompany 63
Hecker, Guy 18, 19, 21, 29, 30, 33, 41, 43, 50, 61, 62, 63, 64, 68, 69, 71, 74, 98, 127, 128, 161
Heib, Mike 179
Hemming, George 33, 127
Hendrix, Tim 174
Herman, A. 129
Herman, Billy 167, 169
Hill, William "Still Bill" 92
Hillerich & Bradsby 40, 42, 43, 46, 59, 93, 98, 133, 159, 160, 161, 166, 169
Hillerich, J.F. 41, 46
Hillerich, John A. "Bud" 41, 42, 46, 98, 133, 160, 161
Hite, Billy 179
Holley, Ed 175

Horton, Ricky 179
Householder, Charlie 62, 97
Houston, Allen Polk 95
Hoy, Dummy 33, 34, 94
Hudson, Nat 26, 29
Hughes, Michael 87
Hughson, Tex 168
Hulbert, William Ambrose 8, 9

–I–

Inks, B. 129
Iron City 16
Irwin, Tommy 175

–J–

J.F. Hillerich & Son Company 39, 46, 93, 99
Jackson, Joe 161
Jackson, Judge William 27
Jackson, William L., Jr. 130
Jennings, Hughie 29, 33, 108
Johnson, Albert "Abbie" 54, 57, 92
Johnson, Darrell 167
Johnson, Lance 168
Johnson, Walter 6, 74, 93, 98, 161
Jones, Michael 81

–K–

Kaline, Al 6
Kansas City 49, 66, 71, 90, 128
Kasko, Eddie 167
Kaye, Amy 27
Kearns, Christina 6
Keefe, Tim 19, 74, 98
Keeler, Wee Willie 32, 33
Keener, Jeff 179
Kelly, John 68
Kelly, Mike "King" 12, 17, 54, 57, 90
Kentucky Derby 25, 26, 96
Kepshire, Kurt 179
Kerins, Jack 64, 66, 67, 68

Kilroy, Matty   33, 64, 109, 129

Kimmel, Ralph   169

King, Silver   26, 29, 137, 138

Kirke, Jay   168, 174

Knebelkamp, Bill   174

Knight, Lon   19

Kocher, Brad   174

Koenig, Charles Frederick   137

Koob, Ernie   175

Koufax, Sandy   6

–L–

Lafferty, Frank   44

Lajoie, Nap   161

Lakeland, Ky   43, 59

Landrum, Tito   179

Lankford, Ray   168

Latham, Arlie   29, 67

Latham, Juice   13

Leach, Tommy   35, 92, 94, 99, 161

League Park   15

Lehan, T.   42

Lewis, Oliver   26

Lindell Hotel   43

Lindeman, Jim   168

Lofton, Kenny   6

Lonborg, Jim   168

Long, Herman   37

Long, Tommy   174

Lord Baltimores   25

Louis XVI   15

Louisville   9, 12, 13, 15, 16, 17, 19, 21, 27, 31, 33, 44, 46, 48, 55, 56, 58, 62, 66, 68, 73, 74, 75, 77, 79, 84, 97, 98, 99, 125

Louisville & Nashville Railroad   16

Louisville Baseball Park   14

Louisville Club   50, 66

Louisville Colonels   6, 15, 161, 164, 165, 169, 170, 171, 175, 176, 179, 183

Louisville Eclipse   15, 20, 44, 45, 46, 62, 97

Louisville Falls Citys   25

Louisville Fire Department   72

Louisville Grays   12, 13, 15, 19, 44, 45, 161

Louisville Hotel   10, 11, 77, 160

Louisville Redbirds   161, 167, 176, 179, 182

Louisville Slugger   42, 46, 52, 53, 55, 93, 98, 99, 133, 160, 166

Louisville Slugger Museum   6

Louisville Water Company   91

Lovett, Tom   78, 79, 86, 87

Lowdermilk, Grover Cleveland   168

Lowe, Bobby   31, 66

Lugosi, Bela   43

Luque, Dolf   168

Lutenberg, Luke   58

Lyon, William L.   51, 130

–M–

Mabry, John   168

Mack, Connie   35, 140, 161

Mack, Denny   61

Mack, Reddy   74, 98

Magee, Bill   92, 129

Malzone, Frank   168

Mantle, Mickey   6

Marquard, Rube   74, 98

Maskrey, Leech   61, 64

Mathewson, Christy   93, 161

Mays, Al   64

Mays, Carl   99, 158

Mays, Willie   6

McBride, Joseph   140

McCarthy, Joe   167, 174, 175, 182

McCarthy, Tommy   29, 31

McCloskey, John   12, 27, 37, 38, 58, 91, 158, 162

McCormick, Jim   12, 17

McCreery, Tom   92, 99, 127, 129

McDermott, Maurice   168

McDonald, Allan   95

McDonald, Kenneth   95

McGee, Willie   168

McGinnity, Joe "Iron Man"   37

McGraw, John   33, 43, 161

McGuire, Deacon 21

McGunnigle, William 87

McKain, Archie 168

McKnight, Denny 40

McKune, Jerry 179

McLaughlin, Tom 64

McPhee, Bid 52, 90, 134, 135, 136, 160

McQuaid, John 77, 84

Meakim, George 78, 81, 85, 87

Meekin, J. 129

Menefee, J. 129

Meyer, Bill 174

Miller, Dyar 179

Miller, Joe 64

Milliken, Jamie 6

Milliken, Rev. Michael 6

Mississippi River 15, 16

Missouri River 16

Mitchell, Bobby 13

Montgomery, John 69

Montreal Expos 62, 97

Morgan, Joe 6

Mozzali, Joe 179

Muir, Thomas 95

Mullane, Tony 18, 33, 61, 62, 63, 66, 97, 127, 128, 133

Murphy, Isaac 24, 26

Mutuals 44, 45

–N–

Nash, Cotton 6, 158

Neal, William 96

Nemec, David 6, 43, 80, 138

New Orleans 10, 15

New York 9, 19, 47, 58, 77, 96

New York Giants 74, 93, 97, 99

New York Gorhams 25

New York Yankees 99, 162

Nichols, Al 13, 96

Nichols, Kid 6, 31

Niekro, Phil 168

Nieto, Tom 179

Night Riders 15

Northrup, Jake 168

Nottebart, Don 168

–O–

Oakley, Annie 140

Oberlin 20

Oberlin College 21

O'Brien, William "Darby" 86, 87

O'Connor, Dan 81

Oenbey, Ricky 179

Ogilvie, Ben 168

Ohio River 15

Oil City, Pa. 63

Oklahoma 34

Okrent, Daniel 90

Olivo, Freddy 168

O'Neill, Tip 28, 29, 40, 49

O'Neill, J. Palmer 56

Orr, Davey 19, 54, 138, 139

Osborne, W. 95

–P–

Pacific Coast League 37

Pacific Northwest League 37

Pagnozzi, Tom 168

Paige, Satchel 161, 168

Palmer, Edward 50

Palmero, Emilo 174

Parkway Field 161, 167, 168

Parsons, Lawrence S. 77, 130

Pendleton, Terry 168

Perez, Tony 6

Pesky, Johnny 168

Pfeffer, Fred 12, 17, 31, 57, 89, 127, 160

Pfeiffer, Charles 42

Pfiester, Jack 37, 42

Phelps, Amy Kaye 28

Phelps, Zack 26, 27, 28, 130, 161, 162

Philadelphia 9, 14, 18, 19, 51, 67, 70, 77, 92, 98, 99, 128, 137

Philadelphia Athletics   74, 134
Philadelphia Pythians   25
Philips Exeter Academy   80
Phillippe, Deacon   31, 33, 35, 92, 94, 99, 127, 129, 161
Phoenix Hotel   72
Piersall, Jimmy   168
Pike, Lipman   13
Pinckney, George   86, 87
Pisgah Presbyterian Church Cemetery   163
Pitts, Gaylen   179
Pittsburgh   15, 16, 18, 21, 63, 92, 94, 128, 129, 132
Pittsburgh Keystones   25
Pittsburgh Pirates   35, 89, 99, 161
Pizarro, Juan   168
Plank, J.H.   130
Players' League   40
Polly, Nick   168
Portland Canal   15
Powell, Abner   71
Preuss, William   96
Princes of the City   76
Pulliam, Harry C.   89, 130, 162
Puttman, Ambrose   168

–Q–

Quaker City   69
Quest, Joe   142

–R–

Rajsich, Gary   168
Ramsey, Toad   21, 23, 53, 64, 65, 66, 67, 68, 71, 127, 128
Rasmussen, Eric   179
Raymond, Harry   69, 80, 81, 85, 87
Reccius, John   42, 61, 64, 162
Reccius, Philip   64, 128, 160
Redding, Frank   96
Reeder, Nick   96
Reese, Pee Wee   20, 158, 161, 167, 169, 175

Regulars   59
Reitz, Ken   179
Reserves   59
Revolutionary War   15
Rhodes, Mike   179
Richardson, Danny   57
Richter, John   96
Ricks, Napoleon   25
Rincon, Andy   179
Rivera, Bombo   179
Roach, John   66, 97
Roberts, Robin   6
Robinson, Jackie   20, 23, 161
Robinson, Wilbert   33, 74, 98
Rochester   74
Rogers, Jimmy   89
Roof, Gene   168, 179
Rowe, Schoolboy   74, 98
Royer, Stan   168
Ruth, Babe   6, 35, 93, 99, 161, 168
Ryan, John B.   80, 85, 87, 96
Ryan, Johnny   36, 37
Ryan, Nolan   21

–S–

Sachs, Vice President   77
Salt Lake City, Utah   27
Sanchez, Orlando   179
Sanders, Ben   33
Santana, Rafael   179
Schenck, Bill   61
Schepner, Joe   175
Schrupp, Todd   6
Selee, Frank   31
Semple, Henry   96
Seymour, Harold   9
Shaffer, George   44
Shaffer, Orator   13
Shannon, Dan   69
Shannon, Maury   175
Shatzkin, Mike   90
Shelby, John   158

Sheppard, Mary Jane   44

Sherlock, Vince   175

Shinnick, Tim   80, 81, 85, 87

Sievers, Roy   6

Simmons Hardware   42

Simms, Willie   26

Simons, Butch   168

Sisker, George   183

Sloane, Mayor Harvey I.   133

Smith, George   78, 86, 87

Smith, Jed   179

Smith, Skyrocket   68

Snyder, Charles "Pop"   19, 36, 37

Sohan, Pat   179

Somerville, Ed   37

Southern League   37

Spalding, Albert   12

Speaker, Tris   161

St. Cloud Hotel   37

St. James Court   14, 96, 161

St. Louis   9, 15, 19, 42, 45, 57, 64, 71, 74, 77, 128, 129

St. Louis Browns   6, 17, 18, 19, 20, 21, 26, 33, 58, 136, 140

St. Louis Cardinals   161

St. Louis Cemetery   162

St. Louis Maroons   93

Stafford, James "General"   92

Standiford Field   161, 166

Stengel, Casey   161

Stennett, Rennie   74, 98

Stern, Aaron   62, 133

Stewart, Bill "Shorty"   174

Stinson, E.B.   96

Stith, Andy   6

Stivetts, Jack   27

Stovey, Harry   19, 137

Stratton, Scott   27, 31, 67, 68, 69, 71, 72, 73, 74, 75, 77, 78, 79, 80, 81, 85, 87, 98, 127, 128, 129, 163

Strick, John   61

Stuckey, Dr. T. Hunt   130

Sullivan, Dan   61, 64

Sunday, Arthur   140

Sunday, Billy   12, 142

Syracuse   74

–T–

Tannehill, Jesse   158

Tartabull, Jose   168

Tasby, Willie   168

Taylor, Harry   33, 80, 81, 85, 87, 127

Terry, William "Adonis"   78, 86, 87

Tewksbury, Bob   168

Texas League   37

Thompson, Sam   91, 134

Thruman, Harry   95

Tincup, Ben   168, 174, 175

Tinker, Joe   37, 161

Toledo   20, 128, 140

Tomney, Philip   69, 80, 81, 85, 87, 115

Topp, Richard   6

Turner, Tuck   91

Twineham, Arthur   57

Tyson, Ty   175

–U–

Uecker, Bob   168

–V–

Valley Cemetery   163

Van Slyke, Andy   168

Vatter, Phillip   96

Vaughn, Farmer   69

Veach, Bobby   158

von der Ahe, Chris   19, 67, 140

–W–

Waddell, Rube   34, 35, 92, 94

Wadsworth, John   99, 129

Wagner, Honus   18, 31, 34, 41, 92, 93, 94, 99, 161, 175

Wagner, Richard   93

Walker, Moses Fleetwood   20, 21, 40, 97, 98,
    132, 161

Walker, Welday   20, 21, 40

Walsh, Mike   19

Wanderers   15

Wandering Jays   69

Washington   15, 98

Washington Senators   74

Waverly Hotel   72

Weaver, Farmer   27, 69, 74, 77, 80, 81, 85, 87,
    98, 127

Weaver, Jim   175

Weaver, Sam   19

Webb, Sam   65

Weckbecker, Peter   85, 87

Welch, Curt   29, 32, 33

Werden, Perry   92

Werrick, Joe   68

Western League   59

Weyhing, Gus   34, 38, 90, 99, 134, 160, 162

White, Bill   68

White Sewing Machine Company   20

White, Will   135, 136

Whiteford, Mike   141

Williams, Bill   6

Williams, Ted   161, 166

Williamson, Ned   17

Wilson, Bill   92

Winkfield, Jimmy   26

Wolf, Chicken   27, 29, 30, 61, 64, 68, 69, 71,
    72, 76, 79, 80, 81, 85, 87, 127, 128, 160,
    161, 162

Wood, Smokey Joe   74, 98

World War I   26

World War II   26

Worrell, Todd   168

Wortman, Chuck   174

Wrigley Field   136

Wulf, Steve   90

–Y–

Young, Cy   161

Young, Gerald   168

–Z–

Zahner, Fred   96

Zeile, Todd   168

Zimmer, Charles "Chief"   94

Zimmerman, W.   42

www.ingramcontent.com/pod-product-compliance
Lightning Source LLC
Chambersburg PA
CBHW050643150426

42813CB00054B/1165